16.95

D0143820

The Politics of Revenge

TITLES OF RELATED INTEREST

THE POLITICS
OF REVENGE

Fascism and the military in twentieth-century Spain

PAUL PRESTON

London and New York

First published by the Academic Division of
Unwin Hyman Ltd in 1990

First published in paperback 1995
by Routledge
11 New Fetter Lane, London EC4P 4EE

Simultaneously published in the USA and Canada
by Routledge
29 West 35th Street, New York, NY 10001

© 1990, 1995 Paul Preston

Typeset in 10 on 12 pt Garamond

Printed and bound in Great Britain by
Redwood Books, Trowbridge, Wiltshire

British Library Cataloguing in Publication Data

A catalogue record for this book is available from the British Library

Library of Congress Cataloging in Publication Data

A catalogue record for this book has been requested

ISBN 0-415-12000-4

**Cover illustration: printed with the
generous support of the Cañada
Blanch Foundation, London**

For Raymond Carr and James Joll

Contents

Author's note

Some of the ideas developed in this book were first tested in lectures, seminars and earlier articles. Where material has appeared before, it has been very substantially expanded and reworked for inclusion in the present volume to take into account later research by myself and others, to reflect changes in my own views and also to draw out the central themes of the book. What is now Chapter 1 was first given as a lecture at the Universidad Menéndez Pelayo in Santander in 1980. Parts of it were included in my essay on Spain in S. J. Woolf's *Fascism in Europe* (Methuen, London, 1981). I am grateful to Methuen & Co, for permission to reproduce it here. An earlier version of Chapter 2 was given as a lecture at Harvard in 1986 and subsequently published in Harvard University Center for European Studies, Working Paper Series no. 13. Chapter 3 is an extension of the central section of my inaugural lecture as Professor of History at Queen Mary College and has not previously been published. Chapter 4 started life as a paper at the Institute of Historical Research in London. Chapter 5 was given as a lecture at the Maison des Sciences de l'Homme in Paris and originally appeared in Martin Blinkhorn's edited collection *Fascists and Conservatives in Europe* (Unwin Hyman, London 1990). Part of Chapter 6 draws on some material which appeared in my contribution to *Élites and Power in Modern Spain: Essays for Raymond Carr*, edited by Frances Lannon and Paul Preston (The Clarendon Press, 1990). I would like to thank Oxford University Press for permission to reprint it. Chapter 7 on the extreme right is a much extended version of a short article which appeared in *New Society* in 1973. A rather shorter version of Chapter 8 appeared in Christopher Abel and Nissa Torrents, *Spain: Conditional Democracy* (Croom Helm, London, 1983). I am grateful to Croom Helm for permission to reproduce it here.

Preface

The historiography of modern Spain is overwhelmingly, and perhaps inevitably, obsessed with the examination of the causes, course and consequences of the Civil War. The fratricide of the 1930s has given rise to a bibliography which is astonishingly large, disproportionately so when compared with that on the Second World War. Leaving aside the enormous body of propaganda, polemic and personal memoirs, one curious feature of the abundance of writing on twentieth-century Spain is the sheer weight of scholarship about the left. At one level, that is understandable. The revolutionary exploits of Spanish anarchists make passionately interesting reading. The bitter rivalries between Spanish socialists and anarchists are hardly less engrossing. The internecine conflicts between anarchists, socialists and communists lie at the heart of the reasons for the defeat of the Spanish Republic, and with it, the collapse of the great collectivist experiments of the Civil War.

On the other hand, the fascination of the left rather obscures the fact that the Spanish Republic was a short-lived interval, almost an aberration, in a modern history dominated by the right. Accordingly, the immediate justification for this book is the relative lack of serious consideration of the Spanish right in English, or indeed in any other language. Most of those who have written about, or have been sympathetic to, the left have little or nothing to say about the right. A majority of those who have written about the right have tended to be propagandists of its cause, taking for granted that ultimately the justification for the Civil War could be found in left-wing disorder. There are, of course, outstanding and honourable exceptions.[1] Nevertheless, by comparison

---

1 Although I do not always agree with their conclusions, the prolific works on various aspects of Francoism, the army and the right in general by Javier Tusell in Spain and Stanley G. Payne in the United States are indispensable. My own debts to them will be apparent from the footnotes of the present book. The writing of Martin Blinkhorn on Carlism is seminal and, in demonstrating how the ideological well-springs of the Spanish right are to be found in traditionalism, has resonances far beyond its immediate subject. The trail-blazing contributions of Herbert R. Southworth to the study of Falangism in particular and of the wider aspects of Francoist manipulations of its own historical record remain crucial. A short guide to further reading also highlights some important monographic contributions by young Spanish scholars.

with the left, the right has not been the object of an abundant historiography.

During several years living in Spain it was impossible not to be led by my own research into the political conflicts of the Second Republic, and by my everyday observations, to see a Spanish right which seemed harsh, rigid and obstinate, in comparison with the relatively flexible conservatism that then still apparently prevailed in England. I was also much struck by the extent to which the right, in the starkest possible contrast with the left, and despite the considerable ideological, strategic and tactical discrepancies between its component groups, tended to act with unity of purpose. During the Second Republic, the various rightist groups acted as 'regiments in the same army'. The scale of their co-operation throughout the Republic was matched and intensified during the Civil War, something which posed remarkable comparisons with the comportment of the left. The particular development of Spanish history in the twentieth century can be traced in large measure to the right's obstinacy, inflexibility and fear of democracy, just as the country's present progress can in some measure be attributed to the emergence of a modern, moderate and civilized right capable of working within a democratic system.

The remarkable solidarity of the right during the 1930s was crisis-induced and, once the Civil War was won, discrepancies could re-emerge. Those discrepancies formed the basis of the belief that, under Franco, there was a kind of limited pluralism. When the regime once again underwent a major crisis in the mid-1970s, a different kind of unity was re-established by those elements of the Francoist coalition, the army and the Falange, which had evolved least during the years of dictatorship. In the interim between the rightist unity of the Civil War and the rather narrower unity of the 1970s' retreat into the bunker, the right evolved dramatically in different directions under Franco. For many Catholics and monarchists the dictatorship's harsher face became increasingly unacceptable. There were Falangists too who considered the stultifyingly bureaucratic atmosphere of the regime to be a betrayal of their original ideals. The authoritarian Catholic leader José María Gil Robles, the one-time monarchist backer of the Falange, José María de Areilza, the Christian Democrat ex-minister of Franco, Joaquín Ruiz Giménez and the Falangist poet Dionisio Ridruejo were the most striking cases of the evolution of right-wingers who came to oppose the dictatorship. There were to be many others, Francoist functionaries, of whom Adolfo Suárez is merely the most celebrated, who evolved to a point where they were to work for the transition from dictatorship to democracy. There were, of course, those who developed in other, more retrogressive, ways.

The chapters of this book attempt to provide some sense of the unity and the development of the hard-line right. What they do not do is discuss the evolution of a democratic, constitutional right, whose components I have examined at length in my book *The Triumph of Democracy in Spain* (Methuen, London, 1986). Nor, except marginally, are they concerned with the political role of the Catholic Church. This book centres rather on various closely linked aspects of the relationship between fascism and the military in the fifty years from the birth of the Second Republic in 1931 to the despairing military coup of 1981. It examines the roles of fascism and the military as instruments of right-wing dominance in twentieth-century Spain. It does so with particular regard to General Franco and his ongoing preoccupation with his own survival. The total identification between the Caudillo and his regime ensured that neither he nor most of his followers saw any contradiction between his personal interests and those of the servants and backers of the dictatorship. Nevertheless, by the 1970s, some of its most powerful supporters saw the regime as an anachronism and were therefore prepared to open negotiations with the forces of the moderate left. Because Franco had used the instruments of his dictatorship entirely in the interests of a narrowly partisan view of his own and the regime's interests, they found themselves divorced from the sectors of society for whom they had fought between 1936 and 1939. The greatest victim in this regard was, paradoxically, the army. Its interests should have transcended the immediate protection of a transitory dictatorship. That is one of the recurring themes of this volume.

The book opens with a chapter on the nature of fascism in Spain. Attempts to define Spanish fascism have been bedevilled by the fact that the one undisputably fascist party in the 1930s, the Falange, was numerically weak and overshadowed by the army. Chapter 1 examines the Spanish variant of fascism both in its long-term historical context and as merely one of the various units among the rightist forces. In this sense, its argument is that to confine the search for fascism in Spain to the pre-Civil War Falange Española is a meaningless exercise. It suggests rather that a more fruitful object of examination is the broad counter-revolutionary alliance of the parties which supported the Francoist cause, forcibly formalized as Falange Española Tradicionalista y de las Juntas de Ofensiva Nacional-Sindicalista in April 1937. Although merely a part of a wider whole, FET y de las JONS was to give a fascist veneer to the wider Francoist coalition. Chapter 2 explores the ways in which the collective memory of the Spanish Civil War was manipulated by the dictatorship, through the Falangist propaganda machine and its Youth Front, in schools and in military academies, through cultural artefacts and censorship. It examines the crude construction of an ideological hegemony which aimed to keep together the Francoist coalition by dividing the population into victors and vanquished.

Three pairs of matching chapters follow. The first concerns two related aspects of General Franco's survival in the period when he was most vulnerable both to internal political machinations and to overthrow by an external power. Chapter 3 examines the temptation of General Franco by the Axis in the Second World War. It considers the way in which he survived both his own and the Falange's enthusiasm for the new Hitlerian world order. It suggests that the exquisitely careful diplomacy or *hábil prudencia* seen by Franco's admirers as the reason for Spain's wartime neutrality played less of a part than did good fortune and the errors of judgement of Hitler and Ribbentrop. That examination of pro-Axis inclinations within the Franco camp is balanced by Chapter 4, which traces the Caudillo's skilful deflection of the tentative efforts of his generals to restrain his dictatorial inclinations. The second pair of chapters is made up of broad surveys of the evolving roles of both the military and the Falange under the Franco regime. In each case, these two instruments of the dictatorship were radically changed, even distorted, by the way in which they allowed themselves to be exploited by the dictator himself. The final pair of matched chapters considers the efforts of both fascists and soldiers to resurrect the past in the aftermath of Franco's death. They examine the subversive activities of the civilian and military 'bunkers' during the break-up of the dictatorship and the transition to democracy.

In the course of preparing this volume, I derived incalculable benefit from the encouragement and criticisms of Enrique Moradiellos, Florentino Portero and Ismael Saz, with all three of whom I discussed at length many of the specific ideas elaborated here. I would like to thank Chris Ealham for preparing the index. Other debts are more diffuse and range back over time. For twenty years, I have learned an enormous amount about the workings of Spanish politics from Elías Díaz. For almost as many years, Angel Viñas has been a limitless fount of information and insight into the structures of Francoism. Sheelagh Ellwood continues to teach me much about the Falange, its inner workings and the personalities of its leaders. My earliest researches into the Spanish right benefited from the help and hospitality of Herbert R. Southworth. For many years, he has made available to me with boundless generosity the resources of his library and his incomparable knowledge of the Falange and Francoism. The book is dedicated to Raymond Carr and James Joll, with gratitude for their unstinting support in all my academic enterprises.

Chronology

1892	4 December	Birth of Francisco Franco Bahamonde in El Ferrol.
1898		Defeat of Spain by USA. Loss of Cuba, Puerto Rico and Philippines.
1905	25 November	*Cu-Cut* incident. Army officers attack offices of satirical weekly in reprisal for the publication of an anti-military joke.
1906	20 March	Army secures military jurisdiction over offences against the *patria* and the armed forces.
1917		Military Defence Juntas, formed to protest about low pay and to protect the system of promotion by strict seniority, become involved with industrialists and trade unionists in a national reform movement, yet violently repress a socialist general strike.
1923	13 September	Military coup led by General Primo de Rivera.
1930	30 January	Primo de Rivera replaced by General Dámaso Berenguer.
1931	14 March	Foundation of fascist newspaper *La Conquista del Estado* by Ramiro Ledesma Ramos.
1931	14 April	Departure of Alfonso XIII and the foundation of the Second Republic.
1931	26 April	Foundation of Catholic authoritarian party, Acción Popular.
1931	10 October	Foundation of fascist party, Juntas de Ofensiva Nacional-Sindicalista by Onesimo Redondo and Ramiro Ledesma Ramos.
1931	15 December	Foundation of Alfonsine monarchist society and journal Acción Española.
1933	28 February	Acción Popular unites with other legalist rightist groups to form the Confederación Española de Derechas Autónomas.
	1 March	Acción Española creates political front organization, Renovación Española.
	29 October	José Antonio Primo de Rivera launches Falange Española.
	19 November	José Antonio Primo de Rivera elected parliamentary deputy for Cádiz.

1934	11 February	Falange Española merges with the Juntas de Ofensiva Nacional-Sindicalista to become FE de las JONS.
	6 October	General strike, left-wing uprising in Asturias and brief declaration of Catalan independence, both crushed by army.
1936	16 February	Popular Front wins elections.
	14 March	FE de las JONS outlawed and its leadership, including José Antonio Primo de Rivera, arrested.
	18 July	Military uprising; Civil War starts.
	20 November	Execution in Alicante of José Antonio Primo de Rivera.
1937	19 April	Franco unites Falange, Carlists, CEDA and Renovación Española into Falange Española Tradicionalista y de las JONS and suppresses the radical Falangists under Hedilla.
1939	1 April	End of Civil War.
1940	13 June	Spain moves from neutrality to non-belligerency.
	14 June	Spain occupies Tangiers.
	17 September	Ramón Serrano Suñer visits Hitler and Ribbentrop.
	19 October	Himmler visits Madrid and inaugurates collaboration of Gestapo in reorganization of Spanish police.
	23 October	Franco meets Hitler at Hendaye.
1941	12 February	Franco meets Mussolini at Bordighera.
	14 February	Franco meets Pétain at Montpellier.
	27 June	Spain moves from non-belligerency to 'moral belligerency' in the Axis orbit.
	25 November	Serrano Suñer visits Berlin and renews Anti-Comintern Pact.
1942	3 September	Serrano Suñer dismissed as Foreign Minister.
1943	3 October	Spain abandons non-belligerency and readopts neutrality.
1944	28 January	Spanish failure to stop wolfram deliveries to Germany leads to American oil embargo.
1945	11 September	Fascist salute no longer obligatory greeting in Spanish public life.
	18 September	Spanish withdrawal from Tangiers.
1946	13 December	United Nations recommends withdrawal of ambassadors from Madrid.
1947	1 April	Ley de Succesión defines Spain a kingdom.
1950	4 November	UNO approves possible Spanish membership of international organizations.
1953	27 August	Concordat with Vatican.
	26 September	Pact of Madrid with USA provides for American bases in Spain in return for military equipment.
1955	8 December	Spain accepted into UNO.
1956	February	Student troubles mark major reverse for Falange.
1957	25 February	Opus Dei technocrats enter Franco's cabinet.
1962	March-May	Strike wave in Asturias, Basque country and Catalonia.
1963	20 April	Execution of Communist Julián Grimau.

	28 December	Introduction of first Development Plan.
1970	3–28 December	Burgos trials of Basque revolutionary separatists of ETA.
1971	March-April	Emergence of ultra-rightist terror squads.
1973	8 June	Admiral Carrero Blanco made head of government.
	20 December	Carrero Blanco assassinated by ETA.
1974	April	Emergence of liberal military pressure group Unión Militar Democrática.
1975	20 November	Death of Franco.
1976	March	Trials of army officers implicated in Unión Militar Democrática.
1976	22 September	Resignation of Minister of Defence in protest at legalization of trade union.
1977	15 June	First democratic elections since 1936.
1978	17 November	*Operación Galaxia*, failed military coup involving Colonel Antonio Tejero.
1981	23 February	Colonel Tejero seizes parliament and the entire political élite as the first stage of an elaborate, and ultimately abortive, military coup.

Part I

DEFENDING THE PAST

1

Resisting modernity: fascism and the military in twentieth-century Spain

In the summer of 1936 important sections of the officer corps of the Spanish army rose against the Second Republic. The officers involved were convinced that they were acting to save their country from the breakdown of law and order, the disintegration of national unity and waves of proletarian godlessness provoked by foreign agents. They believed themselves to be acting disinterestedly, inspired only by the highest patriotic values.[1] In fact, the military uprising, the consequent protracted war effort between 1936 and 1939 and the dictatorship which institutionalized the eventual victory of the rebels all shared a socially and politically partisan function. The function, if not the explicit intention, of the military rebels of 1936 and the military rulers of Spain after 1939 was, in addition to rooting out regionalism and reasserting the hegemony of institutionalized Catholicism, the protection of the interests of the agrarian-financial-industrial élites. In particular, that meant shielding the reactionary landed oligarchy from the challenge to Spain's antiquated economic structures embodied in the reforms of the Second Republic.

In 1936, for a number of complex reasons, the military uprising could count on a substantial amount of popular support that was, in the crudest terms, broadly equivalent to the combined electoral strengths of the major right-wing parties of the Second Republic.[2] That civilian support was consolidated in the course of the Spanish Civil War because of religious convictions reinforced by the Catholic Church's commitment

---

1 Gabriel Cardona, *El poder militar en la España contemporánea hasta la guerra civil* (Madrid, 1983), pp. 197–247.
2 Although there is a massive bibliography of regional electoral studies, there exists no satisfactory study of the electoral geography of the 1930s Spain as a whole. Jean Bécarud, *La segunda República española 1931–1936: ensayo de interpretación* (Madrid, 1967) remains the best overview. See pp. 97–104, 125–41, 155–83. Javier Tusell, *Las elecciones del Frente Popular*, 2 vols (Madrid, 1971) is the best study of the last elections before the military uprising, see Vol. II, pp. 22–58. For the largest mass party of the right, the CEDA, whose rank and file made up a large part of Franco's armies, there is the comprehensive study by José R. Montero, *La CEDA: el catolicismo social y político en la II República*, 2 vols (Madrid, 1977). See Vol. II, pp. 271–336.

to Franco, fear fuelled by political terror, the geographical loyalty of those whose survival instincts dictated that they adhere to the Nationalist cause, the wartime intensification of passions and hatreds provoked by atrocities in both zones, and the victorious dictatorship's capacity to disburse patronage and preferment. This is not to say that the Franco dictatorship was as popular as its propagandists claimed but simply to recognize that it had an autonomous base of mass support and was not merely the instrument of an isolated clique of soldiers and plutocrats.[3] The mechanism whereby the military mobilized and channelled that civilian backing was the sprawling umbrella organization of the right, the *Movimiento* or, more formally, the Falange Española Tradicionalista y de las Juntas de Ofensiva Nacional-Sindicalista, artificially created by the forced unification of the pro-Franco political parties in April 1937.[4]

The *Unificación* merely formalized the fact that the Franco regime was built upon a coalition of interlocking and overlapping forces, Falangists, Carlists, authoritarian Catholics and aristocratic monarchists. The Nationalist coalition was legitimized by the Catholic Church and dominated by its own praetorian guard. There would always be a certain rivalry for power between the component groups although the jostling was usually restrained, exploding into violence but rarely and then on the smallest scale. Inter-regime hostilities were kept within bounds by an awareness of the need to cling together against the recently defeated left. It is often said that General Franco's supreme skill was the ability to manage in his own interests the competition between his supporters. Nevertheless, it would be wrong to imply that they were not willing collaborators in his political juggling act. After all, the Caudillo's own position was never seriously threatened in thirty-eight years of dictatorial power.

The fact that Franco was so infrequently challenged reflected both the power of the army within the Spanish right and the care which he devoted to his own relationship with the military. Although it was ultimately to be diminished by its part in the dictatorship, the army maintained a privileged position, to an extent *au dessous de la mêlée*. Its only serious challengers for dominance of the Francoist establishment were to be found in the Falange and then only in the early years of the regime. It is not entirely surprising that the two most powerful instruments of Francoism, the civilian and the military, united under pressure during

---

3 The alleged isolation of the Franco clique was a constant feature of Communist Party analyses of its own strategic necessities. See, for example, Partido Comunista de España, *¡Por la Unión Nacional de todos los españoles contra Franco, los invasores germano-italianos y los traidores!* (México D. F., 1941); Fernando Claudín, *Las divergencias en el Partido* (n.p., but Paris, 1964) pp. 9–17.

4 Maximiano García Venero, *Falange en la guerra de España: la unificación y Hedilla* (Paris, 1967); Herbert R. Southworth, *Antifalange: estudio crítico de Falange en la guerra de España* (Paris, 1967).

the Civil War and then again in the last days of the dictatorship, should be rivals in the interim. The tensions between them were to be most acute during the Second World War when the Falange perhaps appeared stronger than it really was, its ranks flooded by recent recruits from other parties and its influence inflated by the military successes of Hitler and by the machinations of the German embassy.[5] After 1945 its strength was slowly to wane. Throughout the war, however, the Falange was to be a raucous advocate of Spanish entry into the Second World War on the Axis side. Although there was no shortage of fascist army officers, many of the most senior generals, invariably Catholic and often monarchists, adopted a patrician tone and expressed contempt for Falangists as upstart riff-raff. Moreover, in contrast to the ideological zealots of the Falange, the high command was cautious, after the devastation of the Civil War, about making any commitment to the Axis, despite an admiration for German military prowess.

By 1943 the balance in the internal jostling for power was tipping against the Falange. While the army's position remained as strong as ever, after the fall of Mussolini, the voice of the Falange was muted. In the aftermath of the Second World War the political pre-eminence of the Falange within the dictatorship was diminished by Franco. Anxious to clear himself of the stigma of his Axis and fascist connections, he began to look for senior political servants among the ranks of authoritarian Catholics.[6] Nevertheless, the Falange still maintained an important presence in Franco's cabinets. Outside of government it stood astride a substantial, and profitable, power base, controlling a huge national and provincial press chain and the state trade union system, as well as commanding insidious influence through its mass organizations, the Youth Front and the Feminine Section.[7] Over the subsequent decades that influence was to decline inexorably, its fascist rhetoric rendered anachronistic by social and economic changes that were impelling Spain towards ultimate integration in a democratic Europe. Ironically, the military, despite its essentially stronger position was also to lose political relevance. That was to be

---

5 Klaus-Jörg Ruhl, *Franco, Falange y Tercer Reich: España durante la segunda guerra mundial* (Madrid, 1986), pp. 45–74, 167–211. For a highly colourful account, see Aline, Countess of Romanones, *The Spy Wore Red: My Adventures as an Undercover Agent in World War II* (London, 1987), pp. 110–14.

6 Javier Tusell, *Franco y los Católicos: la política interior española entre 1945 y 1957* (Madrid, 1984), pp. 52–79.

7 On the press, see Javier Terrón Montero, *La prensa de España durante el régimen de Franco* (Madrid, 1981) and Justino Sinova, *La censura durante el franquismo* (Madrid, 1989); on the corporative syndicates, see Miguel A. Aparicio, *El sindicalismo vertical y la formación del Estado franquista* (Barcelona, 1980); on the Youth Front, see Juan Sáez Marín, *El Frente de Juventudes: política de juventud en la España de la postguerra (1937–1960)* (Madrid, 1988); on the Sección Femenina, see María Teresa Gallego Méndez, *Mujer, Falange y franquismo* (Madrid, 1983).

the price paid for acquiescing in professional decay under Franco in return for political privilege, for putting the defence of the dictatorship before the military defence of the nation.[8] By the late 1950s Spain's economic development was already such that a military dictatorship was demonstrably an obstacle to further growth. The military and the Falange were thus finally thrown together again, a *rapprochement* between them favoured by the fact that the upper ranks of the army were dominated from the 1960s onwards by Falangist sympathizers who had become provisional second-lieutenants, or *alféreces provisionales*, during the Civil War. No longer confident of the popular support which they had seemed to enjoy at the end of the Civil War, isolated generals and Falangists joined in a series of desperate ventures to destroy the democratic regime established after the death of Franco.[9]

The differences between the army officers of 1931–6 and those of 1973–81 are revealing of the enormous changes which had taken place on the Spanish right in the course of the Franco dictatorship. In the 1930s officers could convince themselves that they were the defenders of essential national values, the territorial integrity of Spain, the Catholic Church and landed property against Moscow-inspired threats. Moreover, in assuming the role of defenders of the 'true Spain', they could do so in the conviction of representing far from negligible sectors of society. When the uprising took place on 18 July 1936 the highly politicized, modern press networks of the right had been unreservedly behind them for months, if not years. That more or less guaranteed the mass support discernible in the electoral geography of the right under the Second Republic. The bulk of the church hierarchy gave them their blessing. Bankers and industrialists looked to them as saviours. Accordingly, the pride of senior army officers in the 1940s was not born solely of their military victory, but also of the unshakeable confidence that they were playing a hegemonic role in Spanish society with the endorsement of the church, the economic élites and large numbers of ordinary Spanish Catholics.

In contrast, many of the army officers of the final days of the Franco regime were entirely divorced from society. The church had withdrawn its support from the Franco regime in the late 1960s and put its weight behind the growing popular clamour for democracy. The most dynamic sectors of banking and industry were also betting on democratic change. After the death of Franco opinion polls and subsequent elections showed

---

8　On the price paid by the army for its links with the dictatorship, see Chapter 6, 'Destiny and dictatorship'.

9　See Chapter 7 'Into the bunker' and Chapter 8, 'Francoism's last stand'. For the wider political context of the transition to democracy, see Paul Preston, *The Triumph of Democracy in Spain* (London, 1986).

that the hard-line Francoist right would never enjoy more than 3 per cent of popular support, and almost all of that concentrated in the two Castiles.[10] Although the rhetoric of the military plotters of the late 1970s barely differed from that heard in the officers' messes of the 1940s, still shot through with references to the Civil War and hatred of the left, it was uttered now not with pride but with resentment. The conspirators of 1936 could reasonably believe that they were saving Spain, not for all Spaniards, but certainly for those who mattered. In contrast, the rancorous *golpistas* of 1981, for all their arrogant swagger, were embittered that even the Spaniards who mattered were no longer interested in the values of the Civil War.

Transformations in the social structure and in the levels of economic development within Spain itself, together with political changes in the world outside, account for the dramatic evolution of the roles of both fascism and the military within the Francoist repertoire. In the murky political twilight of Franco's senile decay, those changes had rendered obsolete the dictatorship, its Falangist apparatus and its military defences. Nevertheless, both Falangists and army officers bestirred themselves to defend their regime. Thereafter, the civilian and military extreme right, known collectively as the 'bunker', worked desperately to overturn the process of democratization. That some sectors of the army and the apparatus of the *Movimiento* should refuse to fade away along with their Caudillo or seek some *rapprochement* with the constitutional monarchy was the natural consequence of the role allotted to each by the dictatorship.

The relationship between fascism and the military in Spain was one which changed significantly in the course of the dictatorship, moving from the uneasy alliance of the Civil War years to something more symbiotic in the 1970s. In fact, the political pre-eminence of the army in taking the lead in the assault on the Second Republic and throughout the Franco dictatorship has been used to absolve Francoism of accusations that it was fascist. However, the co-operation of the Spanish army and the Falange during the Civil War and in the 1970s was far from being that of master and servant. It was different from that between the Wehrmacht and the Nazi Party or that between the Italian army and the Fascist Party, in that the Spanish army held the upper hand. Yet, in all three cases, the fascist party and the army were important elements of a wider counter-revolutionary alliance. In each country, the balance of forces within that alliance was different, for reasons to do with the particular traditions of the armed forces, their recent history and the

10 *El País*, 3 March 1979, 21 November 1982; Fundación Foessa, *Informe sociológico sobre el cambio político en España 1975–1981*, 2 vols (Madrid, 1981), Vol. I, pp. 503–6; Diario 16, *Historia de la transición*, 2 vols (Madrid, 1984), Vol. II, pp. 466, 580.

special national circumstances of the emergence of counter- revolutionary groups.

The Italian army was more subservient to the dictator than the Spanish. Nevertheless, the ambition of fascist leaders such as De Vecchi, Farinacci and Balbo to *'fascistizzare'* the army was frustrated. The activities of the fascist militia were also restrained.[11] The process whereby Hitler passed from deference towards the German officer corps to a contemptuous domination thereof was a complex one, taking over five years to accomplish. However, although the circumstances were rather different and the consequences slower to materialize, the introduction of Nazi elements as part of the major expansion of the Wehrmacht had its Spanish parallel in the influx of *alféreces provisionales* during the Civil War.[12] Where there is to be found a substantial difference is in the personality and political concerns of the leader of the counter-revolutionary alliance. Accordingly, the exercise of personal control over the military machine by both Mussolini and Hitler ensured that the Italian and German armies would not be restraining elements in the elaboration of foreign policy. Franco was, after all, a general himself and responsive to the efforts of the high command to persuade him to resist the Axis temptation.[13] In the Spanish, German and Italian cases, transactions and servitudes, mutual contempt and hidden resentments were present in the co-operation of patrician backers, army officers and fascist activists along with genuine enthusiasms.

In the field of fascist–military relations, exact scientific definitions are a chimera. One of the attractions of limiting the study of fascism in Spain to the Falange is that it neatly side-steps a number of thorny interpretative and ideological problems. If Spanish fascism can be reduced to the squalid hybrid founded by José Antonio Primo de Rivera then other groups of the authoritarian right, like the CEDA or Renovación Española, can simply be excluded from a discussion of the subject. More important, Franco's post-Civil War emasculation of the Falange lets his regime off the hook of being deemed fascist. It may well be that, in so far as precise definitions are possible, the Franco regime was not strictly fascist. The implication that it was therefore something less morally distasteful, merely 'conservative' or authoritarian perhaps, is misplaced. It may be legitimate to dismiss the regime's fascist veneer and its intimate and dependent relations with

---

11 Giorgio Rochat and Giulio Massobrio, *Breve storia dell' Esercito italiano dal 1861 al 1943* (Turin, 1978), pp. 201–16.

12 Klaus-Jürgen Müller, *The Army, Politics and Society in Germany 1933–45* (Manchester, 1987), pp. 29–41; Sir John Wheeler-Bennett, *The Nemesis of Power: The German Army in Politics 1918–1945* (London, 1953), pp. 289–94; Gordon A. Craig, *The Politics of the Prussian Army 1640–1945* 2nd edn, (New York, 1964), pp. 469–503.

13 See Chapter 3, 'Franco and the Axis temptation' and Chapter 4, 'Franco and his generals'.

Italian fascism and German Nazism as cynical masks or circumstantial alliances. However, its record in terms of the imprisonment, torture and execution of its working-class and liberal enemies invites seriously unfavourable comparison with Italian fascism. Indeed, as Himmler was to observe in 1940, the Franco regime was more brutal in its treatment of the Spanish working class than was the Third Reich in its dealings with German workers.[14]

If style and ideology, rather than social and economic function, are the main criteria for defining fascism then the exclusive choice of Falange Española as the Spanish candidate is inevitable. Its cult of violence contributed to the destabilization of the Second Republic. Its blue-shirted militias, with their Roman salutes and their ritual chants, gave every indication of aping Nazi and Fascist models. However, this chapter argues that the meaningful examination of fascism in Spain is best freed from the constraints implicit in isolated consideration of Falange Española. Instead, it argues from two premises which impel the discussion towards wider chronological and political parameters. The first is that the nature of fascism in Spain cannot be understood without consideration of the country's backward agrarian capitalism and the crisis that it was undergoing in the 1930s. The second is that that crisis stimulated the elaboration of extraordinary political measures in the form of the counter-revolutionary coalition which fought the Spanish Civil War. The Nationalist alliance was analogous to the counter-revolutionary groupings which emerged in Italy and Germany in response to their particular national crises. It differed in its balance of component forces, but it nevertheless played a comparable structural role. Accordingly, it is argued that the search for a Spanish fascism should consider the unified Francoist coalition as a whole. Seen in such a context, Falange Española simply becomes one, albeit the most servile, as the army was another, of the groups which co-operated to defend Spain's beleaguered oligarchy.

The political instability which impelled army officers to plot and then to launch a *coup d'état* in 1936 was real enough. It was partly the product of working-class desperation and internecine conflicts between sectors of the labour movement in the face of economic depression and intransigent oligarchical resistance to change.[15] More immediately,

---

14 Ramón Garriga, *La España de Franco: les relaciones con Hitler* (Puebla, Mexico, 1970), pp. 207–9.
15 For excellent local studies of militancy born of desperation and inter-union conflict, see, among many others, Santos Juliá Díaz, *Madrid, 1931–1934: de la fiesta popular a la lucha de clases* (Madrid, 1984), pp. 147–208; José Manuel Macarro Vera, *La utopía revolucionaria: Sevilla en la segunda República* (Seville, 1985), pp. 156–71, 214–42, 279–305, 446–81; David Ruiz, *Insurrección defensiva y revolución obrera* (Barcelona, 1988), pp. 84–97; Graham Kelsey, 'Anarchosyndicalism, libertarian communism and the state: the CNT in Zaragoza and Aragón, 1930–1937', unpublished PhD thesis (University of Lancaster, 1984).

it was the fruit of a deliberate destabilization programme sponsored by the landowners and industrialists most threatened by reform. Before the army assumed the defence of their interests, they had been guarded by a number of rightist political organizations. For the largest of them, the clerical authoritarian Confederación Española de Derechas Autónomas or CEDA, military intervention signalled the failure of its Trojan-horse tactic of blocking reform within the limits of Republic legality. Nevertheless, in a number of ways, the majority of CEDA members threw in their lot with the uprising. For the others, the troglodytic Carlists of the Comunión Tradicionalista, the radical monarchists of Renovación Española and the blue-shirted fascists of Falange Española, the rising was the fruition of their 'catastrophist' commitment to the violent overthrow of the Republic.[16]

With a few notable exceptions, the rank and file and the leaders of both legalist and 'catastrophist' organizations rallied readily behind the army, providing the cannon fodder of the rebel war effort and the political service class of the rebel zone. This was formalized in April 1937 by the so-called Unificación, when prewar rightist groups were subsumed into Falange Española Tradicionalista y de las Juntas de Ofensiva Nacional-Sindicalista. The fact that this strange amalgam took its title and its tone from the Falange met with little resistance from the other groups which, hitherto, had regarded the Falange as a rowdy street-fighting rabble to be patronized and used. The reasons for such humility were various. A recognition of the urgent political and economic issues at stake in the war inhibited manifestations of ruffled pride which might have disrupted the unity necessary for victory. Moreover, the aid given to the rebels by Hitler and Mussolini was helping to build an enthusiastic belief that the future world order would be a fascist one. In any case, the adoption of a Falangist nomenclature and liturgy did no violence to rightist consciences since, even before the war, a mimetic sympathy for fascism was a common feature of all Spanish right-wing organizations.[17]

It is not surprising, given the fulsome praise heaped on the German and Italian regimes and the proliferation of militarized youth sections, that the left in Spain indiscriminately regarded the parties of the right as fascist. It

16 Paul Preston, *The Coming of the Spanish Civil War* (henceforth *CSCW*) (London, 1978) pp. 188, 200; Javier Tusell, *Historia de la democracia cristiana en España*, 2 vols (Madrid, 1974), Vol. II, pp. 266–83; José María Gil Robles, *No fue posible la paz* (Barcelona, 1968), pp. 729 ff.; Joaquim Lleixá, *Cien años de militarismo en España: funciones estatales confiadas al Ejército en la Restauración y el franquismo* (Barcelona, 1986), pp. 197–247.

17 *El Debate*, 25 July, 28 October 1933; *El Socialista*, 29, 30 October 1933; Paul Preston, 'Alfonsine monarchism and the coming of the Spanish Civil War', *Journal of Contemporary History*, vol. II, nos. 3/4, 1972, pp. 100-2; Preston, *CSCW*, pp. 42–3, 46–50, 88; Martin Blinkhorn, *Carlism and Crisis in Spain 1931–1939* (Cambridge, 1975), pp. 163–81.

is even less noteworthy that the Franco war effort, backed by the Axis powers and with its Falangist façade, was seen by contemporaries, Spanish and foreign, as a fascist enterprise. The subsequent excesses of Nazism and the barbarization of warfare on the Eastern front, together with the assiduous efforts of Franco to dissociate himself from the Axis after 1943, did much to undermine this unqualified identification of Francoism with fascism. Indeed, in the last twenty years, scholars have dwelt on the fact that Francoism was not Hitlerism and have been influenced by the very unfascist development of Spain since 1957.[18] These deliberations have resulted in an increasingly widespread consensus that Francoism was *never* really fascism but rather some variant of limited, semi-pluralistic authoritarianism. The problem is not resolved by postulating, explicitly or implicitly, the view that the meaningful study of fascism in Spain should be limited to Falange Española.[19]

Such an approach is both understandable and unfortunate. It starts from the ostensibly laudable premise that contempt for the more reprehensible features of the Franco dictatorship should not permit the unscientific application to it of the term fascist merely as a means of political abuse. Moreover, while doubts are possible with regard to the fascist content of Renovación Española, the Comunión Tradicionalista and the CEDA, the fascist nature of the style, ideology and myths of the Falange are unquestionable. Accordingly, the narrow identification of Spanish fascism with Falange Española obviates the need for examination of the fascist features of other rightist groups and of the Franco regime itself. It is unfortunate because it renders Spanish fascism insignificant and uninteresting except for a period of about twelve months. Before the spring of 1936 the Falange Española was a diminutive organization of students and taxi-drivers. After April 1937 it was emasculated into a bureaucratic and patronage-dispensing machine in the service of Franco. As the Caudillo, in an uncharacteristic outburst of directness and levity, once explained to one of his ambassadors, 'the Falange is the claque which accompanies me on my journeys through Spain'. The easy relegation of the Falange to the fringes of the debate, whether by Franco himself or by scholars, is to forget both the fascist trappings and Axis alliances of Francoism and the activities of its repressive machinery between 1937 and 1945.

---

18 An extreme example of this tendency is Charles W. Anderson, *The Political Economy of Modern Spain: Policy-Making in an Authoritarian System* (Madison, Wisconsin, 1970).
19 Curiously, two authors of differing viewpoints have given titles to their studies of the Falange which imply that Spanish fascism is to be found exclusively in the Falange. Nevertheless, both imply a continuity between the pre-1937 FE de las JONS and the much wider post-1937 amalgam of FET y de las JONS. See Stanley G. Payne, *Falange: A History of Spanish Fascism* (Stanford, 1961) and Sheelagh M. Ellwood, *Spanish Fascism in the Franco Era* (London, 1987). See also the fascinating article by Juan J. Linz, 'An Authoritarian Regime: Spain' in E. Allardt and Y. Littunen (eds), *Cleavages, Ideologies and Party Systems* (Helsinki, 1964).

This is not the only reason for suspicion of the exclusivist definition of fascism in Spain. Awareness that fascism can be a term of abuse as well as of political definition cuts both ways.[20] An eagerness to exonerate the Franco regime from the taint of fascism can go with a readiness to forget that, after coming to power through a civil war which claimed hundreds of thousands of lives and forced hundreds of thousands more into exile, the dictatorship executed at least a quarter of a million people, maintained concentration camps and labour battalions and sent troops to fight for Hitler on the Russian front. Under any circumstances, the confident exclusion both of prewar Spanish rightists other than the Falange and of the Franco regime from a discussion of fascism could be justified only if fascism is taken to be synonymous with Nazism at its most extreme, complete with racialist bestiality. Such a view, since it leads logically to the suggestion that Mussolini's Italy was not really fascist, is so rigid as to be useless.[21]

It is a basic assumption of this chapter that the paradigmatic movement and regime which must be considered generically fascist are those of Mussolini. That is not to say that the search for Spanish fascism should be inflexibly restricted to the quest for similarities with Italy. After all, for all their common features, most fascist movements, except those created in the wake of German occupation, were responses to national crises and drew on national traditions. Thus, if Nazism and Fascism, with all their differences, can be accepted as the German and Italian counter-revolutionary responses to crises of German and Italian society, then a case can be made for the rightist groups which backed the rebels in the Civil War to be considered collectively as the equivalent Spanish counter-revolutionary response to a crisis of Spanish society. The deep structural problems of Germany, Italy and Spain between the 1870s and the First World War did, after all, demonstrate a degree of similarity. Despite enormous differences in terms of levels of economic development, all three experienced the tensions consequent upon a backward political regime fending off challenges from both a dynamic bourgeoisie and a militant working class.[22]

This is not to forget significant differences. Unlike Germany and Italy, Spain did not participate in the First World War. In consequence, there simply did not exist masses of demobilized veterans to swell the ranks

20 Arno J. Mayer, *Dynamics of Counterrevolution in Europe: An Analytical Framework* (New York, 1971), p. 1.

21 See Stanley G. Payne, *Fascism: Comparison and Definition* (Wisconsin, 1980) pp. 101–4.

22 Hans-Ulrich Wehler, *The German Empire 1871–1918* (Leamington Spa, 1985), pp. 71–99; David Blackbourn and Geoff Eley, *The Peculiarities of German History* (Oxford, 1984), pp. 91–7, 238–41 and *passim*; John A. Davis, *Gramsci and Italy's Passive Revolution* (London, 1979), pp. 11–61.

of paramilitary organizations. Nor was there a national psychosis of defeat. Both of those factors contributed to the biggest difference of all – the pre-eminent political role played by the army in the defence of right-wing interests against leftist challenges. On the other hand, the war brought massive social and economic dislocation to an already conflictive Spain, albeit not quite on the scale of Germany and Italy. The subsequent revolutionary ferment in the industrial North and the rural South deeply traumatized Spain's ruling classes. In many respects, the Spanish crisis of 1917–23 is analogous to the Italian crisis of 1917–22. That crisis was merely anaesthetized by the dictatorship of General Primo de Rivera. It re-emerged with greater intensity in the conditions of the economic depression of the 1930s. The belief gained currency in Spain, as it had done earlier in Italy and Germany, that the existing political order could no longer adequately guarantee the economic interests of the middle and upper classes. It was then that the search was renewed for some extraordinary means of defending those interests. Since the Spanish army had already assumed that role in the late nineteenth century, and done so even more after the loss of Cuba in 1898, it was hardly surprising that its services should be called upon in 1917, in 1923 and again in 1936.

It is often pointed out that Spain did not suffer the same crisis of national identity as that undergone by Italy and Germany as a result of the inadequacies of their unification processes and of their respective disappointments in the aftermath of the First World War. On the other hand, the shock of defeat in the Spanish-American War and the loss of the last remnants of empire had far-reaching effects. The Regenerationist movement which grew up in the wake of the disaster had a profound influence on the thinking of the Spanish right well into the Franco years. Nostalgia for empire was common to all rightist groups in the 1930s but was fiercest in the Falange. Falangists openly claimed that imperial conquest was a means of diverting the class struggle and were anxious to join the Axis war effort in order to reopen Spain's imperial account.[23] The main legacy of Regenerationism was the belief that defeat in 1898 was the fault of a political system marked by corruption and incompetence. A better future was associated with a patriotic cleansing of politics and reform imposed from above. Ultimately, this was to breed an anti-parliamentary authoritarianism. Early hopes were pinned on the great conservative politician, Antonio Maura. After his withdrawal from political life his followers, including José Calvo Sotelo and Antonio Goicoechea, switched their allegiance to General Primo de Rivera and were later prominent in Renovación Española. Another line from Regenerationism to the Falange, and particularly the imperialist

---

23 José María de Areilza y Fernando María Castiella, *Reivindicaciones de España* (Madrid, 1941).

emphasis, passed from the philosopher José Ortega y Gasset, via his manic vulgarizer, Ernesto Giménez Caballero, to the dictator's son, José Antonio Primo de Rivera.

A further important difference between Spain, on the one hand, and Italy and Germany, on the other, resides in the fact that Franco was not defeated in an external war and maintained his dictatorship for thirty years after 1945. Since neither Nazism nor Fascism survived, it would be counter-factual absurdity to speculate that either might have evolved as did the Franco regime. Nevertheless, taking into account such unavoidable contrasts as their dissimilar levels of economic growth before 1930, Marshall Plan aid and their post-1945 polities, the similarities between Italy and Spain are eye-catching. To stress them, given these differences, is no doubt an ahistoric exercise. Yet there is an equally ahistorical assumption involved in the comparisons of Franco and Hitler and Mussolini on the basis of the chronological totality of all three regimes. The fact that the Franco regime, in response to changing international realities, evolved away from its overtly pro-Axis position after 1943 is implicitly taken by some commentators retrospectively to absolve Franco from a fascist past that diminished in importance the longer he lived beyond it. It would of course be foolish not to acknowledge that the Franco regime evolved. However, it is equally absurd to assume that the executions, the concentration camps, the imperialist fantasies and the Axis influence on Spanish politics in the 1940s are somehow massaged away by the Opus Dei developmentalism of the 1960s. *Mutatis mutandis*, like should be compared with like. Franco may be deemed not to have been a fascist, in the strictest scientific terms. Nevertheless it has to be considered that, in the light of the scale of the post Civil War repression, he stands comparison with the cruellest dictators of the century, in Latin America as well as Europe.

Broad areas of coincidence arguably outweigh the specific differences between Spain and Italy, if not Germany. This is true not only of the Franco and Mussolini regimes. There are comparisons also to be made between pre-1922 Italian Fascism and the various Spanish rightist groups before 1936, both individually and collectively. It is not simply a question of the ritual trappings associated with fascism, although Roman salutes, strutting, chanting, rallies and paramilitary formations were common enough in Spain before 1936 as they were to be under Franco. There are more interesting comparisons to be made between Spain and Italy, particularly in the light of the far greater differences existing between Italian Fascism and German Nazism. The Unification of 1937 and the emasculation and bureaucratization of the radical Falange had their parallel in the fusion of fascists, nationalists and monarchists in 1923. There are fascinating similarities between the social support, ideological objectives and crucial importance to their respective causes

14

of the agrarian Fascists and the agrarian CEDA.[24] Equally, there are valid comparisons to be made between Renovación Española and the Italian Nationalist Association, both in their relationships to the more radical, populist Falange and Fascist Party and in the disproportionate role that their theorists were later to play in each of the dictatorships.

Nevertheless, the most striking resemblances are to be found between the two regimes. Here again, the liturgical paraphernalia, the militarized rallies in honour of the leadership principle, although they existed in both regimes and were significant, are not the really important similarities. No more so are the ideological coincidences, the glorification of peasant life, the rhetorical quest for the 'new man'. Far more crucial are the similarities based on political, social and economic realities. The areas in which some commentators have seen Mussolini falling short of 'full-scale' fascism, that is to say, of a notional approximation to Nazism, are precisely where his regime coincides with that of Franco. Just as the existence of political and economic pressure groups created a narrowly restricted pluralism under Mussolini, so too did the Franco regime experience a constant jockeying for power and influence between economic interest groups and between generals, Falangists, Catholics, monarchists, the Opus Dei and other political factions. Needless to say, the relationship of forces was far from identical in both countries. Nevertheless, although differing in detail and emphasis, the role of the army, compromise with the church, the harnessing of party radicalism and the subordination of Fascist and Falangist syndicates to business interests all point to the survival of the pre-crisis establishment forces in each case. The rapidity with which Fascists and Falangists were to bewail the failure of their 'revolution' is a clear symptom of the extent to which both regimes, beyond their rhetoric and their professed intentions before gaining power, found their central functions in the protection and fostering of the existing economic order. The biggest difference between Spain and Italy was the importance of the parts played in each country by the army and fascist party in both the seizure of power and the subsequent regime.

In this regard, the opinion of contemporary fascists, both Italian and Spanish, is revealing. Virtually to a man, they accepted that Renovación Española and the CEDA shared the economic, social and political goals of fascism. In that regard, they believed that the conservative right had tried to modernize itself by 'fascistizing' its rhetoric and methods of operation. Where they saw differences was in the élitist disdain for mass mobilization

---

24 Three studies, out of many, on the agrarian origins of Italian fascism, which provoke startling comparisons with the social conflicts of southern Spain and with activities of the CEDA in Old Castile are Paul Corner, *Fascism in Ferrara 1915–1925* (Oxford, 1975); Frank M. Snowden, *The Fascist Revolution in Tuscany 1919–1922* (Cambridge, 1989); Anthony L. Cardoza, *Agrarian Elites and Italian Fascism: The province of Bologna 1901–1926* (Princeton, 1982).

of the monarchists of Renovación Española and in the Vaticanist loyalties of the CEDA. Mussolini did not believe that reliance on the army – which was shared by almost all groups on the Spanish right, including the Falange – was a properly 'fascist' way of proceeding. The Italian ambassador, Raffaele Guariglia, criticized the ideology of the CEDA as 'prehistoric', despite acknowledging that in its success with mass recruiting it might have been the basis for a Spanish fascist party. Guariglia saw José Calvo Sotelo as a 'filofascist'.[25] Gil Robles was, to put it mildly, ambiguous in his attitudes. He visited Italy in January 1933, frequently praised the achievements of Mussolini and permitted his own youth movement, the Juventud de Acción Popular, to behave like a fascist party, with its uniforms, mass rallies and adoption of fascist slogans. However, he had reservations about fascist pantheism. Even so, Gil Robles's participation in the 1933 election campaign during which he spoke of founding a New State and purging the fatherland of 'judaizing freemasons' led José Antonio Primo de Rivera to praise his fascist principles and to applaud the 'fascist warmth' of his style. Yet, in the same prewar parliamentary debate in which Calvo Sotelo declared himself a fascist, Gil Robles expressed doubts about what he saw as fascism's elements of state socialism.[26] For Ramiro Ledesma Ramos, the radical founder of the Juntas de Ofensiva Nacional-Sindicalista, it was a question of traditional conservatives 'fascistizing' themselves, impregnating their rhetoric with fascist elements in order to deceive the masses into supporting them. Even during the Civil War both Mussolini and his first ambassador to Franco, Roberto Cantalupo, were happy to encourage Franco's efforts to 'fascistize' Spain.[27] What this implies is that Calvo Sotelo, Gil Robles and Franco did not merit the seal of approbation of Mussolini or that of Ledesma Ramos. Plainly, none of the three could plausibly emulate the self-perception of Mussolini and Ledesma Ramos as real revolutionaries. That does not wipe away the broad area of coincidence between their social, economic and political ambitions.

Having widened the scrutiny of fascism in Spain beyond the narrow confines of Falange Española, the inquiry should not in any case be limited to the accumulation of similarities between Italy and Spain. Each national counter-revolutionary project must be permitted its individual characteristics. These derived in part from the country's particular traditions of patriotic and conservative rhetoric. More fundamentally, however, the essential character of a given fascist movement and an institutionalized

---

25 Raffaele Guariglia, *Ambasciata in Spagna e primi passi in diplomazia 1932–1934* (Naples, 1972) pp. 259, 321, 347; Ismael Saz Campos, *Mussolini contra la II República* (Valencia, 1986) pp. 51, 57–66.

26 *El Debate*, 17 October 1933; Preston, *CSCW*, p. 214; *Diario de las Sesiones de Cortes*, 19 May 1936.

27 Ramiro Ledesma Ramos, *¿Fascismo en España?* (Barcelona, 1968) pp. 70–3; Saz, *Mussolini contra la II República* p. 222.

fascist regime arose out of the special nature of the crisis that it was their function to resolve. Inevitably, the existence of Soviet communism gave all fascisms a common focus of fear and enmity, just as the vicissitudes of the international economy gave rise to other points of coincidence. Every bit as important as those influences, however, were the national circumstances of social and economic crisis which led to traditional conservative forces being deemed no longer adequate to defend oligarchical interests within bourgeois democracy. The chronological moment at which that happened and the extent to which the threat that they faced came from real or perceived revolution or simply from the achievements of reformist socialism at a time of economic contraction varied from one country to another. Accordingly, any account of a national counter-revolutionary alliance must be informed by an awareness of the nature and development of the corresponding capitalism to which it was linked.

In the fifty years prior to the emergence of fascism Spanish capitalism experienced even greater imbalances than its Italian counterpart.[28] There were modern and dynamic banking and industrial sectors but they were isolated and anything but hegemonic. The dominant force in Spanish capitalism was the agrarian oligarchy. It exerted a virtual monopoly of national politics and, until 1917, controlled an uneven partnership in which industrialists and bankers were the junior partners. That monopoly was built upon the twin pillars of a system of electoral falsification based on the social power of local landlords and the repressive power of the forces of order: the Civil Guard and, at moments of greater tension, the army. Challenges to the system arose in the wake of the country's industrialization. Despairing rural uprisings were supplanted by the strike actions of a militant industrial proletariat. However, when the inevitable explosion came, it was precipitated not by the working class but by the industrial bourgeoisie. The economic boom consequent upon Spain's economically advantageous position as a neutral during the First World War saw coalmine-owners, steel barons, shipbuilders, and textile magnates enjoying the takeoff of Spanish industry. The balance of power within the economic élite shifted somewhat. Agrarian interests remained pre-eminent but industrialists were no longer prepared to tolerate their subordinate political position and even toyed with making a bid for political modernization.

The reforming ambitions of industrialists and bankers enriched by the war coincided with an intensification of militancy amongst a proletariat impoverished by wartime shortages and inflation. The Socialist Unión General de Trabajadores and the anarcho-syndicalist Confederación

---

28 There is a growing bibliography on the agrarian problem and capitalist underdevelopment in Spain. For a provocative recent survey, see Enrique Prieto, *Agricultura y atraso en la España contemporánea* (Madrid, 1988).

Nacional del Trabajo were drawn into an uneasy revolutionary alliance in the hope that a joint general strike would overthrow a corrupt system. While industrialists and workers pushed for change, middle-rank army officers were protesting at low wages, antiquated promotion structures and the political corruption which they blamed for colonial defeat and military inefficiency. Voicing their complaints in the rhetoric of 1898 Regenerationism, the officers were acclaimed as the figureheads of a great national reform movement. Had the movement been united in purpose it might well have supplanted the Restoration system and established a democratic polity capable of permitting social adjustment and defusing the embittered class conflicts of the day. As it was, its contradictions were easily exploited by the establishment. The officers were peeled off from the reform movement by concessions on their complaints about pay and the promotions system. The UGT and the CNT were split by the skilful provocation of a premature strike of socialist railway workers. Again at peace with the system, the army was happy to defend it in August 1917 by crushing the striking socialists, thereby causing considerable bloodshed. Alarmed by the prospect of proletarian revolution, industrialists and bankers muted their own demands for political reform and, lured by promises of economic modernization, joined in a national coalition government in 1918 with the old oligarchical Liberal and Conservative Parties. The readiness with which the army had protected the system ensured that the great revolutionary crisis of 1917 led merely to a readjustment of the power balance between the landed oligarchy and the industrial and banking bourgeoisie.[29]

The fact that the industrial bourgeoisie renewed its partnership with the landed oligarchy guaranteed that, from 1918 onwards, Spain would be divided starkly into two fiercely hostile social groups, with landowners and industrialists on one side and workers and landless labourers on the other. For five years, until the army intervened again, social ferment sporadically reached the scale of undeclared civil war. During the 'three bolshevik years' from 1918 to 1921 uprisings by anarchist day-labourers in the South were put down by the combination of the Civil Guard and the army. In the North too, as industrialists in Catalonia, the Basque country and Asturias tried to ride the immediate postwar recession with wage cuts and lay-offs, there were violent strikes and, in Barcelona, a terrorist spiral of provocations and reprisals.[30] The Restoration political system was perceived as having ceased to be an adequate mechanism for defending the economic interests of the ruling classes. At this point, the

29 Juan Antonio Lacomba Avellán, *La crisis española de 1917* (Madrid, 1970); Carolyn Boyd, *Praetorian Politics in Liberal Spain* (Chapel Hill, 1979); pp. 44–93; Gerald H. Meaker, *The Revolutionary Left in Spain 1914–1923* (Stanford, 1974), pp. 62–98.
30 A revealing, often inadvertently so, account of the yellow union, the *Sindicatos Libres*, which contributed considerably to the break-down of law and order in Barcelona,

army intervened again, a *coup d'état* being carried out by General Primo de Rivera.[31]

As Captain-General of Barcelona, intimate of Catalan textile barons and himself a large southern landowner, Primo was the ideal praetorian defender of the reactionary coalition of industrialists and landowners consolidated after 1917. Primo's regime was mildly repressive, outlawing the CNT, but securing Socialist co-operation. Moreover, the dictatorship enjoyed a degree of prosperity deriving partly from a general European upturn but also from a massive investment in infrastructural development. Accordingly, the Primo de Rivera period came to be regarded in later years as a golden age by the Spanish middle and upper classes. The idea of a successful military monarchy became a central myth of the reactionary right, cherished by the ideologues of Francoism.[32] Ironically, its short-term effect was to discredit the idea of authoritarianism in Spain. Primo's attempt to perpetuate his authoritarian system by means of a single party, the Unión Patriótica, was a resounding failure although it did provide a link from the military monarchy to the right-wing parties of the Second Republic.[33] In addition to his failure to create an enduring apparatus of authoritarianism, the dictator's amiably paternalist improvisations inadvertently alienated landowners, industrialists, the church hierarchy and some of the élite officer corps of the army. A window of opportunity opened for the left. Crucially, Primo's attempts to reform the military and in particular .to standardize promotion machinery ensured that the army would stand aside when a great coalition of socialists and middle-class Republicans swept to power on 14 April 1931.

The nostalgic rightists who had served the dictatorship were impelled to reflect on the importance of the army. Through the journal *Acción Española* and the party Renovación Española, they were to form the general staff of the extreme right in the Second Republic and were to provide much of the ideological content of the Franco regime. It was not lost on them that the army had defended rightist interests in

---

is Colin M. Winston, *Workers and the Right in Spain, 1900–1936* (Princeton, 1985). See also León-Ignacio, *Los años del pistolerismo* (Barcelona, 1981); Manuel Casal Gómez, *'La Banda negra': el orígen y la actuación de los pistoleros en Barcelona (1918–1921)* (Barcelona, 1977); Angel Pestaña, *Terrorismo en Barcelona: memorias inéditas* (Barcelona, 1979).

31 On the coup, see the recent study by Javier Tusell, *Radiografía de un golpe de Estado: el ascenso al Poder del general Primo de Rivera* (Madrid, 1987). On the regime, see Shlomo Ben Ami, *Fascism from Above: The Dictatorship of Primo de Rivera in Spain 1923–1930* (Oxford, 1983).

32 The Primo de Rivera dictatorship was seen as 'the selfless effort of one man to save Spain from the chaos of democracy', *Acción Española*, 1 February 1932: Eduardo Aunós, *Primo de Rivera: soldado y gobernante* (Madrid, 1944); Raúl Morodo, *Los orígenes ideológicos del franquismo: Acción Española* (Madrid, 1985), pp. 31–9.

33 José María Pemán, *El hecho y la idea de Unión Patriótica* (Madrid, 1929); Shlomo Ben Ami, 'The forerunners of Spanish Fascism: Unión Patriótica and Unión Monárquica', *European Studies Review*, vol. 9, no. 1, January 1979.

1917 and 1923 and, by failing to do so in 1931, permitted the bloodless establishment of the Republic. Accordingly, they began to court the army, directing their efforts to persuading officers that an uprising was both legitimate and necessary. The failure of Primo's dictatorship had found the upper classes temporarily bereft of political formations capable of defending them from the adjustment of social and political privilege implicit in the coming of the Republic. The political strategists of the right were determined that the same mistake should not be repeated. After all, the consequences of military passivity in 1931 were enormous. The elections of April and June 1931 saw political power pass to the socialists and their urban middle-class allies, the republican lawyers and intellectuals. They intended to use this suddenly acquired share of state power to create a modern Spain by destroying the reactionary influence of the church and the army but, above all, by far-reaching agrarian reform. This was intended not only to improve the immediate conditions of the wretched *braceros* but also to create a prosperous peasantry as a future market for Spanish industry.

In this sense the Republic was potentially the agent of the economic take-off that Spain's bankers, merchants and industrialists had been historically incapable of realizing. Yet the new regime could not count on their support. This was partly because of the close historic ties between industry and land which had been intensified during the revolutionary upheavals of 1917–23. It was also a reflection of the immediate conditions of the Second Republic. The combination of a context of world depression and a substantial increase in the size and influence of trade unions was hardly likely to encourage adventurism among industrialists. In Catalonia and the Basque country the enthusiasm for the Republic's reformism and federalism among liberal intellectuals and regional nationalists was not shared by the economic élites. At best there was some grudging tolerance for the Republic among the more progressive light industrialists. However, their tentative welcome to the Republic, extended with trepidation and often instantaneous regret, was countered by the reactions of the *hautes bourgeoisies* of Catalonia and the Basque country.[34] Most industrialists and bankers agreed with the rightist press that the Republic was a dangerous revolutionary regime. This was confirmed both by the legal activities of industrial employers' pressure groups which were disruptive and subversive and by the fact that Basque industrialists were almost as prominent

---

34 Bernat Muniesa, *La burguesía catalana ante la II República española*, 2 vols (Barcelona, 1985), Vol. I, pp. 180–255 and Vol. II, *passim*; Antoni Jutglar, *Historia crítica de la burguesía en Cataluña* (Barcelona, 1984), pp. 437–58; Manuel González Portilla and José María Garmendia, *La guerra civil en el País Vasco* (Madrid, 1988) pp. 84–94; Manuel González Portilla and José María Garmendia, *La Posguerra en el País Vasco: política, acumulación, miseria* (San Sebastián, 1988), *passim*.

as landowners in the financing of both Renovación Española and the Falange.[35]

Thus the Republic faced the unremitting hostility of both partners in Spain's reactionary coalition. The economic power of industrialists and landowners remained undiminished by the transition from monarchy to Republic. On the other hand, they had lost their monopoly of political power and were determined to use all the social and economic weapons at their disposal to regain their control of the apparatus of the state. As a result of the relatively honest elections of 1931 the working classes and the urban petty bourgeoisie were now in a position to fulfil their minimal social and political aspirations. Within months of the foundation of the new regime, the Republican-socialist coalition government had introduced reforms which fundamentally challenged the pre-1931 social and economic structure. The intention behind this initial social legislation had been to alleviate the misery of the southern day-labourers or *braceros*. However, the inefficient latifundia system depended for its economic survival on the existence of a reserve army of *braceros* paid starvation wages. The introduction of the eight-hour day where previously men had worked from sun-up to sun-down, and of arbitration committees to regulate wages and working conditions, infuriated the *latifundistas*. With the depression forcing down agricultural prices, the consequent wage increases, minimal though they were, signified a potentially significant redistribution of wealth. Traditional means of keeping wages down, the introduction of cheap outside labour and the rural lock-out, were rendered difficult by the decrees of municipal boundaries and obligatory cultivation. With day-labourers flooding into the UGT's Landworkers' Federation and UGT leader Francisco Largo Caballero as Minister of Labour, the southern landowners felt as besieged as did those of the Po valley when faced with the ambitious advances of the Federterra after the First World War.[36]

Although Catalan textile manufacturers and light industrialists benefited from the increase in the peasantry's disposable income, heavy industrialists in the Basque country and mine-owners from Asturias were as badly hit as the *latifundistas* by the depression and by the increase in trade union power and confidence. They rapidly began to seek new ways of defending economic interests which had never before been subject to legal threats such as those mounted by the Republic. The methods adopted to combat the problems posed by the establishment of a functioning mass democracy took two forms, one legal, the other violent. Despite the

---

35 Mercedes Cabrera, *La patronal ante la II República: organizaciones y estrategia* (Madrid, 1983), pp. 274–86; Javier Jiménez Campo, *El fascismo en la crisis de la segunda República española* (Madrid, 1979), pp. 197–215.
36 Paul Preston, 'The agrarian war in the south' in Paul Preston (ed.), *Revolution and War in Spain 1931–1939* (London, 1984); Manuel Pérez Yruela, *La conflictividad campesina en la provincia de Córdoba 1931–1936* (Madrid, 1979), pp. 108–214.

ostensible differences between them, especially in terms of day-to-day tactics, their overall strategies were complementary and their long-term objectives virtually identical. The legal defence of oligarchical interests involved the mobilization of a mass rightist movement to match the numerical strength of the left. That led eventually to the creation of the Catholic authoritarian Confederación Española de Derechas Autónomas. In contrast to its attempt to gain power and establish a corporative state by electoral means, the so-called 'catastrophists', the Carlists, the monarchists of Renovación Española and the Falange were explicitly committed to the outright destruction of the parliamentary regime.

Given the bitterness of class conflict in Spain, there was never much possibility of any significant section of the working classes being mobilized by rightist groups. All efforts made in that direction during the Second Republic were failures. The one substantial social group that was susceptible to right-wing manipulation consisted of the rural lower middle classes. Efforts to mobilize smallholders against the rising power of the urban and rural working class had already achieved considerable success. The Confederación Nacional Católico-Agraria, financed by big landowners, had half a million members before the Primo de Rivera dictatorship seemed to render it superfluous.[37] Its influence was, however, inherited by Acción Nacional, a mass Catholic political organization founded within a week of the fall of the monarchy and devoted to resistance against any change in the religious, social, or economic order. Under the dynamic leadership of the young monarchist, José María Gil Robles, Acción Popular, as it became in 1932, undertook blanket propagandda campaigns to convince the conservative smallholders that the Republic's attempts to break the social power of the Church constituted outright religious persecution and that projected agrarian reform was directed at them as much as at the big landowners.

Vast sums of money were spent convincing these poor but proud farmers that the Republic would proletarianize them. When Acción Popular absorbed similar rightist organizations in early 1933 and became the CEDA, it could count its support in millions. These supporters were consistently presented with the most virulently anti-Republican propaganda as part of a process whereby they were being groomed to fight the left for what Gil Robles called 'possession of the street'. Mass rallies were staged at which the audiences were pushed to rabid hostility to the parliamentary regime. In 1937, and also in his memoirs, Gil Robles claimed that the reserves of anti-Republican belligerence thus created made possible Franco's Civil War victory.[38] Despite the intensity of its anti-Republicanism the CEDA

---

37   The outstanding study of the CNCA is Juan José Castillo, *Propietarios muy pobres: sobre la subordinación política del pequeño campesino* (Madrid, 1979).

38   *Sur* (Málaga) 25, 28 April 1937; Gil Robles, *No fue posible*, pp. 64–5, 719, 728–30.

remained within the bounds of legality. However, an open admiration for both Italian fascism and German Nazism indicated the fragility of its legalism. Hitler and Mussolini were admired for fulfilling the tasks that the CEDA had set itself: the destruction of socialism and communism, the abolition of liberal parliamentarism and the establishment of the corporative state.[39]

Gil Robles's short-term aim was to block the reforming ambitions of the Republic. Before his considerable electoral success in 1933, this was done by a skilful programme of parliamentary filibustering. Afterwards, when he had sufficient strength to control the policies of a series of Radical and Radical-CEDA ministries, it took the form of a sweeping abolition of the Republic's social legislation. Gil Robles's objective before the 1933 elections had been the legal establishment of the corporative state as a permanent defence against the left. When his victory was insufficient he switched to the more sinuous tactic of gradually breaking up the Radical Party by means of a series of well-orchestrated cabinet crises, in the hope that he would eventually be called upon to form a government. At the same time the savage reversal of working-class living standards was a second string to his bow. If a left-wing rising could be provoked a corporative state could be imposed in the aftermath of its suppression.[40] In the event, the insurrection of October 1934 was put down with such difficulty that hopes for a rapid introduction of the corporative state were dropped in favour of a return to the slower legalist tactic. Gil Robles's hopes were finally dashed in late 1935 when a miscalculated cabinet crisis led not to his becoming prime minister but to the calling of elections.[41]

The relative success of Gil Robles in reasserting the pre-1931 social order created the left-wing unity that was to be the foundation of the Popular Front's electoral victory in February 1936. The Asturian insurrection of October 1934 had already indicated the impossibility of a peaceful imposition of a corporative state. The Popular Front elections signified the definitive failure of the CEDA's efforts to use democracy against itself. Henceforth the landed and industrial oligarchies sought a less hazardous and permanent form of protection. They began to switch their financial support to the 'catastrophist' right. At the same time the uniformed masses of the CEDA's radical youth movement began to flood into the Falange and, to a lesser extent, the Carlist movement.[42] The paymasters of catastrophism, of course, had pinned their hopes on the army.

39 *El Debate*, 4, 17, 25 August 1933, 2, 8, 10, 11, 22 March 1934.
40 Gil Robles, *No fue posible*, p. 131; Preston, *CSCW*, pp. 122–6.
41 Joaquín Chapaprieta Torregrosa, *La paz fue posible: memorias de un político* (Barcelona, 1971) pp. 207–332; Preston, *CSCW*, pp. 162–9.
42 Payne, *Falange*, pp. 104–5; Blinkhorn, *Carlism*, p. 257; Ramón Serrano Suñer, *Entre Hendaya y Gibraltar* (Madrid, 1947), p. 25.

The end of illusions about the legal establishment of corporativism by the CEDA gave a welcome lease of life to the ailing Falange. It made little difference to the other 'catastrophist' organizations, Renovación Española and the Carlist Comunión Tradicionalista, except to confirm what they had long predicted. The Carlists in particular were little affected by day-to-day developments in Republican politics. Maniacally anti-modern and devoted to the establishment of a theocratic monarchy, their commitment to the violent destruction of the laic Republic was unswerving. Locked in their Navarrese strongholds, they tended to stand aloof from the rest of the right, although they did make two significant contributions to it. The more obvious was the provision of their fanatical militia, the *Requeté*, to the right-wing cause in the Civil War. The less obvious one was to provide a body of indigenous reactionary doctrine which permitted other rightists to defend fashionable authoritarian and fascist notions as authentically Spanish.[43]

Gil Robles's defeat provided the context for the military rising to which the main activities of Renovación Española were directed. Like Gil Robles and José Antonio Primo de Rivera, its leaders had been members of Primo's Unión Patriótica and of the Unión Monárquica Nacional, founded in 1930 to fill the gap left by the demise of the oligarchical parties of the restoration period. Once young activists of the pre-1923 monarchical political élite, they believed that the monarchy failed because it was tainted with liberal constitutionalism. Accordingly, they sought new means of defending upper-class interests. Devotees of General Primo de Rivera, their ideal was a corporative state under a military monarchy although they were receptive to other solutions to the problem of the rise of the left-wing masses. Sporting a small radical youth movement and even belonging to Acción Popular until late 1932, the authoritarian monarchists were repelled by populist politics and inclined towards incisive and élitist schemes to deal with the leftist threat. Renovación Española was thus conceived of as a front organization to spread the idea of the legitimacy of a military rising against the Republic, to inject a spirit of rebellion into the army and to provide a cover for fund-raising, arms purchases and conspiracy. That the defence of the social order had priority over the preservation of the monarchy was made clear by the group's plans for the future, which were a remarkably prophetic blueprint for the Franco regime. Intensely sympathetic to Italian fascism, Eduardo Aunós and José Calvo Sotelo had travelled widely in search of models for the defence of the existing order and had returned enthusiastic advocates of the corporative regimentation of labour and the economy.[44] However, their disdain for

---

43 Blinkhorn, *Carlism*, pp. 141–82.
44 Preston, 'Alfonsine monarchism', pp. 103–4; Eduardo Aunós, *Calvo Sotelo y la política de su tiempo* (Madrid, 1941), pp. 115–55.

the masses, whom they held responsible for the excesses of democracy, restrained any inclination that they might have had towards full-scale fascist populism.

It was not surprising that members of the Renovación Española group should be happy to subsidize the Falange. Having no mass base themselves, the monarchists saw the Falange as potential cannon fodder for street fighting with the left and as an instrument of political destabilization to spread an atmosphere of insecurity and provide justification for a military rising.[45] In addition, the presence of the dictator's son José Antonio at the head of the Falange was a useful guarantee to industrialists and particularly to landowners. The sort of reassurance that the aristocratic young Primo de Rivera provided to southern landlords was duplicated for the Basque *haute bourgeoisie* by the wealthy Bilbao engineer José Maria de Areilza. In fact, for all its anti-conservative rhetoric, the limits of Falangist radicalism were clear enough. The more outspoken lumpenproletariat elements from the Juntas de Ofensiva Nacional-Sindicalista, with which the Falange merged in early 1934, were quickly brought under control. Moreover, even Jonsista criticisms of the moral and spiritual mediocrity of the bourgeois establishment never extended into attacks on the capitalist system of production. The emptiness of the Falange's revolutionary sloganizing was revealed by its participation in the repression of the left after the October 1934 rising and, most blatantly, by its role in the Civil War.[46]

Before 1936 the Falange was unable to develop a significant mass following because its natural constituency, the rural lower middle classes, had already been recruited by the CEDA. It was to lose the financial backing of the monarchists of Renovación Española, not because of any rhetorical left-wing sloganizing, but simply because of the personal rivalries between José Antonio Primo de Rivera and José Calvo Sotelo. Although other allegedly radical elements of the Falange were happy to do so, José Antonio refused to join Calvo Sotelo's rightist coalition, the Bloque Nacional. Ramiro Ledesma Ramos, for instance, was not so intransigent as to refuse the gift of a motor bike from the monarchists.[47] Unable to recruit the masses and shorn of financial support, the Falange managed to survive in part thanks to cash from the Italian government, although this should not be taken as an exclusive seal of fascist approval since both the Carlists and Renovación Española were also objects of Mussolini's goodwill.[48]

---

45 For a wider theoretical discussion of the relationship between traditional conservatives and radical fascisms, see Mayer, *Dynamics*, pp. 98–101.
46 Ricardo Chueca, *El fascismo en los comienzos del régimen de Franco: Un estudio sobre FET-JONS* (Madrid, 1983) *passim*; Ellwood, *Spanish Fascism*, pp. 29–47.
47 Ismael Saz, 'Tres acotaciones a propósito de los origenes, desarrollo y crisis del fascismo español' in *Revista de Estudios Políticos* (Madrid) Nueva Epoca, No. 50, Marzo-Abril 1986; Pedro Sainz Rodríguez, *Testimonio y recuerdos* (Barcelona, 1978), p. 220.
48 Saz, *Mussolini contra la II República*, pp. 64–85.

While the Falange was in the doldrums the main burden of oligarchical effort was directed towards bringing the CEDA masses within the more aggressive orbit of Renovación Española. This was to be done through the device of the Bloque Nacional. Under the leadership of Calvo Sotelo the Bloque Nacional in theory perfectly anticipated the Francoist Unificación. In practice, both Gil Robles and José Antonio Primo de Rivera stood aside. There was a strong element of personal rivalry at work in this. José Antonio resented the way in which Calvo Sotelo had stolen his ideological baggage in advocating fascist solutions to the Spanish crisis. Aristocratic disdain was revealed in his judgement that Calvo Sotelo could never lead a movement of national salvation because of his inadequate horsemanship.[49] Personal friction also existed between Gil Robles and Calvo Sotelo. However, if formal unity was hindered by personal considerations, the left-wing triumph in the elections of Feburary 1936 created a context in which practical unity became an urgent necessity.

The left was now determined to carry out the reforms which had been so successfully thwarted by the CEDA. The obvious challenge to oligarchical interests led to a remarkable closing of ranks on the right. Renovación Española's leadership intensified pressure for military intervention and diverted funds to the Falange for a programme of political destabilization. Attacks on the left by the Falange and members of the Juventud de Acción Popular were used by Gil Robles and Calvo Sotelo as the basis for spine-chilling parliamentary speeches which alleged that Spain was in the grip of anarchy. The middle and upper classes were thereby terrorized into a belief that only the army could save them. The roles of Carlists, Falangists and Renovación Española in the final preparations for the long-awaited catastrophe were almost predictable. More interesting was the behaviour of the CEDA. Although it was the most successful mass political party of the right, and had been created specifically to counter the left in the electoral arena, when the crisis came, most of its leaders and the bulk of its rank and file reverted to the reflex response of the Spanish right under threat. Along with the catastrophists who had been trying to pave the way for a *coup d'état*, they turned to the army. Having once accepted that legalism had failed, Gil Robles did nothing to stop the flow of his followers to more extreme organizations. He handed over the CEDA's electoral funds to the army conspirators and ordered the party's rank and file to place itself under military orders as soon as the rising began. He praised fascist violence as a patriotic response to the alleged crimes of the left. Although much praised for his legalism, Gil Robles did

49   Ramiro Ledesma Ramos, *¿Fascismo en España?*, 2nd edn (Barcelona, 1968) pp. 161–5; Ian Gibson, *En busca de José Antonio* (Barcelona, 1980), p. 108; Payne, *Falange*, pp. 61–8; Juan Antonio Ansaldo, *¿Para qué. . .? (de Alfonso XIII a Juan III* (Buenos Aires, 1951), pp. 76–8.

not hesitate to throw his weight behind those who aimed to establish the authoritarian corporative state by violence.

The smooth orchestration of the efforts of both 'catastrophists' and legalists in the spring of 1936 induced many on the left to see the CEDA, Renovación Española, the Carlists and the Falange as regiments in the same army. Throughout the Republic, leaders of each rightist group had addressed the meetings of the others and had usually been well received. Space was made available in party newspapers for favourable reports on the activities of rivals. All sections of the right shared the same determination to establish a corporative state and to destroy the effective forces of the left. They were all the servants of the landed and heavy industrial oligarchies in so far as they depended on them for financial backing, and all their political activities were directed towards the protection of oligarchical interests. There were, of course, differences of opinion and they occasionally led to public polemic. Nevertheless, they rarely went beyond discussions over tactics, and then usually over what seemed to the others to be the excessive legalism of the CEDA. These groups rarely broke unity in parliament, at election times or, most crucially, during the Civil War – a stark contrast with the divisions that split the left both in peace and in war. Indeed, it was not uncommon, particularly among the provincial rural bourgeoisie, to belong to more than one, or in some cases all, of these organizations.

Both separately and together, all these groups constituted attempts to resolve the crisis in which the Spanish landed and industrial oligarchies found themselves as a result of left-wing pressure for change. The acuteness of that crisis was partly a consequence of the international situation but it was even more the result of the landed oligarchy's success in holding back change for nearly a century. After the collapse of restoration politics and the ultimate failure of the Primo de Rivera dictatorship new methods had to be sought to defend oligarchical privilege. It is primarily in this sense that the rightist organizations may be seen variously, and after February 1936 in conjunction, as manifestations of the peculiar Spanish counter-revolutionary alliance. The primordial role of the army has sometimes been seen as suggesting that the nationalist uprising was not in any meaningful sense fascist. In fact, like other sections of the traditional right, the army had, to an extent, allowed itself to be 'fascistized'. Some army officers were card-carrying Falangists, the conspiratorial organization Unión Militar Española was unashamedly fascist in its rhetoric and, throughout the Civil War, the politics of the army were indistinguishable from contemporary fascisms.

Various differences and similarities between the Italian and Spanish experiences have already been outlined. One crucial difference which underscores similarities in other areas is the fact that the Spanish crisis came to a head fourteen years after Mussolini attained power. The Spanish left had learnt the lesson of Italy, as it had learnt those of Portugal, Germany and Austria. There was no possibility of breaking the left with skirmishing *squadristi* in Spain. The Civil War was, in that context, the inevitable culmination of the attempt to impose adequate counter-revolutionary, authoritarian solutions, in more or less fascist style, to the Spanish crisis. In other words, not only historical tradition and existing patterns of civil–military relations, but also the strength of the Spanish working class and its determination to resist what it saw as fascism, dictated that the principal role in the defence of right-wing interests would be played by the army.

The fact that in the event the defence of the oligarchy led to all-out war inevitably gave the army an influence in the Franco regime that was not paralleled in Italy. For this reason the rhetoric of anti-oligarchical novelty was rather more subdued under Franco than under Mussolini. Nevertheless, with the rightist groups of the prewar period formally united into a single party, the Franco regime achieved the goals to which they all aspired – the corporative state, the abolition of free trade unions, the destruction of the left-wing press and political parties. Large numbers of working-class cadres were executed and many more put into concentration camps. The social domination of the big landlords was restored intact. Francoist economic policy in the 1940s consistently favoured the landed oligarchy, as was only to be expected.[50] This identification with the traditional oligarchy is one reason why the Franco regime is often assumed not to have been fascist. The continuing political dominance of the Spanish army throughout the dictatorship is another. However, it should not be forgotten that the officer corps was swamped by Falangists during the Civil War or that important regime functions, press, propaganda and syndical organization were in the hands of the Falange until the 1970s.

It is not without irony therefore that the Franco dictatorship, inadvertently fulfilling the modernizing function associated with fascist regimes, was to preside over the eclipse of the landed oligarchy and the final triumph of the industrial oligarchy. The repressive labour relations of the regime led to an accumulation of capital; its rabid anti-communism led to American aid. The combination of the two, in the favourable context of the late 1950s, led to Spain's second, and definitive, industrial take-off. By the 1970s the industrial élite came to regard the Franco regime as an irksome anachronism. Accordingly, industrialists and bankers were to be found coinciding with the democratic opposition in the quest for change. A right which had been sufficiently ruthless and versatile to use both Falangists and soldiers had changed. To safeguard the economic development of the

---

50 Eduardo Sevilla Guzmán, *La evolución del campesinado en España* (Barcelona, 1979), pp. 149–76.

1960s and 1970s the oligarchy was prepared to contemplate co-operation with the moderate left to permit the establishment of democracy. It is hardly surprising that bewildered ultra-rightist civilians and Falangist army officers huddled together in defence of a rhetorically fascist concept of the regime and in defiance of the wishes of the overwhelming majority of the population.

2

The politics of revenge: Francoism, the Civil War and collective memory

The historiography of modern Spain has been concerned with three major issues – the origins of the Spanish Civil War, the course of the Spanish Civil War and the aftermath of the Spanish Civil War. In the interior, history under the Francoist dictatorship was a direct instrument of the state, written by policemen, soldiers and priests, invigilated by the powerful censorship machinery. It was the continuation of the war by other means, an effort to justify the military uprising, the war and the subsequent repression.[1] In contrast, among Republican emigrés and in the oblique writings of those who wrote from a kind of internal exile, there was an all-consuming quest for an explanation, rather than a justification, of the national tragedy. Examinations were undertaken of the Spanish 'mind', to explain the country's plethora of civil wars. Apparent continuities were easy enough to find. The idea that political problems are best settled by violence is a commonplace of Spanish history and literature. The aridity of the land, the harshness of the climate and the stark division of the country by mountain ranges were grist to the mill of this kind of *Kulturgeschichte*. Pre-Civil War political discourse was peppered with a vocabulary of bloody struggle and exhilarating conquest, legacies both of the reconquest of Spain from the Moors and of the colonial experience. The imagery of a broken Spain and of two Spains was habitual in the nineteenth century.

The consequent cultural/national character interpretations provided implicitly, and sometimes explicitly, teleological versions of Spain's history, characterizing the national past in terms of a propensity to pitiless blood-lust and savage discord. They fed off the similar attempts by the

---

1   See my article 'War of words: the Spanish Civil War and the historians' in Paul Preston (ed.), *Revolution and War in Spain 1931–1939* (London and New York, 1984). The most penetrating examination of Francoist historiography remains Herbert R. Southworth, *El mito de la cruzada de Franco* (Paris, 1963).

'generation of 1898' to grapple with the so-called *problema nacional*. The turmoil of frequent civil wars in the nineteenth century, the revolution of 1868, the chaos of the First Republic in 1873 and the loss of Cuba in 1898 had stimulated an endless picking through the national entrails. Spanish history was presented variously as an eternal contest between the orthodox and the heterodox, between Spain and anti-Spain, between the traditional and the modern, between *hispanidad* and *europeismo*, between Catholic and liberal values. After the Civil War of 1936–9 such brooding speculations were renewed with greater intensity. Among exiled Republicans it produced the monumental scholarly polemics of Américo Castro and Claudio Sánchez Albornoz.[2] The concerns of historians and philosophers were a reflection of those of the population as a whole. The scale of the trauma caused by the war rendered these later obsessions entirely comprehensible. They bore fruit even among repentant Falangist intellectuals.[3]

Less serious but altogether more pervasive were the products of regime propagandists who delved into the writings of 1898 at random for their own partisan selection of the cultural and racial components of 'Spanishness'. They found their most extreme forms in two pro-Francoist interpretations of Spain's history emanating from the Falange and the church. For the Falangists, what the past proved was that 'the Spanish way of being has always, in the finest hours of its history, been struggle'.[4] The idea that deep in the national character lay a propensity to exaltation, paroxysm, impetuousness, violence and aggression was joyfully reiterated by Francoist propagandists. The Caudillo and the Falange had seized upon it during, and in the immediate aftermath of, the Civil War when an Axis-dominated world order seemed to be in the offing. It was fashionable to claim that the spirit which made the Civil War possible and which indeed secured victory for the Nationalists was one of imperialist conquest which harked back to the greatest days of Spain's history.[5] This linked up with the vision of the more militant clergy that the Civil War had been a religious war, a

---

2 An intriguing albeit vehemently partisan survey of such polemics can be found in Vicente Marrero, *La guerra española y el trust de cerebros* (Madrid, 1961), especially pp. 366–7. See also Salvador de Madariaga, *Spain: A Modern History* (London, 1961); Claudio Sánchez Albornoz, *España, un enigma histórico*, 2 vols (Buenos Aires, 1957); Américo Castro, *La realidad histórica de España*, 2nd edn (México D. F., 1962); Martin Blinkhorn, 'Spain: the "Spanish problem" and the imperial myth' in *Journal of Contemporary History*, vol. 15, no. 1, 1980.

3 Pedro Laín Entralgo, *España como problema*, 2nd edn (Madrid, 1957); Dionisio Ridruejo, *Escrito en España* (Buenos Aires, 1961); Pedro Laín Entralgo, *Descargo de conciencia (1930–1960)* (Barcelona, 1976).

4 Marrero, *La guerra*, p. 473; Ernesto Giménez Caballero, *Genio de España*, 7th edn (Madrid, 1971), pp. 167–78.

5 José María de Areilza and Fernando María Castiella, *Reivindicaciones de España* (Madrid, 1941) p. 23.

vision underwritten by a narrow interpretation of the past as a series of crusades.[6]

That was also, in 1939, a view shared by the Vatican. The telegram of congratulation from the newly elected Pius XII to Franco on his victory made identical historical assumptions: 'Lifting up our hearts to God, we sincerely thank Your Excellency for the desired Catholic victory in Spain. We pray that this most beloved country, once again at peace, will return with renewed vigour to the ancient and Christian traditions which made her great.' In an effusive broadcast message to the Spanish people on 16 April 1939 the pope declared that

the designs of Providence, beloved children, have once more been made manifest over heroic Spain. The nation chosen by God as the principal instrument of the evangelization of the new world and as the impregnable bulwark of the Catholic faith has just given the proselytes of materialist atheism in our century the most sublime proof that the eternal values of religion and the spirit rise above all else.[7]

Although in fact diplomatic relations between Madrid and the Vatican were decidely cool at this time these messages were taken as a seal of approval for a savage repression presented as an effort to rechristianize Spain. The most obvious successes by way of rechristianization were chalked up by prison chaplains. They secured the confessions and sometimes the conversions of condemned men who were thus deemed to have died in a state of grace.[8]

The more or less racist vision which linked the Civil War to the crusading spirit of the wars between Christians and Moors and to the evangelical imperialism of the conquest of America was to be inflicted on Spanish society with varying intensity for more than twenty years under the banner of *Hispanidad*. The Falange's corporative structures, the military's obsession with national unity, the regime's militant Catholicism could all be wrapped up in archaic liturgies and justified by the notions of *Hispanidad* as somehow linked to a timeless national destiny.[9] Eventually, as a side effect of the renewal and expansion of universities which accompanied the process of economic modernization in Spain, a more empirical

---

6 Félix G. Olmedo, *El sentido de la guerra de España* (Bilbao, 1938), pp. 18-19.

7 Norman B. Cooper, *Catholicism and the Franco Regime* (Beverly Hills, 1975), p. 12; Antonio Marquina Barrio, *La diplomacia Vaticana y la España de Franco 1936-1945* (Madrid, 1983), pp. 159–60.

8 The most malignant statement of this view may be found in F. Martín Torrent, *¿Qué me dice Usted de los presos?* (Barcelona, 1942), *passim*. On the death row conversions, see *ibid.*, pp. 67–79.

9 See Eduardo González Calleja and Fredes Limón Nevado, *La Hispanidad como instrumento de combate: raza e imperio en la prensa franquista durante la guerra civil española* (Madrid, 1988).

and less philosophical approach to the past began to challenge regime historiography, albeit within the confines of the censorship. Nevertheless, even then, most works of history and philosophy either focused on, or existed in the shadow of, the Civil War.[10] The underlying anxiety was redolent of the comparable German obsession with the long-term origins of the Third Reich. However, there was an important difference. Spanish destructiveness was contained within the national boundaries and inflicted on Spaniards themselves, unlike the more widely cast German variant, with the result that the consequent trauma was one of pain rather than of guilt. That is one important reason why it is difficult to imagine the Spanish historical profession being rent asunder by the sort of *Historikerstreit* which has caused such controversy in West Germany.[11]

For the Spaniards, denied liberation in 1945, the question of coming to terms with the past has been rendered difficult by the fact that 'the past' continued for nearly forty years after the war's conclusion and indeed beyond. It was a deliberate policy of the dictatorship that it should be so. One of the earliest and most perceptive of the cultural historians, José Castillejo, had foreseen that when he wrote that 'war, panic, hatred, misery and the recollection of hideous crimes are sure to hamper freedom for a long time'.[12] Fear of a repetition of civil war vied with unrequited desires for a settling of old scores. In the event the general urge after the death of Franco to contribute by whatever means, first to the re-establishment, and then to the consolidation, of democracy had its effect on the historical profession as it did on the population at large. The renunciation of revenge was an unspoken agreement across the entire political spectrum with the exception of the lunatic fringes. This 'pact of oblivion' found its reflection among the historians in a cautious determination to avoid judgements which might suggest grounds for a settling of accounts.[13] The shadows of the Civil War and of the Francoist repression hang over Spain but they do not lour as menacingly as that of the Third Reich does over West Germany. The trend in post-Franco Spain was towards the accumulation of empirical

---

10 Santos Juliá, 'Segunda República: por otro objeto de investigación', in Manuel Tuñón de Lara *et al.*, *Historiografía española contemporánea* (Madrid, 1980).

11 For expositions of a debate complex in its political implications if not in its empirical content, see Richard J. Evans, 'The new nationalism and the old history: perspectives on the West German *Historikerstreit*', *Journal of Modern History*, vol. 59, no. 4, December 1987; Gordon A. Craig, 'The war of the German historians', *The New York Review of Books*, 15 January 1987; Geoff Eley, 'Nazism, politics and the Image of the Past: Thoughts on the West German *Historikerstreit* 1986–1987', *Past and Present*, no. 121, 1988; Charles S. Maier, *The Unmasterable Past: History, Holocaust and German National Identity* (Cambridge, Mass, 1988); Richard J. Evans, *In Hitler's Shadow: West German Historians and the Attempt to Escape from the Nazi Past* (New York, 1989).

12 José Castillejo, *Wars of Ideas in Spain: Philosophy, Politics and Education* (London, 1937), p. 158.

13 See, for example, a right-wing attempt to play down the scale of the repression, Ramón Salas Larrazabal, *Pérdidas de la guerra* (Barcelona, 1977), pp. 359–95, and a

evidence to the exclusion of all else. The Civil War remained the overriding issue, but there was great reluctance to draw any conclusions which might in some way reopen old wounds. This was reflected in a refusal by the socialist government to sanction any official commemoration of the fiftieth anniversary of the Civil War in 1986.[14]

It is the purpose of this chapter to examine two interlinked and apparently contradictory questions. Why is the Spanish Civil War still an issue that sells books and fills lecture halls? Why did the determination of the dictatorship to keep the Spanish Civil War a living issue fail to prevent the re-establishment of democracy in 1977? Interest in the Spanish Civil War remains undimmed, vividly remembered by participants and eagerly studied by the young in Spain and elsewhere. Yet there is little sense in Spain as there seems to be in Germany of what Ernst Nolte has called 'the past that will not pass away'. The Franco regime used a distorted historical memory as a major weapon in its propaganda armoury. Its purpose was to cow the defeated Republicans and to reward its own supporters, and also to remind them that they must cling to the dictatorship to prevent a resurgence of the left. In fact such policies were only partially successful; they were rejected entirely by the defeated, accepted by some regime supporters but, despite constant streamlining, scorned by the younger generations.[15] After the Caudillo's death, the fruits of such propaganda were to be harvested only in the efforts of nostalgic army officers to reaffirm the nationalist victory in the Civil War by destroying democracy. Despite the regime's politically motivated rewriting of the past, the war was finally relegated to history, at least sufficiently to permit the process of dialogue and consensus by which Spain emerged from its long authoritarian nightmare.

One symptom of the extent to which passions were exhausted despite the regime's efforts is the fact that Spanish historians now eschew cultural and national character interpretations. That is largely a reflex against the

---

left-wing comment on it which pays tribute to General Salas's honesty and understates the extent to which detailed research has demolished Salas's modest figure, Manuel Tuñón de Lara, Julio Aróstegui, Angel Viñas, Gabriel Cardona and Josep M. Bricall, *La guerra civil española cincuenta años después* (Barcelona, 1985), p. 423. For more critical views, see Josep Fontana, 'Naturaleza y consecuencias del franquismo', in Josep Fontana (ed.), *España bajo el franquismo* (Barcelona, 1986), pp. 22–4, and Alberto Reig Tapia, *Ideología e historia: sobre la represión franquista y la guerra civil* (Madrid, 1984), pp. 25–6.

14 The determination to produce a 'value-free' history of the Civil War as part of the tacit no-revenge pact of the transition period is made explicit in Juan Luis Cebrián, 'Para una nueva cultura política', his introduction to the fiftieth anniversary collection of articles published in the newspaper of which he was editor, *El País*, *La guerra de España 1936–1939* (Madrid, 1986). The scale of the empiricist tendency may be seen in the fiftieth anniversary history produced by *Historia 16*, Julio Aróstegui *et al.*, *La guerra civil*, 24 vols (Madrid, 1986–8). See also R. A. Stradling, 'The propaganda of the deed: history, Hemingway, and Spain', in *Textual Practice*, vol. 3, no. 1, Spring 1989.

15 Preston, 'War of Words', pp. 3–4.

inanities of regime historiography. In part too, it is a measure of the influence on the profession of Jaime Vicens Vives, the Barcelona scholar who virtually alone carried the banner of modern history inside Spain in the 1950s. Historians now seek to establish the Spanishness of the Spanish Civil War in terms of long-term socio-economic structures rather than of some national propensity to violence. Curiously, what they have not done is to establish the war's Europeanness. It is precisely in its wider dimension that some of the main reasons for the burning interest in the Civil War should be sought. It is true that, until the military uprising of 18 July 1936, the conflicts which were simmering were Spanish ones, for all that they were flavoured by the fashionable contemporary language of fascism and communism. However, the local conflicts were overshadowed once the intervention of Hitler and Mussolini turned what was meant to be a rapid army coup into a long-drawn-out war.

The refusal of Britain and France to intervene to save the legally elected government, the readiness of the Axis powers to fish in troubled waters, and the Byzantine intervention of the Soviet Union did more than convert Spain into the nodal point of Europe. The reactions of the powers also placed Spain in a continuum which dated back to the Bolshevik revolution. Spain became the latest battleground in an ongoing European civil war whose previous battles had been Vienna in 1934, Berlin in 1933, Lisbon in 1926, Rome in 1922. These are not terms in which inward-looking Spanish historians tend to think. Nor are they ones which have exercised the minds of the most influential historians of the origins of the Second World War, the paucity of whose consideration of the Spanish war is lamentable. It is astonishing that the most respected surveys of the origins of the Second World War tend either to ignore the Spanish conflict almost entirely or else to describe it in terms which suggest that its events ran separately from the central drift of international relations. This is to ignore the extent to which the timing of Hitler's central European ventures was calculated on the basis of Nationalist fortunes in Spain and of the reactions of the Western powers to the vagaries of the Francoist cause. The only possible explanation can be the general inclination of historians other than Spaniards and Hispanists to consider Spain a backwater.

In contrast, for politically aware non-Spaniards at the time, the wider implications of what was at stake were altogether clearer. Volunteers left their homes and families to fight in Spain. Many who could not go took part in political demonstrations and participated in 'Aid Spain' campaigns. They did so because they felt that Spain was the battlefield on which a challenge had to be mounted to the growing threat of fascism.[16] Accordingly the subsequent, and largely successful, efforts of the Franco

---

16 Abe Osheroff and Bill Susman (eds), *¡No Pasarán! The 50th Anniversary of the Abraham Lincoln Brigade* (New York, 1986), p. 3.

regime to keep memories of the Civil War simmering for its own political purposes would also work to its detriment by maintaining international opprobrium. Eventually, the regime's vehement anti-communism would help undermine some of that hostility. Nevertheless, the survival until the 1970s of interest in the Spanish war and of sympathy for the defeated Republic owes much to the association of the Nationalists and their Caudillo with the Axis.

That already clear association was proudly and theatrically trumpeted to the world on 19 May 1939 when 120,000 troops took part in Franco's victory parade through Madrid. The parade was headed by the band of the Carabinieri, a battalion of Italian Black Shirts, and mechanized and cavalry units of the regular Italian army. Thereafter, for five hours, Falangists, Carlist *Requetés* carrying huge crucifixes, regular Spanish troops, foreign legionaries and Moorish mercenaries filed through the streets. The rear was brought up by the Portuguese volunteers who had fought for Franco and, led by General Von Richtofen, Hitler's Condor Legion. Overhead, an aeroplane wrote the name of Franco in smoke.[17] The choreography of close association with the Axis cause was carefully restaged in the summer of 1939. On 1 June a naval convoy took Franco's close collaborator, his Minister of the Interior and brother-in-law, Ramón Serrano Suñer, to Italy along with several generals and 3,000 troops, who paraded through the streets of Rome. Six weeks later an Italian flotilla brought Mussolini's son-in-law and Foreign Minister, Count Galeazzo Ciano, to Barcelona for a reciprocal visit.[18]

Sympathy for the Axis cause in the Second World War, although never translated into outright belligerence against the Allies, earned Franco the hostility of many Western democrats and not just those of the left. In the last resort Franco did not join Hitler because the Führer could not pay his price. Nevertheless, the Caudillo's passage from neutrality to 'non-belligerence' and then to 'moral belligerence' made it difficult to avoid a postwar association with the defeated cause. During the war refuelling and other facilities in Spain had been made available to the German and Italian navies, intelligence assistance had been freely given and, until mid-1944, invaluable exports of wolfram sent to Germany.[19] It is hardly surprising, in view of Francoist Spain's close involvement in the

---

17 For a vivid description of the parade, see Daniel Sueiro and Bernardo Díaz Nosty, *Historia del franquismo*, 2 vols, 2nd edn (Barcelona, 1985), Vol. I, pp. 22–4. See also Ricardo de la Cierva, *Francisco Franco: un siglo de España*, 2 vols (Madrid, 1973) Vol. II, p. 186.

18 Xavier Tusell and Genoveva García Queipo de Llano, *Franco y Mussolini: la política española durante la segunda guerra mundial* (Barcelona, 1985) pp. 30–40. This book is the best account available of the effusive relations between Franco and Mussolini.

19 The immensely controversial debate over Franco's 'real' intentions in the Second World War has given rise to an enormous literature. The best recent summaries are Tusell and Garcia Queipo de Llano, *Franco y Mussolini*; David Wingeate Pike, 'Franco

Axis cause, that the subsequent survival of interest in the Spanish Civil War should feed off the activities and the ultimate longevity of its victor. The fact that Franco continued for nearly forty years to enjoy a dictatorial power seized with the aid of Hitler and Mussolini and that he had made blatant bids to be part of a victorious Axis world order remained an affront to opponents of fascism until his death in 1975.

For all the regime's propaganda about 'the long years of peace', the Civil War continued to traumatize Spanish life long after the end of formal hostilities. April 1939 did not see the beginnings of peace or reconciliation but rather heralded the institutionalization of full-scale vengeance against the defeated left. For a variety of reasons Franco worked harder than anyone to keep the war a festering issue. In official language, there were only 'victors' and 'vanquished', 'good Spaniards' and 'bad Spaniards', 'patriots' and 'traitors'. The Primate of Spain, Cardinal Gomá, had a pastoral letter censored on 9 August 1939 for using the word 'reconciliation' instead of the officially sanctioned 'recuperation'.[20] The term meant redemption, after due punishment, for those who recanted their liberal heresies and accepted the entire political and moral value system of the victors.

The year 1939, once 'III Triumphal Year' in the Francoist calendar, became enshrined as the 'Year of Victory'. Until the mid-1960s the Falangist hymn, *'Cara al sol'* 'Face to the sun' was regularly heard on public occasions and at close-down every evening on Spanish radio. Every church in Spain had painted or carved on its walls the name of the Falangist leader, José Antonio Primo de Rivera, *el ausente* (the absent one). Spanish public buildings had, and some still have, scrolls of honour for the war dead, but only for those of one side, the *Caídos por Dios y por España* (those who fell for God and for Spain). National holidays in Spain other than saints' feast days were victory festivals: 1 April – 'the Day of Victory', 17 April – 'the Day of the Unification' (to celebrate the forcible unification of all political parties into the Falangist-dominated single party, the *Movimiento*), 18 July 'the Day of the Uprising', 1 October – 'the Day of the Caudillo', 29 October – 'the Day of the Fallen'. It was only in the 1980s that monuments began to sprout up to *'los caídos por la libertad* (those who fell for freedom).

Memories of the war and of the bloody repression which followed it were carefully nurtured in order to keep together the uneasy Francoist

---

and the Axis stigma', *Journal of Contemporary History*, vol. 17, no. 3, July 1982; Denis Smyth, 'The Moor and the money-lender: politics and profits in Anglo-German relations with Francoist Spain, 1936–1940', in Marie-Luise Recker (ed.), *Von der Konkurrenz zur Rivalität: Das Britische-Deutsche Verhaltnis in den Landern der Europaischen Peripherie 1919–1939*, (Stuttgart, 1986); Charles B. Burdick, *Germany's Military Strategy and Spain in World War II* (Syracuse, 1968); Victor Morales Lezcano, *Historia de la no-beligerancia española durante la segunda guerra mundial* (Las Palmas, 1980). See also Chapter 3, 'Franco and the Axis temptation' in this volume.

20 Frances Lannon, *Privilege, Persecution, and Prophecy: The Catholic Church in Spain 1875–1975* (Oxford, 1987), pp. 215–16.

coalition. Gory atrocity literature and purple hymns of praise to Nationalist military exploits were directed at those who belonged to the disparate alliance of regime supporters. It consisted of soldiers and prelates, of landowners, industrialists and bankers, of what might be called the 'service classes' of Francoism, those members of the middle and working classes who, for whatever reasons (opportunism, conviction, or wartime geographical loyalty), threw in their lot with the regime, and finally of ordinary Spanish Catholics who supported the Nationalists as the defenders of religion and law and order.[21] Reminders of the war were useful to rally the wavering loyalty of any or all of these groups. They also, gratifyingly, served to intensify the misery of the defeated whose own deeds of heroism and endurance were distorted into the inhuman acts of the puppets of communism. Within months of the end of hostilities, a massive 'History of the Crusade' was being published in weekly parts, glorifying the heroism of the victors and portraying the vanquished as the dupes of Moscow, as either squalidly self-interested or the blood-crazed perpetrators of sadistic atrocities. Even after the defeat of the Axis, and until well into the 1960s, a stream of publications, many aimed at children, presented the war as a religious crusade against communist barbarism.

This process was continued in school textbooks in various disciplines. Political indoctrination courses under the heading '*Formación del Espíritu Nacional*' were compulsory for all schoolboys. They aimed to imbue the idea of 'true' national character associated with the nationalist victory: aggressive, violent, imperialist. Girls were obliged to take '*Enseñanza del Hogar*', a domestic studies course which purveyed a particularly submissive role for women as the wives and mothers who kept hearth and home ready for virile Falangist warriors. Well into the 1960s, all classrooms had a picture of Franco and a crucifix hanging side by side. At the beginning of the school day the children of the entire school in military formation would raise the Spanish flag, then pray, then sing the Falangist hymn '*Cara al sol*', then file into their single sex classrooms singing one of the anthems of the Falangist Youth Front. The process would be repeated in reverse at the end of the school day, concluding with the lowering of the flag.[22]

---

21 The notion of 'service classes' is derived from Eduardo Sevilla Guzmán and Salvador Giner, 'Absolutismo despótico y dominación de clase: el caso de España', in *Cuadernos de Ruedo Ibérico*, (Paris) nos 43–5, enero-junio 1975. The Francoist coalition is best analysed in Amando de Miguel, *Sociología del Franquismo* (Barcelona, 1975).

22 *Formación política: Lecciones para flechas* (Madrid, n. d.); José María Pemán, *La Historia de España contada con sencillez: Para los niños. . . y para muchos que no lo son* (Cádiz, 1939); Joaquín Arrarás Iribarren, (ed.), *Historia de la Cruzada española*, 36 vols (Madrid, 1939–1943). See also Rafael Valls Montes, *La interpretación de la Historia de España, y sus orígenes ideológicos, en el bachillerato franquista (1938–1953)* (Valencia, 1984) and Fernando Valls, *La enseñanza de la literatura en el franquismo 1936–1951* (Barcelona, 1983); Pamela O'Malley, 'Reservoirs of dignity and pride: schoolteachers and

Those who were more directly implicated in the regime's networks of corruption and repression, the beneficiaries of the killings and the pillage, were especially susceptible to hints that only Franco stood between them and the revenge of their victims. They were to make up what in the 1970s came to be known as the 'bunker', the die-hard Francoists who were prepared to fight for the values of the Civil War from the rubble of the Chancellery.[23] A similar, and more dangerous, commitment came from the praetorian defenders of the legacy of the nationalist uprising and subsequent victory, which Spanish rightists refer to broadly as *el 18 de julio* (from the date of the military rising of 1936). Army officers had been educated since 1939 in academies where they were taught that the military existed to defend Spain from communism, anarchism, socialism, parliamentary democracy, and regionalists who wanted to destroy the nation's unity. Franco used the army not as an instrument of national defence but as a mechanism for guaranteeing the survival of his regime. Promotion, preferment and decorations were used as devices to secure the personal loyalties of potential enemies. Low levels of professionalism hardly mattered in a force whose primordial function was to block political opposition.

The three service academies, the Academia General Militar, revived on 27 September 1940, the Escuela Naval Militar, founded on 15 August 1943 and the Academia General del Aire, founded on 15 September 1945, provided a military education in which ideology prevailed over strategy and technology. A generalized and highly partisan interpretation of Spain's history, and particularly of the years immediately preceding the Civil War took up so much of the curriculum that it virtually squeezed out technical training. The Academia General Militar was concerned, according to its regulations, to educate the cadets 'not only militarily, but also in religious, moral and social terms, channelling and directing all the acts of their lives towards the attainment of becoming perfect Christian Spanish soldiers'. There were virtually no cadets from the regions with historic aspirations to independence, Galicia, the Basque country and Catalonia, and therefore no one to counter the idea that in the regions resided the enemy within. Accordingly, after Franco's death, under an aconfessional Constitution which granted devolution to the regions, and enraged by Basque terrorism, the bunker and its military supporters were to attempt with monotonous frequency to destroy democracy in Spain in the name of the Nationalist victory in the Civil War. They did so in 1978, in 1979, in 1980,

---

the creation of an educational alternative in Franco's Spain', unpublished PhD thesis (Open University, 1989), pp. 62–3, 261.

23 On the 'bunker', see 'Luis Ramírez' (pseudonym of Luciano Rincón), 'Morir en el bunker', in *Horizonte español 1972*, 3 vols (Paris, 1972), Vol. I, pp. 1–20. See also Chapter 7 'Into the bunker' in this volume.

most notably on 23 February 1981, and again on the eve of the elections of October 1982. For these ultra-rightists, Nationalist propaganda efforts to maintain the hatreds of the Civil War were perhaps gratuitous.[24]

In the long term the propagandistic efforts to make eternal the 'values of 18 July 1936' were in vain. In the developing and increasingly Europeanized and indeed Americanized Spain of the late 1960s the maintenance of an idealized notion of the Civil War as a medieval religious crusade was ever more anachronistic. That point was made starkly when the church changed sides and withdrew its support from the regime. Individual priests had been criticizing the regime since the early 1950s and Catholic workers' associations had long been part of the opposition to the dictatorship. However, after the Second Vatican Council and in response to the encyclicals of Pope John XXIII, even the ecclesiastical hierarchy began a gradual process of dissociating itself from the Franco regime.[25] This became startlingly obvious in September 1971, when a joint assembly of Spanish bishops and priests issued a declaration rejecting the dictatorship's Civil War ideology and begging the forgiveness of the Spanish people for the clergy's failure to be 'true ministers of reconciliation'.[26]

The church was recognizing something to which the regime remained blind. The manipulation of the popular memory of the Civil War was a meaningless exercise for the majority of Spaniards born since 1939. A series of opinion polls held in 1983 in Spain suggested that, far from seeing the Civil War as a glorious crusade to defend true religion against the blood-crazed hordes of Moscow, 73 per cent of Spaniards regarded it as 'a shameful period of Spanish history that was best forgotten'. Only about 20 per cent of Spaniards alive in the mid-1980s were aged thirteen or over in 1936. Leaving out women and those under sixteen, that meant that fewer than 7 per cent of the then Spanish population could have fought in the war. Nevertheless, the impact of the war was still felt. One in four Spaniards has a relative who was killed in the war; one in ten had a relative who was forced into exile in 1939; two out of three had a relative who fought. It was hardly surprising then that nearly 60 per cent regarded the Civil War of 1936–9 as the most formative event in modern Spanish history. There were inevitably high levels of ignorance: 35 per cent of respondents could not say on which side the International Brigades fought; 41 per cent were equally unsure as to the side on which

---

24 The cultivation of a hermetic military mentality and the consequent emergence of *golpismo* is dealt with in Colectivo Democracia, *Los ejércitos... más allá del golpe* (Barcelona: Editorial Planeta, 1981); Julio Busquets, Miguel Angel Aguilar and Ignacio Puche, *El golpe: anatomía y claves del asalto al congreso* (Barcelona: Editorial Ariel, 1981). See also Chapter 8, 'Franco's Last Stand', in this volume.

25 Lannon, *Privilege, Persecution, and Prophecy*, pp. 246–50.

26 Cooper, *Catholicism*, pp. 28–41; José Chao Rego, *La Iglesia en el franquismo* (Madrid, 1976), pp. 150–202.

the German Condor Legion fought. On the international aspects of the war, 24 per cent were ignorant of which side was supported by Hitler, 37 per cent of which side was supported by Stalin.[27]

However, the underlying memory of the horrors of the war was such that, although personal hatreds still survived, the post-Franco political consensus was built on a collective agreement to renounce revenge. The hatreds were subsumed into what has been called 'a militant pacifism'. The consequences of that were to be of the greatest importance for the survival of Spain's new democracy. Over 70 per cent of Spaniards described themselves in the late 1970s as belonging to a broad continuum from centre-right to centre-left. In none of the four elections held between 1977 and 1986 did parties of the extreme left or right gain more than 3 per cent of the vote. The Communist Party, at its most moderate and Eurocommunist, never gained more than 10 per cent and in 1982 was fortunate to gain 4 per cent. The corollary was that 40 per cent of Spaniards claimed to have no interest whatsoever in politics, as opposed to 50 per cent in Italy, 28 per cent in Britain, 26 per cent in France and 14 per cent in West Germany.[28] On the other hand, after the abortive military coup of 23 February 1981, millions of Spaniards were sufficiently concerned for the fate of democracy to take to the streets to demonstrate against Colonel Tejero's efforts to repeat the experience of 1936.

That implicit moderation was in large part a reaction against the Francoist attempt to keep alive the hatreds of war and a reflection of a collective horror of what the war meant. Only the most militant Falangist and military supporters of the dictatorship could continue to glory in the 'values of the 18 July' and of the 'Crusade'. The bulk of the population was appalled by what had happened, was determined to avoid its repetition and was repelled by the regime's relentless reiteration of bloody events. At least 300,000 Spaniards were killed during the hostilities: 440,000 went into exile; 10,000 of them were to die in Nazi concentration camps. Another 400,000 in Spain spent time in prison, in concentration camps, or labour battalions. A Law of Political Responsibilities decreed on 9 February 1939 provided blanket justification for the repression. A Special Tribunal for the Repression of Freemasonry and Communism was created on 1 March 1940. Until 1964, when it was replaced by the Tribunal de Orden Público, it carried out the gory selection of victims. Among them were the flower

---

27 'Encuesta guerra civil', *Cambio 16*, nos 616–19, 19 September-17 October 1983.
28 For detailed analyses of Spanish electoral behaviour, see Juan J. Linz *et al.*, *Informe sociológico sobre el cambio político en España 1975–1981* IV Informe FOESSA Vol. 1 (Madrid, 1981); Howard R. Penniman and Eusebio Mujal Leon (eds), *Spain at the Polls, 1977, 1979 and 1982* (Durham, North Carolina, 1985); Juan J. Linz and José R. Montero (eds), *Crisis y cambio: electores y partidos en la España de los años ochenta* (Madrid, 1986); and Richard Gunther, Giacomo Sani and Goldie Shabad, *Spain after Franco: The Making of a Competitive Party System* (Berkeley, 1986); especially chapters 4 and 8.

of the country's cultural life and the nation's university teaching and research staff virtually in their entirety. Seven thousand schoolteachers were imprisoned. The Republic's journalists were systematically purged, many being executed and almost all losing the opportunity to work.[29]

Until Franco's death Spain was governed as if it were a country occupied by a victorious foreign army. The training, deployment and structure of the Spanish army under Franco was such as to prepare it for action against the native population rather than an external enemy. That was entirely in keeping with the Caudillo's view, expressed in 1937, that he had been fighting a 'frontier war'. From 1937, collective trials lasting a matter of minutes had been held with only the most cursory observance of legal procedure. Thereafter, folders of death sentences were taken to Franco by the Juridical Assessor to the Army, Colonel Lorenzo Martínez Fuset. Contrary to the regime myth of a tireless and merciful Caudillo agonizing late into the night over death sentences, the reality was harsh. In fact, after lunch, over coffee, the Caudillo would sign sheafs of them, often without reading the details but nonetheless specifying the most savage form of execution, strangulation by *garrote*. Occasionally, he would compound the pain and humiliation of the victims' families by writing *garrote y prensa* (garrote with press coverage).[30]

Killing had gone on for some years after the war. In addition to the routine of executions there were occasional orchestrated rituals of revenge. In November 1940, for ten days and ten nights, a massively choreographed torch-lit procession escorted the mortal remains of the Falangist leader José Antonio Primo de Rivera from Alicante to the Escorial, the resting place of the kings and queens of Spain. It was the most spectacular of many deliberate attempts to link Francoism and Falangism to the historical glories of Philip II. Every section of the Falange was involved: youth, women, syndicates, and also regular troops. Along the route the procession was greeted by huge bonfires and church services. Falangists from every province took their turns as pall-bearers. As they were relieved, artillery salutes and bell-ringing broke out in all the towns and villages of Spain. All school classes and university lectures were interrupted for teachers and professors to raise their arms in the

---

29 On the repression and the exile, see Reig Tapia, *Ideología e historia*; Josep M. Solé i Sabaté, *La repressió franquista a Catalunya* (Barcelona, 1985); *Catalunya sota el règim franquista: informe sobre la persecució de la llengua i la cultura de Catalunya pel règim del general Franco* (Paris, 1973); Antonio Vilanova, *Los olvidados: los exiliados españoles en la segunda guerra mundial* (Paris, 1969); Vicente Fillol, *Los perdedores* (Caracas, 1971); Avel·lí Artís-Gener, *La diáspora republicana* (Barcelona, 1975).

30 Ramón Garriga, *Los validos de Franco* (Barcelona, 1981) pp. 42–3, 72–3; Ramón Serrano Suñer, *Entre el silencio y la propaganda, la historia como fue: memorias* (Barcelona, 1977) pp. 243–4; Fernando González, *Liturgias para un Caudillo* (Madrid, 1977) p. 75; Philippe Nourry, *Francisco Franco: la conquête du Pouvoir* (Paris, 1975) p. 541; interview of the author with Ramón Serrano Suñer in Madrid in 1977.

fascist salute and shout 'José Antonio ¡Presente!'. When the cortège arrived in Madrid, it was received by the high commands of the armed services and representatives from Nazi Germany and Fascist Italy. At the Escorial Palace of San Lorenzo there were monumental wreaths from both Hitler and Mussolini. Prisons had been attacked along the way and Republican prisoners assaulted and in at least one case, murdered.[31]

The last official victim of Francoist revenge against the Republican side was the Communist Julián Grimau, executed on 20 April 1963 for crimes allegedly committed during the Civil War. His trial and execution was widely perceived as a deliberate gesture by the regime to revive memories of the war. There were major demonstrations outside Spanish embassies in London, Rome, Moscow, Copenhagen and Paris. In Brussels the embassy was stoned and the one in Mexico City sacked by a mob. The regime press quickly blamed world communism and drew comparisons with the devastation of the Civil War, equally presented as communist-inspired.[32] Grimau was not, however, to be the last political prisoner put to death by the dictatorship. The anarchists Francisco Granados Gata and Joaquín Delgado Martínez were executed by *garrote vil* on 17 August 1963. The anarchist Salvador Puig Antich was executed, also by *garrote vil*, on 2 March 1974. Two militants of the Basque revolutionary separatist organization ETA and three of the Marxist-Leninist faction Frente Revolucionario Antifascista y Patriota were shot by firing squads on 27 September 1975.

For the captured Republicans who escaped the executioner there remained the appalling conditions of massively overcrowded prisons. Sentences were expected to be 'redeemed by work'. In the 1940s captive Republicans were formed into 'penal detachments' and 'labour battalions' to be used as forced labour in the construction of dams, bridges, and irrigation canals. Many were hired out to private firms for work in construction and mining. Twenty thousand were employed, and several were killed or badly injured, in the construction of the Valle de los Caídos, a gigantic mausoleum for Franco and a monument to those who fell in his cause.[33] The Valle de los Caídos was merely one of several

---

31 Ian Gibson, *En busca de José Antonio* (Barcelona, 1980) pp. 246–8; Sueiro and Díaz Nosty, *Franquismo*, I, pp. 176–82.

32 On the deliberate nature of the efforts to maintain memories of the war, see the article by Dionisio Ridruejo in *Le Monde*, 24 April 1963 and Salvo Mazzolini, 'La guerra civile non è ancora finita', *L'Espresso* (Rome) 28 April 1963. On the destruction of the Spanish embassy in Mexico City, see *Excelsior* (México D. F.) 21 April 1963. For the regime's exploitation of the attacks on embassies, see *Diario de Barcelona*, 19 April 1963; *La Vanguardia Española* (Barcelona) 21 April 1963. For a general survey, see Amandino Rodríguez Armada and José Antonio Novais, *¿Quién mató a Julián Grimau?* (Madrid: Ediciones 99, 1976), *passim*.

33 Martín Torrent, *Los presos*, pp. 109–115; Daniel Sueiro, *El Valle de los Caídos: los secretos de la cripta franquista* (Barcelona: Editorial Argos Vergara, 1983), *passim* and especially pp. 61–7 and 195–205.

efforts to perpetuate the memory of the Francoist victory in permanent form. The war-ravaged wreckage of the town of Belchite was left standing as a Nationalist monument. The ruined Alcázar of Toledo was rebuilt as a symbol of the Nationalist heroism displayed during its three-month siege. In Madrid the entrance to the University City, the site of the savage battle for the capital, was marked by a gigantic Arch of Victory. The Valle de los Caídos, however, dwarfed them all.

The monument was Franco's brainchild, conceived as the Pharoahs had conceived the pyramids, revealing both his own messianism and his determination to intimidate the population with his memorial of the war. The decree announcing its foundation on 1 April 1940 declared that

> the dimension of our Crusade, the heroic sacrifices which victory involved and the transcendental importance which this epic had for the future of Spain cannot be perpetuated with the simple monuments with which the outstanding events of our history and the glorious deeds of her sons are usually commemorated in towns and villages. It is necessary that the stones which rise up should have the grandeur of ancient monuments, that they challenge time and forgetfulness and constitute a place for meditation and rest where future generations will pay tribute to those who bequeathed them a better Spain.

When finally complete, the Valle de los Caídos was to be Franco's pride and joy. His hope was that it would establish a Francoist imperial architecture which would eternally link his regime and his victory with the triumphs of Charles V and Philip II.

The Caudillo, having personally searched for and found a site in 1940, expected the monument to be completed within a year of the first announcement. In fact, it took nearly twenty years to dig the 262-metre-long basilica, to construct the monastery – carved into the hillside of the Valle de Cuelgamuros in the Sierra de Guadarrama to the north-east of Madrid – and to erect the immense cross which towered 150 meters above it. The arms of the cross were as wide as a two-lane highway. The entire enterprise cost Spain almost as much as had Philip II's Escorial in a more prosperous era. The original notion was that it would be the final resting place for those who died fighting on the Nationalist side or as victims of 'red terror' in the Republican zone. By 1958 the regime had evolved sufficiently for the vaults, in theory at least, to be open to those who fought on either side, provided they were Spaniards and Catholics. The latter condition excluded many Republicans. In any case, considerable, other, obstacles were placed in the way of the burial of Republicans.[34]

---

34   Sueiro, *El Valle de los Caídos*, pp. 8–12, 118–43, 184–92.

The architectural style of the Valle de los Caídos emphasized the extent to which Franco, like most activists of the Spanish right, was obsessed with Spain's fall from imperial greatness. They saw the Civil War as the first step back to past glories achieved before Spain was corrupted by the ideas of Erasmus, Voltaire and Montesquieu. Franco rarely missed an opportunity to eliminate the legacy of the Enlightenment, the French Revolution and other symbols of progress. The flowering of liberal values in Spain was for the Caudillo merely the visible sign of what he called 'the great invasion of evil'. Spanish history since Philip II consisted only of three 'calamitous centuries' that brought decadence, corruption and freemasonry. His eternal delays in restoring the monarchy were excused on the grounds that the Bourbon dynasty was no longer capable of emulating the virile 'totalitarian' monarchy which had expelled the Jews and the Moriscos and conquered America. Present-day monarchists were hampered by liberal prejudices inherited from the nineteenth century, a period which Franco fervently desired 'to wipe from our history'.[35] Leaping over the three awkward centuries of decadence meant creating a political model by fusing medieval despotism and Axis totalitarianism. Accordingly, when his acolytes referred to Fernando el Católico as the first authentic Caudillo, they were implying that Franco was part of a line of great leaders that had been interrupted after Philip II.[36]

The reality of what this meant in terms of wiping out the visible signs of modernity was seen throughout the 1940s. In the context of the material damage caused during the Civil War, an economic system born of a bizarre fusion of medieval ideas with fascist autarky guaranteed stagnation and hardship. The war had destroyed 60 per cent of Spain's railway rolling stock. The proportion of the labour force employed in agriculture reverted to the levels of the turn of the century. National income was overall at the levels of 1914 but, given population increases, the per capita figures corresponded to the late nineteenth century. Real wages were barely at 50 per cent of 1936 levels a decade after the war had finished. There was rationing until 1952 and the rations alone were insufficient to maintain human existence. There sprang up a huge and all-embracing black market system, the *estraperlo*, wherein anything could be obtained. Food prices were about ten times the officially sanctioned figures. The consequences were widening gaps in living standards. Dyptheria, typhoid

---

35   See speeches by Franco on 14 May 1946, 19 October 1946, 28 March 1950, 13 June 1958, 2 October 1961, 1 April 1964 quoted in Agustín del Río Cisneros (ed.), *Pensamiento político de Franco*, 2 vols (Madrid: Ediciones del Movimiento, 1975), Vol. I, pp. 78–93. Franco's view of history is expounded in a letter of 12 May 1942 to the pretender to the throne, Don Juan de Borbón, reprinted in Alfredo Kindelán, *La verdad de mis relaciones con Franco* (Barcelona: Editorial Planeta, 1981), pp. 42–6.
36   Valls, *La enseñanza*, p. 67. See also C. H. Cobb, 'Recuperación': An Aspect of the Cultural Policy of the Franco Regime', *Iberian Studies*, vol. VIII, Autumn 1979.

and tuberculosis were rampant. Infant mortality increased. In 1942, in the Andalusian province of Jaén, it was 347 per 1,000. There was a massive increase in prostitution. In 1950, milk delivered to Madrid was watered down by 50 per cent. Prewar per capita consumption of meat was not reached until 1971.[37]

Just as wages were being effectively slashed, strikes were treated as sabotage and made punishable by long prison sentences. The trade unions were destroyed, their funds, their printing presses and other property seized by the state and the Falange. Travel and the search for jobs were controlled by a system of safe conducts and certificates of political and religious reliability. This effectively made second-class citizens of those defeated Republicans who escaped imprisonment. The Franco regime was especially committed to the maintenance of the rural social structure which had been threatened by the Republic. Rural labourers were forced to work the soil under conditions even more inhuman than those they had known before 1931. With no social welfare safety net, not to work was to starve. The Civil Guard and armed retainers employed by the big landowners, the *latifundistas*, maintained a brutal vigilance of the estates against the pilfering of hungry peasants.

The repressive labour relations of the 1940s and 1950s contributed to higher profits and the accumulation of native capital. It was also a contribution, along with Franco's much-vaunted anti-communism, to the process of making Spain attractive to foreign investors. Foreign capital flooded in. The boom years of European capitalism saw tourists pouring south as Spanish migrant labourers headed north, from where they would send back their foreign currency earnings. Gradually, within the antiquated political strait-jacket of Francoist Spain, there began to grow a new, dynamic, modern society. The pro-fascist 'New State' of the 1940s gave way to the authoritarian despotism of the 1950s, but that too was to find itself overtaken by circumstances.[38] Surrounded by sycophantic courtiers as obsessed as he was with the perpetuation of the victory of 1939, the increasingly senile Franco withdrew ever more into his El Pardo palace.[39] By the time of the energy crisis of the 1970s many Francoists were beginning to wonder if their own survival did not lie in some sort of accomodation with the forces of the democratic opposition.

The more progressive of his supporters were shocked into accepting the need to come to terms with the present by the executions of political prisoners authorized by Franco in March 1974 and September 1975.

---

37 Sueiro and Díaz Nosty, *El franquismo*, I, p. 134; Rafael Abella, *La vida cotidiana en España bajo el régimen de Franco* (Barcelona, 1985), pp. 49–56.
38 This idea is developed more fully in Paul Preston, *The Triumph of Democracy in Spain* (London, 1986) chapter 1.
39 For a gruesome account of the atmosphere therein, see Vicente Gil, *Cuarenta años junto a Franco* (Barcelona, 1981), p. 139 ff.

Franco's blood-lust, in the face of international opprobrium, provoked fear and distaste among the waverers. By 1977, only two years after his death, Franco's worst nightmares had begun to be realized. King Juan Carlos appointed as prime minister an apparatchik of the Francoist single party, the *Movimiento*, Adolfo Suárez. His job was to exploit the intricacies of the Francoist pseudo-constitution to permit a bloodless transition to democracy.[40] The operation to bring together the progressive elements of the regime and the moderate majority of the democratic operation was to be backed by an overwhelming consensus of right and left. Franco's legacy was the memory of the Civil War and the spirit of revenge. It was rejected by the vast majority of Spaniards and most crucially by Franco's heir, Juan Carlos, who became a national symbol of reconciliation. On 23 February 1981, against the wilful minority of nostalgic conspirators, the king was to risk his throne and his personal safety in the cause of a democracy for all Spaniards.[41] The cherished Francoist divisions between victors and vanquished, Spain and anti-Spain, were finally exposed as meaningless.

40   This process is analysed fully in Preston, *Triumph, passim*.
41   There is already a huge bibliography on the 1981 coup. The most comprehensive surveys are Colectivo Democracia, *op. cit.*; José Oneto, *La verdad sobre el caso Tejero* (Barcelona, 1982); Pilar Urbano, *Con la venia... yo indagué el 23F* (Barcelona, 1982).

Part II

SURVIVING THE PRESENT

3

Franco and the Axis temptation

As an openly declared enemy of liberal democracy and Bolshevism Franco could not conceal his sympathies when Hitler unleashed his war to exterminate both. In the last resort, however, the Caudillo's natural inclinations in foreign policy were restrained by two overriding considerations: his own domestic survival and Spain's economic and military capacity for war. In both of those areas he was obliged to pay considerable heed to the views of the army high command. The army was the most powerful player within the complex game of power rivalries between the component groups of the recently victorious Nationalist coalition.[1] At the beginning of the Second World War military conviction of an inevitable German victory was virtually unanimous. However, the likelihood of Spanish generals acting on the basis of that conviction was diminished both by their awareness of Spain's shattered economic and military capacity and by their monarchist sympathies. From the autumn of 1940 onwards the generals showed increasing scepticism about the ultimate Axis triumph. The Falange was a different matter. In its ranks could be found an unrestrained sympathy for German military exploits which was to remain undiminished until the last days of the war. Ideological affinities with the Third Reich immeasurably strengthened the Falange in the internal power struggle within Spain. The military and the Falange were the two major influences on Franco in the making of his foreign policy during the Second World War. Aristocratic royalists and middle-class Catholics were more ambiguous in their views, at first grateful for German assistance in the Civil War and envious of the Third Reich's success but increasingly suspicious of its religious policies and fervent anti-monarchism.

The views of all the Nationalist groups, with the exception of the most hard-line Falangists, inevitably evolved in relation to the shifting fortunes of war. Franco, always sensitive to the moods of his most powerful supporters, similarly adapted his responses to changing wartime developments. However, at the beginning of the Second World War,

---

1 On the military in this period, see Chapter 4, 'Franco and his generals 1939–45'.

flushed with success in the Civil War, fired by solidarity with the Axis allies who had played such a crucial role in achieving his victory, Franco was anything but cautious. Indeed, he very nearly took Spain into war on the Axis side in the course of the summer of 1940. By the autumn of that year, though, the unexpected survival of Britain had helped Franco's natural caution to reassert itself. However, even then, had it not been for the offhand way in which both Hitler and Ribbentrop treated him and his brother-in-law Ramón Serrano Suñer, Spain could easily have slid into war. Moreover, after the most acute danger of Spanish belligerence had passed in late 1940, Franco went on experiencing what might be called the Axis temptation, most intensely after the German invasion of Russia in the summer of 1941.

Accordingly, it understates the case to say that, in the course of the first year of the Second World War, Franco made less use of his characteristically careful ambiguity with regard to international relations than he was later to do. As early as 20 February 1939 the Caudillo had agreed to join the Anti-Comintern Pact, a secret act of solidarity with the Axis made public on 6 April.[2] On 8 May he pulled Spain out of the League of Nations. When Hitler and Mussolini signed the Pact of Steel at the end of May 1939, Franco, in a further gesture of virile bellicosity, sent troops to the Gibraltar area. The Spanish dictator's relations with Hitler were cordial, informed by gratitude for German aid during the Civil War but tinged too with the caution provoked by the Führer's brutal arrogance. With Mussolini there were no reservations but rather an effusive warmth and sympathy. In the course of the summer of 1939 relations between Spain and Italy grew ever warmer. In early June 1939 Franco's closest collaborator, at the time Minister of the Interior, Serrano Suñer, told both Mussolini and Count Ciano that Spain needed two or preferably three years in order to complete her military preparations. However he said, when war broke out, 'Spain will be at the side of the Axis because she will be guided by feeling and by reason. A neutral Spain would, in any event, be destined to a future of poverty and humiliation'; never free or sovereign until she had regained Gibraltar and captured French Morocco.[3]

Ciano and Mussolini both felt that Serrano was 'undoubtedly the strongest Axis prop in the Franco regime'.[4] There is little doubt about Serrano Suñer's enthusiasm for fascist Italy. It was widely supposed, especially in Spanish military circles and among the diplomatic community in Madrid, that he was equally committed to Nazi Germany. The Germans eventually

---

2 Malcolm Muggeridge (ed.), *Ciano's Diary 1939–43* (London, 1947) pp. 32–3; *Documents on German Foreign Policy* Series D, XIII vols (London, 1951–64) (henceforth *DGFP*), vol. III, pp. 880–1.

3 *Ciano's Diary 39–43*, pp. 99–100; Ramón Serrano Suñer, *Entre Hendaya y Gibraltar*, (Madrid, 1947) pp. 91–118.

4 *DGFP*, Series D, vol. VI, pp. 695–7; *Ciano's Diary 39–43*, pp. 97, 102.

came to regard him as an enemy and he later spent considerable energy portraying himself as the man who worked skilfully to keep Spain out of the war. What is absolutely certain is that he bitterly hated the British and the French, partly because he abhorred liberal democracy and more particularly because their embassies in Republican Madrid had refused sanctuary to his brothers – who shortly afterwards died in gaol.[5] Serrano Suñer should not, however, be made the scapegoat for the pro-Axis activities of the Francoist establishment in these years. There were few senior figures in civilian or military life who did not participate in a generalized enthusiasm for the new political order that seemed to be in the process of being forged. General Kindelán, head of the Spanish air force, had arrived in Italy shortly after Serrano Suñer, accompanying Italian airmen who had fought during the Civil War. The reputedly pro-British Kindelán gave an interview to *La Stampa* on 15 June in which he stated that, if Italy were involved in war, 'none of the Spanish Armed Services, the Air Force least of all, will be able to remain impassive'. Franco told the Italian ambassador, Count Viola, on 5 July 1939 that Spain needed 'a period of tranquillity to devote herself to internal reconstruction and the achievement of the economic autonomy indispensable for the military power to which she aspired'. At the same time he asserted that he planned to keep a large army mobilized to prevent Spain being imposed upon by the British and the French. Such a force would 'permit him to make Spain's weight be felt in the unfolding of events and possibly to take advantage of circumstances'. France, he boasted, 'would never be able to feel easy with regard to Spain'. As part of Spanish efforts to discomfort France, the Spanish ambassador in Paris, José Félix Lequerica, was passing on to the Germans information about French policy intentions which he had been given in confidence.[6]

Ciano arrived in Barcelona on 10 July for a reciprocal visit. Franco told him that Spain needed five years of peace for economic and military preparation before she could identify completely with the totalitarian states. In the event of war, he would prefer neutrality but would be on the Axis side because he did not believe that his regime could survive a victory by the democracies in a general war. Accordingly, with apparent lack of concern about Spain's bankruptcy, he speculated about a major

---

5 *Ciano's Diary 39–43*, p. 100; Maurice Peterson, *Both Sides of the Curtain: An Autobiography* (London, 1950), pp. 223–4; Sir Samuel Hoare, *Ambassador on Special Mission* (London, 1946), pp. 56–8; Serrano Suñer, *Entre Hendaya y Gibraltar*, pp. 108–9.

6 *DGFP*, Series D, vol. VI, pp. 830–2, vol. VIII, p. 24; *The Times*, 17, 21 June 1939; Marc Ferro, *Pétain* (Paris, 1987) pp. 51–2; Javier Tusell and Genoveva García Queipo de Llano, *Franco y Mussolini: la política española durante la segunda guerra mundial*, (Barcelona, 1985) p. 37; on Lequerica, see Juan Avilés Farré, 'Lequerica, embajador franquista en París', *Historia 16*, no. 160, August 1989, pp. 12–20.

rearmament programme for both the navy and the air force.[7] Franco was in fact worried that, if the Axis won the coming war without his participation, the world would be reconstructed without respect for his ambitions. So he began, within the very narrow possibilities open to him, to rearm. Efforts were made to fortify the Pyrenees and financial and technical help was requested from Italy for the rebuilding of the Spanish navy and air force.[8] In August Franco told General Gastone Gambara, the head of the Italian Military Mission in Spain, that he intended to destroy the British installations in Gibraltar with heavy artillery. Plans for a state visit by Franco to Rome in September 1939 and to Berlin later in the autumn were postponed only because of the outbreak of the Second World War.[9] The Caudillo had been warned by Ciano in August that war was likely between Germany and Poland. He responded with troop movements and the building of fortifications near the French border and on the frontier between Spanish and French Morocco. He had also set up a new Gibraltar command of one division. All of these measures, he informed both Italian and German ambassadors, were by way of helping the Axis.[10]

Franco's awareness that war was imminent found an immediate reflection in the cabinet changes of 9 August 1939 in the replacement of the Anglophile Minister of Foreign Affairs, the Conde de Jordana by Colonel Juan Beigbeder Atienza, an early adherent of the Falange. A keen *Africanista*, Beigbeder shared Franco's imperial ambitions in Morocco. Nevertheless, he was an erratic operator. Accordingly, after hostilities had begun, the German ambassador in Madrid, Baron Eberhard Von Stohrer, tended to by-pass Beigbeder and to liaise with Serrano Suñer, who promised to influence the attitude of the Spanish press completely in favour of the German cause.[11] This he did so effectively that it became an important Axis propaganda weapon in Spain. The willing Falangist press apparatus was supplied by the German embassy with Nazi propaganda material, which was then relayed as news. Pro-Allies material virtually never appeared except in response to specific diplomatic protests.[12] In fact German influence over the press was just one of the many ways in which Spain was heading towards becoming an informal German colony. The police were strongly influenced by the Gestapo. Embassy and ministry

7   Galeazzo Ciano, *Ciano's Diplomatic Papers*, edited by Malcolm Muggeridge (London, 1948) pp. 290–5; Tusell and Garcia Queipo de Llano, *Franco y Mussolini*, pp. 38–9.

8   Tusell and Garcia Queipo de Llano, *Franco y Mussolini* p. 40.

9   *DGFP*, Series D, vol. VI, p. 882; Series D, vol. VII, p. 57.

10   *DGFP*, Series D, vol. VII, pp. 388–9.

11   *DGFP*, Series D, vol. VII, pp. 501–2; Peterson, *Both Sides*, pp. 191–2.

12   Hoare, *Ambassador* pp. 54–5; Serrano Suñer, *Entre Hendaya y Gibraltar*, p. 132; Javier Terrón Montero, *La prensa de España durante el régimen de Franco* (Madrid, 1981), pp. 41–54.

telephones were tapped by Germans with official acquiescence, secured either by bribery or ideological affinity.[13]

When war did break out on 3 September Franco, like Mussolini, lamented the fact that it had happened too soon. The best that either could do was to proffer surreptitious help and take advantage where possible. Officially, Franco announced that 'the most strict neutrality' would be required of Spanish subjects.[14] In private, his attitude was far from neutral. Both he and Serrano Suñer believed that Spain had been kept in humiliating subjugation by the arrogance of Britain and France. Accordingly, they were looking for any opportunities provided by the war to help Spain achieve her place among the European powers.[15] Beigbeder regularly provided the German embassy with information received from Spain's diplomatic missions abroad. Reports from France were to be especially useful during the Franco-German hostilities in June 1940. The Spanish Foreign Ministry also regularly obtained for the Germans reports on the effect of Luftwaffe bombing raids on Britain.[16]

As eager spectators of the phoney war, Franco and Mussolini were drawn together even more. The warmth of their relations was underlined by Italian generosity in the settlement of Spain's war debts. Eventually, the Duce, ever restless and unwilling, as he put it, to sit on the sidelines while history was being written, decided to enter the war. He had given Franco two months notice of his plans, on 8 April 1940. After her exhausting enterprises in Abyssinia, in Spain and in Albania, Italy was barely in better shape than Spain for a military escapade. Serrano Suñer and Beigbeder both told Stohrer in the first half of April that Spain was on Germany's side and that Italy's imminent entry into the war would ensure that Spain would be 'automatically drawn in'. However, even Serrano Suñer was pessimistic about Spain's chances of waging war given the parlous state of her reserves of fuel and grain. Nevertheless, he and Franco were sorely tempted by the prospect of Spanish belligerence leading to the acquisition of Gibraltar and Tangiers.[17] What distinguished Mussolini and Franco at this time was that the Caudillo by temperament lacked the Duce's irresponsible rashness, had a less sycophantic general staff and as a soldier himself had a much more realistic notion of his country's capabilities.

---

13 Paul Reynaud, *Au coeur de la mêlée 1930–1945* (Paris, 1951) p. 919; Peterson, *Both sides*, pp. 191–5.

14 *Boletín Official del Estado*, 4 September 1939. Cf. Serrano Suñer, *Entre Hendaya y Gibraltar*, p. 89.

15 Serrano Suñer, *Entre Hendaya y Gibraltar*, pp. 133–5, 142–3.

16 *DGFP*, Series D, vol. VIII, pp. 324–5, vol. IX, p. 558, vol. X, p. 291, vol. XI, pp. 48, 185; Ferro, *Pétain*, pp. 51–2.

17 *DGFP*, Series D, vol. VIII, pp. 190–2.

In the spring of 1940 Franco was confident of an early German victory.[18] The British were sufficiently worried to replace their ambassador in Madrid, Sir Maurice Peterson, by Sir Samuel Hoare. It was an indication of the importance given to the Madrid embassy that such a senior figure was chosen for this 'special mission'. With France about to fall, it was crucial to prevent Franco throwing in his lot with Hitler and Mussolini. If he did, the loss of Gibraltar and the Spanish Atlantic ports to the Axis would have been a devastating blow to Britain. With the Germans already at Ostend and the retreat at Dunkirk under way, Hoare arrived in Madrid on 1 June; there he found high prices, food shortages, German domination of communications, the press and aviation and his embassy virtually besieged by crowds of Falangists chanting '*Gibraltar Español*'.[19] While the British Expeditionary Force limped back home the Caudillo watched with excitement. He sent his Chief of the General Staff, General Juan Vigón, to Berlin on 10 June with an effusive letter of congratulation for Hitler.[20] In fact, Hitler kept Spain at arm's length, more or less rebuffing Vigón when he saw him at the Castle of Acoz on 16 June 1940, merely acknowledging Spain's Moroccan ambitions. At that stage Hitler had no intention of paying a high price for services which he believed would not be needed since he expected the British to surrender at any moment.

The fact that Spain did not ultimately join in the war on the Axis side has been the basis of claims from apologists of Franco that, with immense statecraft and sheer guile, he outwitted Hitler and Mussolini in favour of the Allies.[21] To say that this was not so is not to underestimate the importance of Spanish neutrality to the eventual outcome of the Second World War. Churchill wrote after the war that 'Spain held the key to all British enterprises in the Mediterranean, and never in the darkest hours did she turn the lock against us'. Gibraltar was crucial to British naval control of the Eastern Atlantic. If German planes had been able to fly from Spanish airfields, they could have wreaked havoc on British convoys. Churchill was sufficiently aware of the danger to hold in readiness for two years an expeditionary force (a brigade and four fast transports) to seize the Canary Islands in the event of losing Gibraltar.[22] Serrano Suñer

---

18 *DGFP*, Series D, vol. IX, p. 396.

19 Peterson, *Both Sides*, pp. 228–33; Hoare, *Ambassador*, pp. 14–18, 30–2; J. A. Cross, *Sir Samuel Hoare: A Political Biography* (London, 1977) pp. 322–8.

20 *DGFP*, Series D, vol. IX, pp. 509–10.

21 See, *inter alia*, Brian Crozier, *Franco: A Biographical History* (London, 1967) pp. 313–75; José María Doussinague, *España tenía razón (1939–1945)* (Madrid, 1949), *passim*; George Hills, *Rock of Contention: A History of Gibraltar* (London, 1974) pp. 428–32.

22 Winston S. Churchill, *The Second World War*, Vol. II, *Their Finest Hour* (London, 1949) pp. 460, 552, 562. For earlier perceptions of Spain's strategic importance, see Denis Smyth, *Diplomacy and Strategy of Survival: British Policy and Franco's Spain, 1940–1941* (Cambridge, 1986) pp. 1–4; Alexander Cadogan, *The Diaries of Sir Alexander Cadogan 1938–1945*, edited by David Dilkes (London, 1971) p. 117; Report by the Chiefs of Staff

argued persuasively in 1947 that, if Spain had joined in the war in June 1940 the outcome would have been very different, although he omitted to comment that she did not do so only because Hitler rejected her offer.[23] So the eulogies bestowed on the Caudillo for his role in the Second World War find their justification in the fact that, although he was in a position to do great damage to British and Allied interests, in the last resort he did not do so. They conveniently play down both the fervour of his pro-German offers of mid-1940 and subsequent recurrences of the Axis temptation.

Inevitably, in 1940, the strategic importance of Spain to the Axis cause made Franco the object of courtship by both sides, the Germans to bring him into the war and the British to keep him out. Despite some internal dispute as to the wisdom of such a policy, the British inclined to using the carrot and stick made available to them by their ability to blockade Spanish trade and to give desperately needed credit. The Germans on the other hand took it for granted in a rather bullying manner, based in part on the presence of German units on the Spanish-French border, that Franco could be expected to do what they wanted without any special wooing. In the last resort, that difference, rather than any skilful diplomacy on Franco's part was the reason for Spain's non-belligerence. In November 1942 Spain's attitude to Operation 'Torch', the code-name for the Anglo-American landings in North Africa, was to have a major impact on the rest of the war. Thousands of Allied troops and tons of equipment were gathered in Gibraltar prior to the landings and eventually they and others were shipped through the straits under Spanish guns on both sides of the Mediterranean. Franco is credited with resisting German blandishments to cut Allied communications and so not hindering Operation 'Torch'. To his admirers, this is proof of his *de facto* 'benevolent neutrality' towards the Allies.[24] In fact, neither Franco nor any of his ministers had any real inkling of what was being prepared. Moreover, German pressure was half-hearted and was exerted only after the event.[25] Churchill, in October 1944, in rejecting an offer by Franco to join in a postwar anti-communist alliance, nevertheless commented on 'the supreme services' which Franco

---

Sub-Committee on the situation in the Western Mediterranean arising from the Spanish Civil War, *Documents on British Foreign Policy*, 2nd Series, vol. XVII (London, 1979), pp. 151–2.

23 Serrano Suñer, *Entre Hendaya y Gibraltar*, pp. 204–5.

24 José María de Areilza, *Embajadores sobre España* (Madrid, 1947) pp. 4–5, 57–8; Hills, *Gibraltar*, pp. 436–8. The definitive demolition of that view is to be found in Smyth, *Diplomacy and Strategy of Survival*. See also David Wingeate Pike, 'Franco and the Axis Stigma', *Journal of Contemporary History*, vol. 17, no. 3, 1982, and Victor Morales Lezcano, *Historia de la no-beligerancia española durante la segunda guerra mundial* (Las Palmas, 1979).

25 Denis Smyth, 'Screening "Torch": Allied counter-intelligence and the Spanish threat to the secrecy of the allied invasion of French North Africa in November 1942', *Intelligence and National Security*, vol. 4, no. 2, April 1989, pp. 335–56. For an account of German pressure, see Doussinague, *España tenía razón*, pp. 133–8.

had rendered the Allied cause 'by not intervening in 1940 or interfering with the use of the airfield and Algeciras Bay in the months before Torch'. It is this in particular which lies behind the oft-propounded view of a cannily shrewd Franco, foreseeing the eventual result and holding off by a charade of pro-Axis rhetoric an invasion of Spain by Hitler to seize Gibraltar.

However, by the time that 'Torch' was on the horizon, it was clear to Franco that the war was going to be extremely protracted and that it might even be won by the Allies. In 1940, however, Franco was seriously committed to entering the war and was held back only by his inability to negotiate acceptable terms with Hitler. Unlike Mussolini, Franco was not tempted by a surge of rash ideological fervour into a precipitate declaration of war without first establishing the price. Although the Caudillo used the rhetoric of Spanish Civil War camaraderie, he was far from pathetically grateful for German assistance during the Civil War. He had deeply resented, for instance, the Nazis' neo-colonial ambitions during that war. The Germans had ruthlessly exploited his temporary dependence on their military aid by 'smash and grab' tactics aimed at entrenching themselves in the Spanish economy, taking over companies, especially those in the mining industry.[26] Franco was outraged by the German insistence that they be paid back for their aid in the war. In his rather self-regarding and pompously messianic way, the Caudillo believed that the Axis was in debt to him since the Spanish Civil War had been an ideological crusade of common interest to all, in which the Germans should have felt honoured to participate.

Franco certainly approached the question of joining the German war effort with more circumspection than did Mussolini. Nevertheless, in the early summer of 1940, the spectacular success of Hitler's drive to the west impelled the Caudillo to uncharacteristic impetuosity. On 3 May 1940 he had sent a 'colourless message' to Mussolini confirming 'the absolute and unavoidable neutrality of a Spain preparing to bind up her wounds'.[27] He knew that an economically prostrate Spain could not sustain a long war effort but, on the other hand, he could not bear the thought that France and Britain might be annihilated by a new Hitlerian world order and Spain still not get any of the spoils. Accordingly, fully convinced in 1940 that German victory was inevitable, Franco sought to make a last-minute entry in order to gain a ticket for the distribution of the booty. His attitude was, however, conditioned by the troubled legacy of his economic relations with Hitler during the Civil War. Ultimately, the

---

26 Denis Smyth, 'The Moor and the money-lender: politics and profits in Anglo-German relations with Francoist Spain', in Marie-Luise Recker (ed.), *Von der Konkurrenz zur Rivalität: Das Britische-Deutsche Verhältnis in den Länden der Europäischen Peripherie* (Stuttgart, 1986); Angel Viñas, *Guerra, dinero, dictadura: ayuda fascista y autarquía en la España de Franco* (Barcelona, 1984), pp. 158–67.

27 *Ciano's Diary 39–43*, p. 243.

common desire of both dictators for co-operation against Britain was to run aground on Hitler's continuing underestimation of Franco's dogged meanness and inflated sense of destiny. If the Führer had been able, as Mussolini had, to make a virtue of enforced generosity over Civil War debts, or if he had lied more daringly over his readiness to give away French North Africa, the outcome would certainly have been different. As it was, Franco had learnt too much about Nazi buccaneering during the Civil War not to have his suspicions and his indignation aroused when in the autumn of 1940 it seemed to him that Hitler was up to his old tricks.

Until he ran into German arrogance and intransigence, Franco's first chosen moment for Spanish entry into the war was shortly after the fall of France when Britain seemed also on the verge of surrender. The second was in the autumn of 1940 when he believed that Operation 'Sealion' was about to be launched and the collapse of England was imminent. On the first of these two occasions, the Germans brushed off the Spanish offer with a cavalier disdain, convinced that they did not need it. On the second, when they did need it, they were indifferent to Franco's sensibilities and in particular to his African ambitions. In early June 1940 the British and French embassies in Madrid were stormed by Falangists and the tightly controlled Francoist press gleefully reported German and Italian sympathy for the return of Gibraltar. After a cabinet meeting on 12 June Franco changed Spain's official neutrality to the much more pro-Axis position of non-belligerence. Franco told the Italian chargé d'affaires in Madrid that 'the present state of the Spanish armed forces prevented the adoption of a more resolute stance but that he was none the less proceeding to accelerate as much as possible the preparation of the army for any eventuality'.[28] The fanatical Serrano Suñer was enthusiastic about German triumphs and keen to take over the reins of Spanish foreign policy. He was already intriguing against Foreign Minister Beigbeder.[29] German submarines were being provisioned in Spanish ports; Franco permitted German reconnaissance aircraft to fly with Spanish markings and a radio station at La Coruña was at the service of the Luftwaffe. In the autumn requests were successfully made for secret night-time refuelling of German destroyers in bays on Spain's northern coast.[30]

With France on her knees and Britain with her back to the wall, Franco felt all the temptations of a cowardly and rapacious vulture. Despite Franco's professed friendship with Pétain, on 14 June, as the Germans poured into Paris, Spain occupied Tangiers having assured the

28 *ABC*, 13 June 1940; Tusell and Garcia Queipo de Llano, *Franco y Mussolini* p. 79; *DGFP*, Series D, vol. IX, p. 560.

29 *DGFP*, Series D, vol. IX, p. 542; Serrano Suñer, *Entre Hendaya y Gibraltar*, pp. 159–60.

30 *DGFP*, Series D, vol. IX, pp. 449–53; vol. XI, p. 445.

French that this action was necessary to guarantee its security. Hitler was delighted, all the more so because Franco 'had acted without talking'.[31] On the day following the French plea for an armistice Franco asserted that the further existence of the French empire in North Africa was now impossible, and so Spain demanded French Morocco, the Oran region of Algeria and the expansion of Spanish Sahara and Spanish Guinea. In the event of England continuing hostilities after the surrender of France, the Caudillo offered to enter the war on the Axis side in return for 'war materials, heavy artillery, aircraft for the attack on Gibraltar, and perhaps the co-operation of German submarines in the defence of the Canary Islands'. He also requested foodstuffs, ammunition, motor fuel and equipment from the French war stocks.[32]

After keeping the Spaniards waiting for nearly a week the German Foreign Ministry rebuffed their offer with a dry acknowledgement of Spain's territorial desires in North Africa.[33] Hitler had responded coolly to Vigón three days earlier, suspicious, in the aftermath of Mussolini's precipitate attack on France, of more unwanted last-minute volunteers for a war which he was convinced was already won. He was not about to prejudice the armistice negotiations with France in order to give gratuitous satisfaction to Spain. Franco, Serrano Suñer and Beigbeder were all, in their different ways, obsequious towards the Third Reich, constantly seeking means of currying favour with Berlin. On 23 June, for instance, Beigbeder offered to detain the Duke and Duchess of Windsor who were passing through Madrid *en route* to Lisbon, in case the Germans wanted to make contact with them. Throughout the summer of 1940 Serrano Suñer and Franco were willing collaborators in German machinations to prevent the Duke of Windsor taking up the post of Governor of the Bahamas in order that he might be used against 'the Churchill clique' in peace negotiations with England. In the hope of persuading the Duke to be a kind of English Rudolf Hess, Serrano Suñer's close collaborator Angel Alcázar de Velasco told him that the British secret service had plans to assassinate him.[34] Serrano Suñer himself was pressing for an official invitation to visit Germany to negotiate Spanish entry into the war.[35]

In contrast to the Spanish efforts at ingratiation with the Third Reich, the Germans at all levels were arrogant and dismissive towards the Spaniards.

---

31 *DGFP*, Series D, vol. IX, pp. 585–8; Reynaud, *Au coeur de la Mêlée*, pp. 855–6.

32 *DGFP*, Series D, vol. IX, pp. 620–1.

33 *DGFP*, Series D, vol. X, pp. 15–16.

34 *DGFP*, Series D, vol. X, pp. 2, 9, 187–9, 199–200, 276–7, 283, 290–1, 317–18, 366–7, 376–9, 397–401, 409–10; Walter Schellenberg, *The Schellenberg Memoirs: A Record of the Nazi Secret Service* (London, 1956) pp. 126–43; Mariano González-Arnao Conde-Luque, '¡Capturad al duque de Windsor!', *Historia 16*, no. 161, September 1989; Michael Bloch, *Operation Willi: The Plot to Kidnap the Duke of Windsor July 1940* (London, 1984), *passim*.

35 *DGFP*, Series D, vol. X, pp. 97–9.

Franco's urgent requests for food were simply dismissed out of hand, on the grounds of the greater needs of Germany and Italy. In contrast, it was assumed by the Germans that essential Spanish raw materials would continue to be exported to the Third Reich.[36] Although Franco was upset by the Führer's offhand response to his offer, he remained anxious to negotiate Spanish entry into the war. Franco declared on 18 July 1940 that Spain had two million warriors ready to fight to revive her past imperial glories and to pursue the mission of retaking Gibraltar and expanding Spanish Africa.[37] The general staff was drawing up plans for an attack on French North Africa and on Gibraltar. Moreover, during this period, Hitler was gradually being forced to give a higher priority to Spanish entry into the war. The unexpected obstinacy of British resistance and the defeat of the Luftwaffe in the Battle of Britain put paid to his invasion plans, Operation 'Sealion'. German thoughts turned to bringing down Britain by means other than frontal attack. On 15 August General Jodl had suggested the intensification of U-boat warfare and the seizure of the nerve centres of her empire, Gibraltar and Suez, in a bid to give the Axis control of the Mediterranean and the Middle East. Already, on 2 August, Ribbentrop had informed the ambassador in Madrid that 'what we want to achieve now is Spain's early entry into the war'.[38] German officials began the process of ascertaining what exactly were Spain's essential civilian and military needs in terms of fuel, grain and other vital goods. The figures produced for civilian uses alone were enormous.[39]

The acute problems of supplying a war machine were skated over in Madrid because of a widely held conviction in official circles that the conflict would be short and the Third Reich swiftly victorious. Beigbeder was certain that Britain would fall within a matter of weeks. The Portuguese had been pressed for an assurance that they would give Spain a free hand for an attack on Gibraltar. Franco told Vigón that he regarded an early entry into the war as useful since, as a result of the British blockade, 'Spain already had one foot in the war'. He also said that he could reconcile himself to a war of longer duration.[40] Serrano Suñer was preparing public opinion for war by carefully orchestrated attacks on England in the state-controlled press. Apprehensive that Berlin's silence with regard to his overtures could mean that Spain would not be invited to share the spoils, Franco had written a buoyant letter, barely a week

---

36 *DGFP*, Series D, vol. IX, pp. 605–6, 608–11.

37 Hoare, *Ambassador*, pp. 48–9.

38 *DGFP*, Series D, vol. X, p. 396; Hoare, *Ambassador*, p. 44; Serrano Suñer, *Entre Hendaya y Gibraltar*, p. 65; Churchill, *Finest Hour*, p. 463.

39 *DGFP*, Series D, Vol. X, pp. 466–7, 499–500, 521; André Brissaud, *Canaris*, (London, 1973) pp. 191–4; Macgregor Knox, *Mussolini Unleashed 1939–1941: Politics and Strategy in Fascist Italy's Last War* (Cambridge, 1982), p. 184.

40 *DGFP*, Series D, vol. X, pp. 514–15, 521.

previously, on 15 August, to Mussolini from Madrid, in which he reminded the Duce of Spanish aspirations and claims in North Africa, declaring that Spain was 'preparing to take her place in the struggle against our common enemies'.[41]

In the early summer of 1940 enthusiasm for Spanish entry into the war had come entirely from Madrid. Since it was blatantly obvious that Franco and Serrano Suñer planned for Spain to take part after the worst of the fighting was over but before the division of the spoils, their offers had been brushed aside ungraciously by the Germans. In the autumn and winter the situation was to change slowly, as Franco gradually came to appreciate the strength of British resistance and as Spain's economic position deteriorated. Although he was never to admit it and always to resent it, Franco was, from the autumn of 1940, to become ever more vulnerable to Anglo-American pressures and blandishments. As the emissary of the British Ministry of Economic Warfare, David Eccles, wrote to his wife on 1 November 1940, 'The Spaniards are up for sale and it is our job to see that the auctioneer knocks them down to our bid'.[42] Another significant factor in the diminution of the Caudillo's warlike fervour was his resentment at Hitler's own demands in relation to Spanish belligerance. At the end of the summer, however, Franco remained sanguine about Spain's possible contribution to the Axis war effort. His optimism was still not shared by the Germans.[43]

That was to be starkly clear when Ambassador Stohrer composed a preliminary draft of a Hispano-German protocol on Spanish entry into the war. Somewhat reworked, with the addition of further opinions from the Oberkommando der Wehrmacht, Stohrer's draft formed the basis of Ribbentrop's brief for discussions with Serrano Suñer who was due to arrive in Berlin in mid-September to reiterate Franco's earlier offers. By its terms, Spain would, in accord with the Axis powers, determine the time of entry into the war. In return for the Reich supplying the necessary military equipment and foodstuffs, Spain would undertake to recognize her Civil War debts to Germany and pay them off through future deliveries of raw materials. French and British mining properties in Spain and Spanish Morocco would be conceded to Germany. Spanish territory on the Gulf of Guinea was to be transferred to Germany. The Spanish economy would be integrated into a German-dominated European economy. Spain would play only a subordinate role, her activities being confined to agriculture, the production of raw materials and industries 'indigenous to Spain'.[44]

---

41 *DGFP*, Series D, vol. X, pp. 484–6; *Ciano's Diary 39–43*, p. 285; Serrano Suñer, *Entre Hendaya y Gibraltar*, pp. 103–4.

42 David Eccles (ed.), *By Safe Hand: Letters of Sybil and David Eccles 1939–42* (London, 1983), p. 180.

43 *DGFP*, Series D, vol. X, p. 561.

44 *DGFP*, Series D, vol. X, pp. 561–5, vol. XI, pp. 37–40, 81–2.

Serrano Suñer arrived in Berlin on 16 September 1940, accompanied by a large party of Falangists, to discuss Spain's contribution to the decisive blow against Britain. Operation 'Sealion' for the invasion of England had been postponed temporarily on 14 September and was about to be postponed indefinitely on 17 September because of the weather and the success of the RAF in the Battle of Britain. The Germans were less than honest with their Spanish guest about this, Ribbentrop telling Serrano Suñer that soon 'there would be nothing left of London but rubble and ashes'. Serrano Suñer described the purpose of his visit as being formally, as a cabinet member and 'the personal agent of Spain', to take discussions on Spanish entry into the war beyond the earlier 'sporadic feelers'. He expressed surprise that the materials necessary for Spain's war effort had not yet arrived from Germany. Reiterating the particular list of items which Spain required, he also reminded Ribbentrop of her determination to acquire all of French Morocco which 'belonged to Spain's Lebensraum' and the area around Oran inhabited by Spaniards. Serrano Suñer and Ribbentrop did not take to each other and this was to have great significance with regard to Spain's ultimate neutrality. The harshness and affectation of the German minister helped to curtail the Spaniard's natural impetuosity and fervour for the Axis cause. Stohrer told Walter Schellenberg of the Reichsicherheitshauptamt that he believed that Ribbentrop's demands were putting the Spaniards off.[45]

Ribbentrop quibbled over the amounts of material requested by Spain but finally agreed that she would receive what was absolutely necessary to her. What Germany wanted in return was stated quite brutally. Aware that the British would respond to the seizure of Gibraltar by taking the Canary Islands, the Azores, or the Cape Verde Islands, the Führer wanted one of the Canary Islands for a German base, and further bases at Agadir and Mogador with 'appropriate hinterland'. He also made substantial economic demands in terms of faster Civil War debt repayment and German participation in mining interests in Morocco. Serrano Suñer regarded this as intolerable impertinence.[46] On the following day, Serrano Suñer was received by Hitler for a one-hour conversation and told him unequivocally that Spain was ready to enter the war as soon as her supply of foodstuffs and war material was secure. Hitler declared enthusiastically how important and easy the speedy capture of Gibraltar would be, something which had, he said, already been the object of minute study by German experts. The Führer also repeated his desire for a base on the Canaries and suggested that he and Franco meet at the Franco–Spanish border. Shortly afterwards, Serrano again met Ribbentrop who pressed

---

45 Schellenberg, *Memoirs*, pp. 135, 143.
46 *DGFP*, Series D, vol. XI, pp. 83–91; Serrano Suñer, *Entre Hendaya y Gibraltar*, pp. 165–71.

him hard on the question of Spain ceding one of the Canary Islands and added that Germany wanted Spanish Guinea and the small Spanish islands off Central Africa in return for letting Spain have French Morocco. Serrano Suñer stressed that Spain would be unable to agree, describing the suggestion as criminal and monstrous. He suggested instead that Germany use Portuguese Madeira.[47]

As a result of his meeting with Serrano Suñer, Hitler wrote to Franco on 18 September outlining his thoughts on the issues raised. The problems with 'Sealion' could be read between the lines, particularly when the Führer stressed that the British blockade of Spain could only be broken by the expulsion of the British from the Mediterranean. This, he claimed, would 'be attained rapidly and with certainty through Spain's entry into the war'.[48] Hitler's demands for a base in the Canary Islands, together with his extensive economic claims in both mainland Spain and Spanish Morocco, took some of the edge off the enthusiasm of both Franco and Serrano Suñer for the Axis cause. It slowly dawned on them that Spain's place in the new order would be 'that of an insignificant and exploited satellite'. Hitler's colonial ambitions for a large Central African empire with bases in the Canary Islands and Spanish Morocco as staging posts to it were of more importance to him than good relations with Franco. Accordingly, he treated Franco in such a way as to sacrifice the Caudillo's co-operation in an attack on Gibraltar. Indeed, the Caudillo wrote to Serrano on 21 September about 'what rightly provoked your indignation and which the pen refuses to write', commenting that the German claims were more appropriate for the treatment of a defeated enemy and were 'incompatible with the grandeur and independence of a nation'.[49] On 24 September Ribbentrop and Serrano Suñer were both back in Berlin for an extremely tough encounter. Adopting a patronizing tone throughout the meeting, Ribbentrop pressed Serrano Suñer for a response to Hitler's territorial requests. After some prevarication, Serrano Suñer replied negatively in all cases. Ribbentrop then raised the question of Spain's Civil War debts to Germany, demanding that British and French business assets in Spain be transferred to Germany and credited to the outstanding debt.[50]

Franco's policy was based on a determination to enter the war as nearly as possible to the end. However, the British capacity to resist made

---

47 *DGFP*, Series D, vol. XI, pp. 93–102; Serrano Suñer, *Entre Hendaya y Gibraltar*, pp. 175–83.
48 *DGFP*, Series D, vol. XI, pp. 106–8.
49 Gerhard L. Weinberg, *World in the Balance: Behind the Scenes of World War II* (Hanover, New Hampshire, 1981) p. 122; Serrano Suñer, *Entre Hendaya y Gibraltar*, p. 183. The two quotations from Franco are from letters reprinted in Ramón Serrano Suñer, *Entre el silencio y la propaganda, la Historia como fue: Memorias* (Barcelona, 1977), pp. 335–7.
50 *DGFP*, Series D, vol. XI, pp. 166–74.

that moment difficult to predict. He had no wish to emulate Mussolini's rashness but neither did he want to miss the boat. Already there was opposition building up within the higher reaches of the Spanish army to entry into the war. The general staff reported that the navy had no fuel, that there was no air force worthy of the name and no effective mechanized units, and that after the Civil War the population would not tolerate more sacrifices. With tensions brewing between monarchists and Falangists, Franco, as a compromise solution, latched on to the idea of the secret protocol with the Axis, which he hoped would guarantee his territorial ambitions yet still leave the precise date of Spanish entry up to him. However, Hitler was neither able nor inclined to pay the Caudillo's price. The harsh demands made by Hitler and Ribbentrop in their meetings with Serrano Suñer in Berlin on 16, 17 and 24 September clinched Franco's determination to enter the war only if he was paid in advance.[51]

Despite the disappointments of his Berlin trip, Serrano Suñer gave Ambassador Stohrer a memorandum which announced Spain's 'readiness to conclude in the form of a tripartite pact a military alliance for 10 years with Germany and Italy'.[52] While in Berlin Serrano Suñer invited Heinrich Himmler to visit Madrid and advise on the modernization of the Spanish secret police.[53] On 28 September Hitler spoke with Ciano in Berlin and he made no secret of his impatience with the Spaniards. He accurately summed up the agreement proposed by Franco and Serrano Suñer as Germany undertaking to supply grain, fuel, military equipment, all the troops and weapons necessary for the conquest of Gibraltar, and all of Morocco and Oran in return for promises of Spanish friendship. In fact, the Führer's main concern was that any agreement over Morocco might leak out to the French and provoke an understanding which might permit the British to establish themselves in North Africa. If the Spaniards were allowed to take over Morocco, they would probably need German help to hold it. He preferred to leave the French there to defend Morocco against the British. With regard to the settlement of Civil War debts, which the Spaniards considered a tactless confusion of economic and idealistic considerations, Hitler said that 'as a German, one feels towards the Spanish almost like a Jew, who wants to make business out of the holiest possessions of mankind'. It was hardly surprising that Hitler should tell Ciano that he opposed Spanish intervention, 'because it would cost more than it is worth'.[54]

---

51 Smyth, 'The Moor', pp. 171–4.
52 *DGFP*, Series D, vol. XI, pp. 199–204.
53 Hoare, *Ambassador*, p. 76.
54 *DGFP*, Series D, Vol. XI, pp. 211–14; *Ciano's Diary 39–43*, p. 294.

On 1 October 1940, on a visit to Rome, Serrano Suñer spoke passionately to Ciano about the Germans' 'absolute lack of tact in dealing with Spain'. Hitler himself was trying to balance the conflicting demands of Franco, Pétain and Mussolini, something which he conceded was possible only through 'a grandiose fraud'.[55] Franco himself was not above a bit of fraud and he was already starting to hedge his bets. The British, for their part, were toying with major concessions to Spain. The American government was considering sending wheat to Spain through the Red Cross. On 7 October General Franco sent a telegram to Roosevelt saying that it was in America's power to take decisive action which would effect the entire course of the war. Spain would stay neutral if only the USA would send wheat. The British agreed to shipments 'on condition that American agents in Spain distributed the wheat, that none was re-exported, that publicity was given to the whole affair, and that wheat ships should go over singly and be stopped by us if anything went wrong'.[56]

On 18 October 1940 Beigbeder was formally replaced as Minister of Foreign Affairs by Serrano Suñer. Mussolini wrote to Hitler on the following day that Franco's cabinet reshuffle 'affords us assurance that the tendencies hostile to the Axis are eliminated or at least neutralized'.[57] However, no reconciliation was effected at the historic meeting between Hitler and Franco at Hendaye on 23 October 1940. Hitler was engaged in his 'grandiose fraud', seeing Laval on 22 October at Montoire-sur-Loire, a remote village railway station near Tours, *en route* to his meeting with Franco and then Pétain on 24 October again at Montoire on his way back. The Führer was preoccupied with the anxiety that Mussolini was about to get involved in a protracted and inconvenient Balkan war by attacking Greece. He was therefore coming round to the view that to hand French Morocco over to the Spaniards was to make them vulnerable to British attack.

Although the Caudillo was unaware of the extent of Hitler's difficulties with regard to both Britain and Greece, he was not inclined to make things easy for him. By this time, it seemed to Franco that a long struggle might be in the offing, a perception which naturally diminished his readiness to go to war in the immediate future. On the other hand, he was still anxious to be in at the death. Always keen to profit from Hitler's successes but determined not to have to pay for the privilege, Franco opened the Hendaye meeting with rhetorical assurances – 'Spain

55 *Ciano's Diary 39–43*, pp. 294–6; Ciano, *Papers*, pp. 393–6; Knox, *Mussolini Unleashed*, pp. 189, 196.

56 Hugh Dalton, *The Second World War Diary of Hugh Dalton*, edited by Ben Pimlott (London, 1986), 7 October 1940, p. 89; *Foreign Relations of the United States 1940*, (Washington, 1957) Vol. II, pp. 812–17, (henceforth *FRUS*).

57 *DGFP*, Series D, vol. XI, pp. 331–4.

would gladly fight at Germany's side', but because of difficulties being made by the USA and Britain, 'Spain must mark time and often look kindly toward things of which she thoroughly disapproved'. More than a conversation, there were opposing monologues. Curiously, in the light of the power balance between the two interlocutors, Hitler was unable to dominate the meeting. He rambled around the point, indulging in a frantic justification of Germany's present difficulties in the war, with particular emphasis on the role of the weather in the Battle of Britain.

Most crucially in terms of the ultimate outcome, Hitler also explained laboriously and rather obliquely why Spain's Moroccan ambitions were problematic, given his need for co-operation with the French. In this regard, he referred to his conversation on the day before with Laval and his forthcoming encounter with Pétain; his theme was that, if France came in with Germany, then her territorial losses could be compensated with British colonies. The bitter pill for Franco was Hitler's statement that

> If co-operation with France proved possible, then the territorial results of the war might perhaps not be so great. Yet the risk was smaller and success more readily obtainable. In his personal view it was better in so severe a struggle to aim at a quick success in a short time, even if the gain would be smaller than to wage long drawn-out wars. If with France's aid Germany could win faster, she was ready to give France easier peace terms in return.

Franco can hardly have failed to notice that his hopes of massive territorial gain at virtually no cost were being slashed before his eyes. It is not therefore surprising that he replied, to Hitler's unconcealed annoyance, with a recital of the appalling conditions in Spain, a list of supplies required to facilitate her military preparations and a pompous assertion that Spain could take Gibraltar alone. The two Foreign Ministers were then left to draw up a protocol.[58] However, after being in Franco's company for nearly nine hours, Hitler told Mussolini later that 'Rather than go through that again, I would prefer to have three or four teeth taken out'.[59] In fact, Hitler had thought to deceive the Spaniards over French Morocco by the seemingly frank admission that he could not give what was not yet his, implying that he would indeed give it when it was in his power to do so. He was, of course, confident of being able to dispose of the French colonial empire as he wished but had no intention of giving it to Franco. That was his 'grandiose fraud'. Serrano Suñer suggested years later that he

---

58 Serrano Suñer, *Memorias*, pp. 283–301; Paul Schmidt, *Hitler's Interpreter: The Secret History of German Diplomacy 1935–1945* (London, 1951) p. 196; Brissaud, *Canaris*, pp. 204–9. For Hitler's statement at Hendaye, *DGFP*, Series D, vol. XI, pp. 371–9.
59 Ciano, *Papers*, p. 402.

had not told a sufficiently big lie. According to the *cuñadísimo*, Franco's *Africanista* obsession with Morocco was such that, if Hitler had offered it, he would have entered the war.[60]

It was fortunate for Franco that Hitler remained unwilling and indeed unable to pay his price. After all, one of the Führer's reasons for wanting Spain's participation was to be able to control North Africa and so preclude a buildup of French resistance there. Yet Franco's price, the cession of French colonies, would almost certainly have precipitated an anti-German movement under de Gaulle that would pave the way to Allied landings. The Hendaye meeting came to a stalemate precisely on this problem. The protocol was signed, committing Spain to join the Axis cause at a date to be decided by 'common agreement of the three Powers' but after military preparations were complete. This effectively left the decision with Franco. Hitler made firm promises concerning only Gibraltar and was imprecise about future Spanish control of French colonies in Africa. The Spaniards would keep their options open. Presumably that is why Serrano Suñer informed the American ambassador on 31 October 1940, and repeated it three times, that 'there had been no pressure, not even an insinuation on the part of either Hitler or Mussolini that Spain should enter the war'.[61]

Franco's offers to join in the war in the early summer of 1940 had been rebuffed by Hitler as gratuitous. The Führer's efforts to get Franco to join the Axis in the autumn of 1940 failed because Hitler did not feel that he had to pay the going rate for the Caudillo's services. Thereafter, in the entire course of the Second World War, Spain came no nearer than she had in 1940 to joining the Axis. That is not to say that Franco was working hard to keep out of Hitler's clutches, as some of his admirers have suggested. There is little doubt that the Caudillo's sympathies continued to lie with Germany and Italy. If Hitler had met the asking price, Franco would almost certainly have joined him. Nevertheless, his own survival was always Franco's paramount ambition; in addition to the fact that Hitler seemed to be seeking Spanish aid on impossible terms, after the cancellation of Operation 'Sealion' the possibility of Axis defeat made the Caudillo ever more circumspect. Moreover, the tensions between the army and the Falange precisely over whether or not to go to war also gave Franco pause. The most obvious example of that circumspection and its link to domestic issues was his non-interference during Operation 'Torch', which took place less than two months after the dismissal of Serrano Suñer. Yet between Hendaye and 'Torch', there was plenty of evidence that Franco still hankered after being part of a victorious Axis coalition.

---

60 Heleno Saña, *El franquismo sin mitos: conversaciones con Serrano Suñer*, (Barcelona, 1981), p. 193. See also the polemic between Serrano Suñer and Antonio Marquina in *El País*, 19, 21, 22, 26, 28, 29 November 1978.
61 *FRUS 1940*, II, p. 824.

In early November 1940, for instance, it looked as if the disappointments of Hendaye had been overcome. Franco took several initiatives which can only be interpreted as a readiness to fight. On 1 November he wrote to Hitler promising to carry out his verbal undertaking to enter the war.[62] On 9 November three copies of the secret German-Italian-Spanish protocol arrived in Madrid and were duly signed by Serrano Suñer and the German and Italian copies sent back by special courier.[63] However, circumstances were changing rapidly in such a way as to curtail Franco's enthusiasm. The economic crisis inside Spain was deepening dramatically and there were ever more frequent signs that the inexorable conveyor-belt of Axis triumphs was slowing down. Hitler, in contrast, shaken by the British naval victory over the Italians at Taranto, was becoming keener to force the pace. To this end, on 11 November, Ribbentrop invited Serrano Suñer to a meeting with himself and Ciano at the Berghof one week later.

The Germans were now ever more convinced of the urgent need for an attack on Gibraltar. On 4 November Hitler told Generals Brauchitsch, Halder, Keitel and Jodl that, having Franco's assurance that he was about to join Germany, it would be possible to seize Gibraltar. Detailed plans were drawn up in mid-November for what was to be called Operation 'Felix', whereby German troops would enter Spain on 10 January 1941 prior to beginning an assault on Gibraltar on 4 February.[64] German troops began to rehearse the assault near Besançon. The problem, as Hitler's chief supply planners quickly discovered, was that Franco had not exaggerated when he had spoken of the prostrate condition of the Spanish economy. The different rail gauges on either side of the Franco-Spanish border, the general disrepair of Spanish track and rolling stock and the limited capacity of the Spanish system were notorious. Moreover, a disastrous harvest meant that Spain needed considerably more grain than specified in her earlier requests to the Germans. With famine conditions developing in many parts of the country, Franco had no choice but to seek to buy food in the United States and that necessarily involved postponing a declaration of war.[65] At the same time the British Government was advocating American food aid for Spain precisely to deprive Franco of the excuse to slip into the arms of the Axis.[66]

The meeting between Hitler and Serrano Suñer took place at Berchtesgaden on 19 November 1940. There was a greater urgency now on Hitler's side and an element of prevarication on Serrano Suñer's. Although he tried

---

62 *DGFP*, Series D, vol. XI, p. 452.

63 *DGFP*, Series D, vol. XI, pp. 478–9.

64 Directive no. 18, 12 November 1940, *Hitler's War Directives 1939–1945*, edited by H. R. Trevor-Roper (London, 1966), pp. 81–7.

65 *DGFP*, Series D, vol. XI, pp. 528–30, 574–6, 581–2; Charles B. Burdick, *Germany's Military Strategy and Spain in World War II* (Syracuse, 1968), pp. 77 ff.

66 *FRUS 1940*, vol. II, pp. 829–38.

to play down the consequences of Mussolini's 'mistake' in Greece, Hitler was blunt about the urgent need to shut off the Mediterranean, at Gibraltar and at Suez. Serrano Suñer reminded Hitler of how disappointed he and the Caudillo were at the vagueness of the promises made in the secret protocol concerning Spain's imperial demands, at which Hitler insisted that Spain would be satisfied in Morocco. The meeting resolved nothing. Hitler perhaps sensed, more than Ribbentrop would do, the difficulties over Spanish entry and, when he saw Ciano immediately after speaking to Serrano Suñer, he suggested that Mussolini use his influence with Franco to clinch Spain's intervention.[67]

Surprisingly, the Germans were convinced, briefly at least, that Spain was about to join them. Hitler therefore sent Admiral Canaris to Spain to discuss the details. As an indication of the inclination of Franco towards the Axis, Serrano Suñer informed Stohrer that the Spanish government had agreed to German tankers being stationed in remote bays on the northern coast for the refuelling of German destroyers.[68] However, it was soon evident that Hitler and the Spaniards had been talking at cross-purposes. On 5 December Hitler met his high command and decided to request Franco that German troops be permitted to cross the Spanish border on 10 January 1941. It was planned for General Jodl to go to Spain to make the necessary arrangements for the attack on Gibraltar as soon as Canaris got Franco's agreement to the target date. Canaris arrived in a freezing, snow-bound Madrid on 7 December. At 7.30 in the evening, he put to Franco, in the presence of General Vigón, the need for Spain's prompt entry into the war, to which the Caudillo replied that she was simply not sufficiently prepared, particularly in terms of food supplies, to be able to meet Hitler's deadline. The deficit in foodstuffs was now estimated by Franco to be 1,000,000 tonnes. The shortages of food were compounded by appalling difficulties on both roads and railways. Franco also expressed his fears that the seizure of Gibraltar would ensure that Spain would lose the Canary Islands and her other overseas possessions. This was a significant admission of doubt about the prospects of an early Axis triumph in the war. General Franco made it clear that Spain could enter the war only when England was almost ready to collapse. On receiving Canaris's depressing report, Hitler decided that Operation 'Felix' should be discontinued. His bitter disappointment was reflected in an end-of-year letter to Mussolini in which he declared that 'I fear that Franco is committing here the greatest mistake of his life'.[69]

---

67 *DGFP*, Series D, vol. XI, pp. 598–606; Serrano Suñer, *Entre Hendaya y Gibraltar*, pp. 235–49; Ciano, *Papers*, pp. 409–11.

68 *DGFP*, Series D, vol. XI, pp. 787–8.

69 *DGFP*, Series D, vol. XI, pp. 812, 816–17, 852–3, 990–4; Heinz Höhne, *Canaris* (London, 1979) pp. 440–1; Brissaud, *Canaris*, pp. 224–6; Serrano Suñer, *Entre Hendaya y Gibraltar*, pp. 258–9.

Throughout November detailed reconnaissance had been carried out, preparations and rehearsals held. However, there was no question of Hitler simply proceeding to attack Gibraltar without the acquiescence of Franco. A frontal sea assault was precluded by the fact that the German navy was already over-committed to protecting Norway and to continuing the Atlantic war. An assault had therefore to be by land. This would involve the German troops in a march of 1,200 kilometres, carrying all their supplies along poor, often unmetalled roads, through narrow, winding mountain passes often affected by fog and ice. Moreover, since Spain was so desperately short of food, there was little hope of the troops either living off the land or purchasing food and fuel as they went. Stohrer reported on 9 December that the intensification of famine conditions had taken precedence over every other issue including entry into the war. He wrote to the Wilhelmstrasse on 11 December of people collapsing in the streets of Madrid from lack of food. He also claimed that 'remonstrances by a number of influential generals have aroused in Franco the fear that the conflict of personalities and issues between S. Suñer and the military could become an acute danger for the regime if the grave misgivings of these generals toward immediate entry into the war, mainly on economic though also on military grounds, are not given heed'. Stohrer was convinced that Franco's change of heart about going to war was entirely the result of the food crisis and his consequent fear for the safety of his regime. He also believed that to overcome Franco's problems would entail economic support of 'tremendous proportions'. To attack without Franco's consent would involve the enormous difficulty of occupying a hostile country. This inspired Churchill with the hope that Hitler would not try to force his way through Spain. As he wrote to General Ismay on 6 January 1941, an invasion in winter was 'a most dangerous and questionable enterprise for Germany to undertake, and it is no wonder that Hitler, with so many sullen populations to hold down, has so far shrunk from it'.[70]

It was the famine, combined with worries over the ongoing hostility between the Falange and his generals, which had caused Franco to pull back at the crucial moment. His regret was no doubt diminished by evidence that the victory of the Axis was at best likely to be delayed and at worst, albeit a remote possibility, no longer certain at all. Nevertheless, that regret seemed to be genuine. When Stohrer told Franco on 20 January 1941 of the view in Berlin that he and the Spanish government were no longer entirely convinced that the Reich would win the war, the Caudillo

---

70 *DGFP*, Series D, vol. XI, pp. 824–5, 847–50; John Lukacs, *The Last European War: September 1939–December 1941* (London, 1976) p. 114; Winston S. Churchill, *The Second World War*, Vol. II, *The Grand Alliance* (London, 1950) p. 7. On military opposition to adventurism in foreign policy see Chapter 4, 'Franco and his generals 1939–45' in this volume.

protested vehemently that his policy was unchanged, that 'his faith in the victory of Germany was also still the same'. Franco insisted that 'it was not a question at all of whether Spain would enter the war; that had been decided at Hendaye. It was merely a question of when.'[71] Deeply stung by a harsh and arrogant message from Ribbentrop, delivered on 23 January, Franco bitterly complained to Stohrer about its accusations of vacillation on his part. With apparent sincerity, he asserted that his position was unswervingly on the Axis side, from gratitude and as a man of honour and insisted that he had not deviated 'one millimetre from his Germanophile course' nor made any political concessions to the Western Allies.[72] When an infuriated Ribbentrop demanded a definitive answer, however, Franco continued to prevaricate. On 5 February 1941 Hitler wrote to Mussolini, lamenting how a great opportunity to seal off the western end of the Mediterranean had been lost by Franco's lack of resolution. The Führer for a second time asked the Duce to try to persuade Franco to change his mind.[73] In fact, with the economic situation in Spain deteriorating daily, there was little possibility of that happening. German consuls were reporting that there was no bread at all in part of the country and there were cases of highway robbery and banditry.

Hitler made a further albeit somewhat half-hearted effort himself in his letter to Franco dated 6 February 1941. After reiterating the reasons why Spain should be linking arms with Germany and Italy, the Führer went on politely to demolish Franco's excuses for delay. There was no specific effort in the letter to get Franco to commit himself other than a general invitation to join in an ideological conflict and an offer of supplies as soon as Spain declared war. Franco replied with an acknowledgement and a separate request for what Stohrer called 'pre-payment'. Drawn up by the Spanish general staff, it amounted to a call for supplies on such a scale as to lead the Director of the Economic Policy Department in Berlin to conclude that the requests were 'so obviously unrealizable that they can only be evaluated as an expression of the effort to avoid entering the war'. Significantly, on the same morning that he received Hitler's letter, Franco had received news of the final annihilation of Marshal Graziani's army by the British at Benghazi.[74] Mussolini having agreed to intercede with Franco, a meeting between the two was arranged for 12 and 13 February at Bordighera.[75] By the time that Franco met Mussolini, public opinion in Spain was moving strongly against any intervention in the war. The Italian

---

71 *DGFP*, Series D, vol. XI, pp. 1140–3.

72 *DGFP*, Series D, vol. XI, pp. 1157–8, 1171–5.

73 *DGFP*, Series D, vol. XII, p. 30.

74 *DGFP*, Series D, vol. XII, pp. 37–42, 51–3, 58, 78–9.

75 Serrano Suñer, *Entre Hendaya y Gibraltar*, pp. 262–3; Roberto Cantalupo, *Embajada en España* (Barcelona, 1951) pp. 240–1.

rout in Cyrenaica by a much smaller British force and the British naval bombardment of Genoa on 8 February had a significant impact in Spain in general, where they caused some malicious anti-Italian merriment.[76]

At Bordighera, Franco told Mussolini of his continued conviction of an ultimate Axis victory. He admitted quite candidly 'Spain wishes to enter the war; her fear is to enter too late'. He complained of German obstruction and made it clear that he was seeking explicit assurance that all Spain's territorial ambitions in Africa would be fulfilled. In this regard, he suggested that Hendaye had been less than successful because of Hitler's concern to draw France into the Axis orbit. Franco was clearly furious about this. He also stated that the attack on Gibraltar should be carried out solely as a Spanish operation. Mussolini was extremely understanding about Franco's difficulties and the enormous responsibility of entering the war. He agreed that Spanish belligerence should be at 'the moment least onerous for Spain and most useful for the common cause', amiably suggesting that 'the date and form of her [Spain's] participation in the war are matters for Spain herself'. The Duce asked Franco if he would declare war if given sufficient supplies and binding promises about his colonial requirements. The Caudillo replied that, even if all the supplies requested were delivered, which was impossible, given Hitler's other commitments, then Spain's military unpreparedness and famine conditions would still mean several months before she could join in the war. Franco summed up the entire question when he stated dryly that 'Spanish entry into the war depends on Germany more than on Spain herself; the sooner Germany sends help, the sooner Spain will make her contribution to the Fascist world cause'. Mussolini was inclined in consequence to stop trying to persuade Franco to join the Axis war effort in the short term. Instead, he believed that Germany and Italy should confine their Spanish efforts to keeping the hesitant Caudillo in the Axis political sphere.[77] The Duce informed Hitler about the Bordighera meeting at about the same time as the German Department of Economic Planning was reporting that Spanish demands could not be met without endangering the Reich's military capacity. Ribbentrop took Bordighera as signifying Franco's definitive refusal to join the war effort. On the assumption that Franco must know, despite his defective military thinking, that Spanish troops alone could never capture Gibraltar, Ribbentrop instructed Stohrer to take no further steps to secure Spanish belligerence.[78]

When finally Hitler contemplated forcing the issue, he had already committed his military machine to rescuing Italy from its disastrous

---

76 Hoare, *Ambassador*, pp. 95, 104.
77 Serrano Suñer, *Entre Hendaya y Gibraltar*, pp. 261–4; for Franco's words, see Ciano, *Papers*, pp. 421–30; Cantalupo, *Embajada*, pp. 249–52.
78 *DGFP*, Series D, vol. XII, pp. 96–7, 131–2.

involvement in the Balkans.[79] In fact, Bordighera showed that Franco was, for the moment, immune to the Axis temptation. He would not entirely put it behind him until late in 1944, but equally he was never again to be drawn by it unequivocally. Hitler simply did not have kingdoms enough to offer. Nevertheless, for a brief moment in mid-1941, with a swift victory over the Soviet Union apparently possible, the Caudillo was once more sorely tempted. When Franco finally replied to Hitler's three-week-old letter on 26 February, the language was effusively supportive of the Axis cause but effectively priced Spanish aid out of the market. It is curious that Hitler accepted Franco's rebuff so calmly. Churchill speculated that 'Hitler was scandalised, but, being now set upon the invasion of Russia, he did not perhaps like the idea of trying Napoleon's other unsuccessful enterprise, the invasion of Spain, at the same time'.[80] For Churchill, Franco's 'exasperating delay and exorbitant demands' were devices, the 'subtlety and trickery' by which he kept Spain out of the war.[81] Writing in the late 1940s, Churchill perhaps thought more highly of the anti-communist Franco than he had done at the time. He was certainly forgetting the immense part played by British economic warfare in twisting Franco's arm.

The changed tone of Hispano-German relations was marked at the end of February by German insistence on the repayment of Spain's Civil War debts, which were agreed at 372 million Reichsmarks.[82] This was to be in marked contrast with the attitude of the Anglo-Saxon powers. On 20 March 1941 Lord Halifax, the British ambassador in Washington, delivered a message from his government to the acting secretary of state Sumner Welles. It suggested that Britain, the United States and Portugal collaborate with economic help for Spain in order both to isolate Serrano Suñer and also to create a western Mediterranean bloc independent of the German continental system. The suggestion was sympathetically received. On 7 April 1941 Britain granted Spain credits of £2,500,000.[83] However, German successes in the spring of 1941 once more wiped away some of Franco's caution.

The German victories in North Africa, Yugoslavia and Greece convinced Franco that his underlying faith in an Axis victory was not misplaced. In a speech commemorating the Unificación on 19 April 1941 he declared that peace was merely a preparation for war, and the latter the normal condition of humanity. After the fall of Crete Franco was confident that Suez would soon be in Axis power.[84] Just as the waning of pro-Axis

---

79 Burdick, *Germany's Military Strategy*, pp. 103 ff.
80 Churchill, *Second World War*, Vol. II, *Their Finest Hour*, p. 468.
81 Churchill, *Finest Hour*, pp. 467–8.
82 *DGFP*, Series D, vol. XII, pp. 194–5.
83 *FRUS 1941*, (Washington, 1959) vol. II, pp. 886–7.
84 *FRUS 1941*, II, pp. 891–903.

enthusiasm in later 1940 had been in part at least a response to internal political tensions within the Francoist coalition, so too the flowering of his fervour in 1941 reflected Franco's permanent preoccupation with his own domestic political position. Throughout the spring of 1941, reports from the Auslandorganization and the Madrid embassy stressed to Berlin both Spain's continually deteriorating economic situation and the intensifying dissatisfaction with Franco's government. This had led to an intensification of the unpopularity of Serrano Suñer, particularly from the military.[85] In search of German support in the internal power struggle which was getting under way, Serrano Suñer vied with Franco for the position of leader of the pro-German claque. At the beginning of May 1941, he told Stohrer that 'we want to and shall enter the war'. At that time, however, Franco had seriously weakened Serrano Suñer's position by the appointment of Colonel Valentín Galarza as Minister of the Interior. There were clashes between the police and members of the Falange and the hostility between the military and the Falange was reaching boiling point.

The Caudillo may not have been in any position to enter a war which showed signs of being prolonged for some considerable time. However, his belief in the ultimate victory of the Axis remained strong. Franco's pro-Axis enthusiasm was inflamed anew by the Nazi invasion of the Soviet Union on 22 June 1941. On being officially informed of the German attack on Russia, Serrano Suñer expressed great enthusiasm and informed Stohrer that, after consultation, he and Franco wished to send volunteer units of Falangists to fight, 'independently of the full and complete entry of Spain into the war beside the Axis, which would take place at the appropriate moment'.[86] At the specific behest of Serrano Suñer, the controlled press rejoiced and printed exaggerated accounts of an exchange of anti-aircraft fire near the Gibraltar border and the British naval blockade. The British embassy was stormed by Falangists on 24 June, after Serrano Suñer had harangued them at the Falange headquarters in Alcalá, declaring that 'history demanded the extermination of Russia'. The assault on the British embassy was facilitated by a truck-load of stones thoughtfully provided by the authorities.

Three days later, Spain moved from non-belligerency to what was described by Serrano Suñer as 'moral belligerency' and preparations began for the creation of the Blue Division of Falangist volunteers to go and fight on the Russian front. This was in addition to the agreement made on 21 August 1941 between the Deutsche Arbeitsfront and the Delegación Nacional de Sindicatos for 100,000 Spanish workers

---

85 *DGFP*, Series D, vol. XII, pp. 611–15; Josef Goebbels, *The Goebbels Diaries 1939–1941*, edited by Fred Taylor, (London, 1982) p. 373.
86 *DGFP*, Series D, vol. XII, pp. 1080–1.

to be sent to Germany. Theoretically 'volunteers', but more often levies chosen by the Falange to fit Germany's industrial needs, between 15,000 and 20,000 were eventually sent.[87] It is now clear that the episode of the Blue Division was not a prelude to a declaration of war on Britain. Indeed, when Ribbentrop thanked Franco for the gesture and invited such a declaration, Franco refused on the entirely plausible grounds that his regime could not survive a full-scale Allied blockade. For him it was a question of keeping an iron in the fire, showing sufficient commitment to the Axis cause to have a say in the future division of the spoils but doing so in a sufficiently remote corner of the war not to alienate the Allies totally.

As Serrano Suñer described the sending of the Blue Division, 'Their sacrifice would give us a title of legitimacy to participate one day in the dreamed-of victory and exempt us from the general and terrible sacrifices of the war.' Franco was heard frequently asserting that the Allies had lost the war. On the fifth anniversary of the outbreak of the Spanish Civil War, 17 July 1941, he addressed the Consejo Nacional of the Falange and expressed his enthusiasm for Hitler's Russian venture at 'this moment when the German armies lead the battle for which Europe and Christianity have for so many years longed, and in which the blood of our youth is to mingle with that of our comrades of the Axis'. 'I do not harbour any doubt about the result of the war. The die is cast and the first battle was won here in Spain. The war is lost for the Allies.' He spoke of his contempt for 'plutocratic democracies', of his conviction that Germany had already won the war and that American intervention would be a 'criminal madness' leading only to useless prolongation of the conflict and catastrophe for the USA. He made an entirely mendacious claim that the USA was holding back grain already purchased by Spain and stated provocatively that her offers of economic aid were a mask for political pressure 'incompatible with our sovereignty and with our dignity as a free people'. He denounced the arrangement made in the autumn of 1940 whereby American warships were sent to Great Britain in return for the concession to the USA of British bases in the Caribbean. 'Gold ends by debasing nations as well as individuals. The exchange of fifty old destroyers for various remnants of an empire is eloquent in this regard.'[88]

Serrano Suñer was rather taken aback by Franco's impetuosity and complained to Stohrer that he had opened the eyes of the English and Americans to 'the true position of Spain'. Previously, according to Serrano Suñer, the British Government in particular kept on believing

---

87 Hoare, *Ambassador*, p. 140; Manuel Espadas Burgos, *Franquismo y política exterior* (Madrid, 1988) p. 123.
88 *FRUS 1941*, vol. II, pp. 908–11.

that only he, the Foreign Minister, was pushing for war, while the 'wise and thoughtful' Caudillo was preserving neutrality unconditionally. 'That illusion has now been taken from them.' Serrano Suñer was absolutely correct in his analysis.[89]

During the summer of 1941, Franco's government continued to display an increasingly pro-German attitude. The controlled press frequently attacked England and the USA and glorified the achievements of German arms. The staff of the British and American embassies were treated coolly. In consequence, imports of essential goods began to dry up as Spain found it harder to get American export licences and British navicerts. Secretary Hull reflected the US reaction when he told the Spanish ambassador Juan Francisco de Cárdenas on 13 September that 'in all of the relations of this Government with the most backward and ignorant governments in the world, this Government has not experienced such a lack of ordinary courtesy or consideration, as it has at the hands of the Spanish Government. Its course has been one of aggravated discourtesy and contempt in the very face of our offers to be of aid.'[90]

Shortages of coal, copper, tin, rubber and textile fibres presaged a breakdown of Spanish industry within a matter of months. In a last desperate bid to avoid falling under Anglo-American economic pressure, the Spanish Minister of Commerce, Demetrio Carceller, was sent by Franco to Berlin in early September. Carceller carried to his hosts the clearly Franco-inspired statement that

> The German General Staff had to determine whether it fitted in with its plans for Spain to enter the war or not, and Germany only had to have full confidence that Spain was and remained at her side. Spain was ready for everything no matter what was planned by the German side. Spain would, without further ado, accomodate herself into the framework of the all-European policy led by Germany; but then she should not be treated like Cinderella and left unnoticed, but should be included in the over-all German economic planning.[91]

Little came of the visit and by 6 October Franco was telling the US ambassador Alexander Weddell of Spain's difficulties in obtaining wheat, cotton and gasoline and made clear his desire to see an improvement of economic relations with the USA.[92] This reflected in part the fact that a significant section of the military now believed that Britain and America

---

89 *DGFP*, Series D, vol. XIII, pp. 353–4, 357–8.
90 *FRUS 1941*, vol. II, pp. 913–25.
91 *DGFP*, Series D, vol. XIII, pp. 444–6, 459–60.
92 *FRUS 1941*, vol. II, pp. 924–9.

would win the war and were already taking their economic revenge on Spain. Moreover, the most senior generals, and even Franco himself, could not avoid the alarming conclusion that Hitler had got himself into serious trouble in Russia.

Even the apparent enthusiasm of Serrano Suñer for the Axis was dented. In the last week of November 1941 a gathering of the Anti-Comintern Pact powers was held in Berlin. On 29 November Serrano Suñer, Ciano, Ribbentrop, Stohrer and Hitler met to discuss the military situation. Serrano Suñer made great play of the attitude of the Spanish press towards the Axis and asserted that Spain 'performed every possible service for the Reich to the modest extent possible to her'. In this regard, he mentioned the Spanish belief that the war would be long and difficult, a significant change from previous declarations of faith in a swift victory.[93] Franco was greatly heartened by the Japanese attack on Pearl Harbour on 7 December 1941, but his joy was short-lived not least because of his considerable misgivings when the Japanese invaded the Philippines.[94] Moreover, Franco's second flowering of pro-Axis enthusiasm withered in the winter of 1941, along with the fortunes of the German armies in Russia. With the entry of the United States into the war and the British victorious in North Africa, the Caudillo seemed finally to have accepted that there were no territorial compensations which could justify the risks now involved in going to war.

Indeed, the unavoidable realization that American involvement meant that the war would be a long and titanic struggle obliged Franco to postpone Spanish entry into the war indefinitely. The precise moment of his so-called *chaqueteo* (or change of coat) is difficult to locate for the simple reason that it was never definitive. Speaking to high-ranking army officers at the Alcázar of Seville in February 1942, Franco declared 'If the road to Berlin were opened then not merely would one division of Spaniards participate in the struggle but one million Spaniards would be offered to help'.[95] Since Franco's own readiness to declare war still depended on guarantees both that British power was irrevocably finished and that prizes from Hitler would be forthcoming, Spain remained at peace. Neutrality then, far from being the result of brilliant statecraft or foresight was the fruit of a narrow pragmatism and what Serrano Suñer called the 'good fortune' that Germany would not or could not pay the price demanded for entry into the war.

93 *DGFP*, Series D, vol. XIII, pp. 904–6; *FRUS 1941*, vol. II, 932–4; *Ciano's Diaries 39–43*, p. 402; Ciano, *Papers*, pp. 461–2.
94 Espadas, *Franquismo*, p. 124.
95 Hoare, *Ambassador*, p. 140.

The internal political situation in Spain had also played its part. Military hostility to Serrano Suñer was reaching boiling point.[96] His days were numbered. The extent of the tension between the traditional right, represented by the generals, and the new right of the Falange, was reflected in Falangist student riots in Madrid in May 1942. Moreover, after his initial enthusiasm for the Japanese assault on the United States, economic and political realism had prevailed with the Caudillo and relations had improved with Washington. Less anti-American material was appearing in the press. Thereafter, Franco remained anxious to maintain good relations with the United States. Nevertheless, from time to time, his real sympathies gleamed through the fog of his rhetoric. On 29 May 1942 he addressed the Sección Femenina of the Falange. He compared his regime with that of Isabel la Católica, referring to her expulsion of the Jews, her totalitarian racial policy and her awareness of Spain's need for *lebensraum* (*espacio vital*).[97]

Throughout the summer of 1942 Franco began to distance himself from Serrano Suñer. Almost at a loose end, and certainly no longer at the centre of affairs, the *cuñadísimo* made a pointless ten-day visit to Italy from 15 to 25 June 1942 leaving Madrid just when the machinations of his enemies were on the verge of success. While in Rome, according to Ciano, Serrano Suñer spoke of Franco 'as one speaks of a moronic servant. And he said this without caution, in front of everyone'.[98] The possibility that his remarks were not reported to Franco is remote in the extreme. The suggestion that Franco's coolness towards his brother-in-law implied a shift towards the Allies ignores the many personal and internal Spanish reasons behind the cooling-off process. There was his own, and perhaps more important, his wife's, resentment of Serrano Suñer's hogging of the limelight. This was compounded by Señora Franco's anger at the fact that Madrid gossip had it that Serrano Suñer was two-timing her sister with the wife of an aristocrat lieutenant-colonel. More important, perhaps, was the intensification of military hostility to Serrano Suñer in the immediate aftermath of the clash between Falangists and Carlists at Begoña in mid-August, which finally suggested to Franco that a change was necessary and now possible.

The Caudillo's great political talent, and indeed the one on which the survival of his regime depended, was his ability to balance the internal forces of the Nationalist coalition. Under Serrano Suñer, the Falange seemed to be growing too powerful, although it too was riven with its own internal rivalries and jealousies. Franco could never afford to

---

96 Lequio to Ciano, 9, 10, 12 January 1942, *I Documenti Diplomatici Italiani*, 9ª serie, vol. VIII (Rome, 1988) pp. 113, 116–17, 123–4; *Arriba*, 13 January 1942.
97 *FRUS 1942*, (Washingon, 1961) vol. III, pp. 288–9.
98 *Ciano's Diary 39–45*, pp. 473.

lose the loyalty of the army. Accordingly, he replaced Serrano Suñer with Jordana as Foreign Minister on 3 September 1942.[99] Neither the Germans nor the Italians expressed much regret at his going, since the broad direction of Spanish policy did not change appreciably, a point made by Franco in a letter which he sent to Mussolini on 18 September 1943. In it, the Caudillo stressed the domestic dimension of the recent political changes, which 'do not in the least affect our position in foreign affairs but are aimed rather at reinforcing our position in domestic politics, giving it greater energy and unity, removing from the party intolerable dualisms and personalisms.'[100]

On the eve of Operation 'Torch', however, the departure of Serrano Suñer certainly favoured the Allied cause, even if that had not been Franco's intention. In the autumn of 1942, when the preparations for Operation Torch showed that an eventual Axis triumph was far from assured, Franco reacted, not with prophetic awareness of ultimate Allied victory, but rather with an entirely reasonable short-term caution. The massing of force on his borders was hardly the best moment to cross swords with perfidious Albion, particularly in the wake of Rommel's failure to conquer Egypt. Franco was intensely conscious of the Allies' power of retaliation. In any case, Allied successes in North Africa were so spectacular as immediately to inhibit any Spanish thoughts of hostile action. When Anglo-American forces entered precisely those French Moroccan and Algerian territories which he coveted, Franco was enough of a realist to instruct his ambassador in London to start a *rapprochement* with the Western Allies. That did not mean that he had lost his belief in an ultimate Axis victory. The *chaqueteo* was to be gradual and to leave options open.

Nevertheless, there could be discerned the beginnings of a slow move back to neutrality, visible for instance in the signing in December 1942 of the Bloque Ibérico agreement with Portugal. By the spring of 1943 it was obvious that the international panorama in which Franco operated had changed dramatically. 'Torch' had shifted the strategic balance, but throughout most of 1943, certainly up to the fall of Mussolini in the summer, Franco remained convinced that the Allies could not win and that their successes in Africa were of marginal importance. However, he did begin to contemplate the possibility that Germany might not gain a clear victory and might indeed be worn down by the sheer weight of Soviet numbers. In a spirit of what seemed to Hoare to be 'impenetrable

---

99   Sheelagh Ellwood, *Spanish Fascism in the Franco Era*, (London, 1987) pp. 84–90; Hoare, *Ambassador*, pp. 140, 164–71; Antonio Marquina Barrio, 'El atentado de Begoña', *Historia 16*, no. 76, August 1982, pp. 11–19.

100   Serrano Suñer, *Entre Hendaya y Gibraltar*, pp. 211–18; Ulrich Von Hassell, *The Von Hassell Diaries, 1938–1944* (New York, 1947) pp. 239–48; Javier Tusell, 'Franco no fue neutral', *Historia 16*, 1988.

complacency', the Caudillo was convinced that he could eventually, after a long war, step in as broker between both sides.[101] Moreover, as part of his own precautions against a possible Axis defeat, he began to present himself as the peacemaker whose intervention could save the West from the consequences of the destruction of the German bulwark against communism. In March 1943 Franco addressed the Cortes, as usual attacking Bolshevism, but also declaring his belief that an early end to the war was unlikely and predicting another six years of hostilities and neither victors nor vanquished at the end of it. In early May he undertook a tour of Andalusia, making speeches on this theme in Cordoba, Huelva, Seville, and Malaga. The culminating moment was reached on 9 May in a speech to the Falange at Almería, in which Franco said 'Neither of the belligerents has the strength to destroy the other.' He called for peace negotiations and a fairer distribution of colonies in the world.[102] None the less, it was not until after June 1944 that Franco removed the pictures of Hitler and Mussolini from his desk.

In the wake of the collapse of Mussolini's regime at the beginning of September and faced with rumblings of discontent from his own high command, Franco made some highly significant moves. On 26 September the withdrawal of the Blue Division was announced, although it was slightly weakened by proposals to permit volunteers to stay on in German units. On 1 October 1943 Franco addressed the Consejo Nacional of the Falange and now described Spain's position as one of 'vigilant neutrality'. That did nothing to prevent incidents such as Falangist attacks on the British vice-consulate in Zaragoza and the American consulate in Valencia.[103] Nor did it inhibit Spanish exports of vital wolfram to the Third Reich.

Wolfram was a crucial ingredient in the manufacture of high quality steel for armaments in general and particularly for machine tools and armour-piercing shells. American policy had been to try to persuade Spain to limit exports to Germany by supplying her with petroleum and buying up Spanish wolfram. On 3 December 1943 Franco spoke to the new German ambassador, Hans Heinrich Dieckhoff, who had arrived at the end of April 1943 after the sudden death in March of Stohrer's original successor Von Moltke. In response to Dieckhoff's complaints that Spain was responding to Allied pressure, particularly in the withdrawal of the Blue Division from Russia, Franco told him of his conviction that his own survival depended on an Axis victory and that an Allied triumph

---

101   Hoare, *Ambassador*, pp. 184–96.
102   On the Bloque Ibérico, see *Dez anos de política externa: A naçao portuguesa e a segunda guerra mundial*, Vol. XII (Lisbon, 1985) pp. 85–96; *The Times*, 23 December 1942; Doussinague, *España tenía razón*, pp. 116–26. On the Andalusian tour, see Doussinague, pp. 207–9 and Pike, 'Stigma', p. 384.
103   Hoare, *Ambassador*, pp. 239–40.

'would mean his own annihilation'. Accordingly, he hoped with all his heart for German victory as soon as possible. It is significant that he never made a similar statement of sympathy with the Allied cause to any British or American diplomat. He explained that he had withdrawn the Blue Division before an Allied request to do so because of growing difficulties about recruiting volunteers and to avoid the humiliation of accepting an Allied ultimatum. The crucial issue was that 'a neutral Spain which was furnishing Germany with wolfram and other products is at this moment of greater value to Germany than a Spain which would be drawn into the war'. At this point the Germans had reason to feel some satisfaction with their Spanish policy because Franco was paying off his Civil War debts with wolfram.[104]

By the beginning of 1944, with the tide of war clearly turning, North Africa secure and Italy out of the war, the USA was altogether less inclined to be patient with Franco. The American military staff was furious about continued Spanish wolfram exports to Germany. A crisis had been reached in October 1943 when Jordana, with Franco's approval, sent a letter of congratulation to José P. Laurel on his installation by the Japanese as puppet governor of the Philippines. They had been pushed into this major ineptitude by pro-German Falangists. There was an uproar in the United States. On 27 January 1944 the British ambassador visited the Caudillo at the Pardo. Hoare's outraged complaints were three. The Spanish government was providing the Third Reich with new and extensive facilities for purchasing wolfram. Secondly, despite the formal withdrawal of the Blue Division, the Falange was still recruiting for the small Spanish legion that remained in Russia and a unit of the Spanish air force was active alongside it. Finally, extensive espionage and sabotage activities were still being carried out in Spain by German agents with the active complicity of Spanish military personnel.[105] The Americans then precipitately curtailed petroleum exports to Spain. A complex process began, with the Spaniards frantic to have the ban lifted. There were differences between the American and British positions, with the Americans inclined to be much tougher with Franco.[106] In the last resort, the Spaniards were worn down to accepting a dramatic restriction of their monthly exports to a near token amount. Finally, with the Germans offering oil in return for wolfram, Churchill persuaded Roosevelt to accept a compromise on the grounds that not do so would

---

104 Department of State, USA, *The Spanish Government and the Axis* (Washington, 1946), pp. 34–7; Hoare, *Ambassador*, p. 258.

105 Hoare, *Ambassador*, pp. 249–56.

106 *Churchill and Roosevelt: The Complete Correspondence*, 3 vols (Princeton, 1984), Vol. II, pp. 725–6, 728, 751; Cadogan, *Diaries*, pp. 602–3; Edward R. Stettinius Jr., *The Diaries of Edward R. Stettinius Jr., 1943–1946*, edited by Thomas M. Campbell and George C. Herring (New York, 1975), pp. 28–9; Hoare, *Ambassador*, pp. 257–62.

slow down the cleaning up of German spy networks in Spain and also threaten British purchases of Spanish iron ore and potash. The eventual agreement with Franco signed on 2 May 1944 encompassed the closing down of the German consulate in Tangier, the withdrawal of all Spanish units from Russia, and the expulsion of German spies and saboteurs from Spain. Needless to say, the Spaniards failed to fulfil their promises in full and throughout the rest of 1944, Hoare protested almost daily at the continued presence in Spain of the German agents. German observation posts and radio interception stations were maintained in Spain until the end of the war.[107]

Franco also ignored totally an unexpected opportunity to diminish the hostility felt towards him in Allied circles which arose in the late summer of 1944. The death of Jordana on 3 August and the need to appoint a new foreign minister made possible a clean break with the pro-Axis past. Instead of seizing the chance to extricate himself from his embarrassing Axis sympathies, he replaced Jordana with the ultra-rightist José Félix Lequerica, the fiercely collaborationist ambassador to Vichy. Franco also removed the pro-Allied under-secretary at the Ministerio de Asuntos Exteriores, Pan de Soreluce. Then, from October 1944, a half-hearted diplomatic initiative was begun to convince the Allies that Franco had never meant them any harm and that his links with the Axis had been only aimed at the Soviet Union. On 18 October 1944 he wrote a letter to the Duke of Alba, the contents of which he was asked to pass on to Churchill. In it, he proposed a future Anglo-Spanish anti-Bolshevik alliance. In Franco's Hitlerian analysis, 'after the terrific test Europe has gone through, those who have shown themselves strong and virile among the nations great in population and resources are England, Spain and Germany'. However, Germany, along with France and Italy were all incapable now of standing up to Russia. American domination of Europe would be disastrous. Accordingly, Britain and Spain together should work to destroy communism. He dismissed his own pro-Axis activities as 'a series of small incidents'. The only obstacle, he claimed, in an astounding act of dogged myopia, to better Anglo-Spanish relations during the previous years had been British interference in Spain's internal affairs, in particular the activities of the British Secret Service.[108]

After some discussion with Eden and Hoare, who favoured a fierce reply to Franco's letter, Churchill eventually approved a somewhat diluted version which was sent on 20 December 1944 and not delivered until early January 1945. In it, while acknowledging that Spain stayed out of the war in June 1940 and during Operation 'Torch' in 1942, Churchill

---

107 *Churchill and Roosevelt: Correspondence*, III, pp. 66–8, 99, 106–8, 114; Cadogan, *Diaries*, pp. 622–3; Hoare, *Ambassador*, pp. 262–8.
108 Hoare, *Ambassador*, pp. 283. The full text is given on pp. 300-4.

reminded Franco of the extent of German influence in Spain and of his own many speeches about how the defeat of the Allies was both 'desirable and unavoidable'. He declared unequivocally that 'it is out of the question for his Majesty's Government to support Spanish aspirations to participate in the future peace settlements. Neither do I think it likely that Spain will be invited to join the future world organisation'.[109]

The Caudillo ultimately avoided war not because of immense skill or vision but rather by a fortuitous combination of circumstances to which he was largely a passive bystander: the skill of British diplomacy; the crude way in which Hitler revealed his contempt for Franco and his price for German aid; the entirely unexpected disaster of Mussolini's entry into the war which both made the Führer wary of another impecunious ally and committed enormous German resources to a rescue operation; and above all to the sheer good luck, if it can be called that, of Spain being economically and militarily shattered by the Civil War. After the war, Serrano Suñer wrote 'Franco and I, and behind us Nationalist Spain, not only betted on a Nazi victory but we desired it with all our hearts. My plan was to enter the war at the moment of Germany's victory.' Letters by General Franco published since his death do nothing to undermine that view.[110] In so far as Franco contributed to his own survival, it was that his instinctive caution and meanness restrained what can now be seen as his real desire to enter the war.

---

109 Slightly differing versions are given in Churchill Papers, 20/138, quoted in Martin Gilbert, *Road to Victory: Winston S. Churchill 1941–1945* (London, 1986), p. 1,071, and Hoare, *Ambassador*, pp. 304–6.
110 Serrano Suñer, *Memorias*, pp. 331–48.

4

Franco and his generals, 1939–45

At the end of the Civil War Franco had an army of 1,020,500 men, including 35,000 Moroccans and 32,000 Italians. It was battle-hardened but in technical and operational terms it was hardly an appropriate force to defend Spain in the major conflagration which was about to break out. The Spanish Civil War had not been a modern war, but rather one which at times was reminiscent of the frontier skirmishes of Spain's colonial wars in Africa, and at others harked back to the trench warfare of the First World War. The modern equipment which had been used and tested by the Germans and Italians was taken back with them when their troops returned home. The Spanish armed forces had virtually no air cover and exiguous mechanized armoured units. There were 850,000 poorly equipped infantrymen to 19,000 artillerymen and the Spanish cavalry was still more dependent on the horse than on the internal combustion engine. In the summer of 1939 a major effort was made to collect and classify abandoned military equipment from the Civil War battle fronts. This helped quantitatively but added to the heterogeneity of material. There was also a partial demobilization, whereby the army's sixty-one divisions were reduced by half. The wartime army was replaced by an army of occupation for which the Caudillo kept over half a million men and 22,100 officers on a war footing. That was 47 per cent more officers than the combined French metropolitan and colonial armies.[1]

Absorbing, in 1941, 45.8 per cent and, in 1943, 53.7 per cent of the state budget, a land army of this size was totally disproportionate to the resources of a country devastated by civil war.[2] The decision not to demobilize fully was not part of a coherent defence policy. Certainly, it reflected the fact that the victory of 1 April 1939 had not definitively put an end to prewar social and political tensions. Sporadic hostilities would

---

1 Carlos Ruiz Ocaña, *Los ejércitos españoles: las fuerzas armadas en la defensa nacional* (Madrid, 1980), p. 113; Report of the German High Command, 10 August 1940, *Documents on German Foreign Policy*, (henceforth *DGFP*) Series D, vol. X (London, 1957), pp. 461–4; Stanley G. Payne, *Politics and the Military in Modern Spain* (Stanford, 1967), p. 421.
2 Julio Busquets and Gabriel Cardona, 'Unas Fuerzas Armadas para el Movimiento' in Justino Sinova (ed.), *Historia del franquismo*, 2 vols (Madrid, 1985), Vol. I, p. 162.

continue until 1951 and an overwhelming military presence was to be part of the apparatus for cowing the population. Moreover, the world war was imminent and Franco and his immediate entourage entertained hopes of being able to get some of the spoils. A central aspect of Falangist and Francoist rhetoric was, after all, imperialistic and colonial ambition.

In the event, neither the excessive size nor the operational inadequacy of the Spanish armed forces made any impact on the outcome of the Second World War. Indeed, the reverse was the case. The progress of the war deeply influenced the domestic conspiratorial activities of the Spanish officer corps. In military terms, the Spanish army was relatively dormant throughout the world war. In political terms, it played a significant role in the crucial years in which Franco was endeavouring to establish his power on a permanent basis. Rumblings of discontent emanated from a tiny but influential minority of officers sufficiently senior to feel able to voice their complaints. Such dissent as there was arose from closely inter-linked issues. Fundamentally, they concerned Franco's persistent failure to restore the monarchy, the danger of an ill-considered Spanish entry into the Second World War and the continuing ascendency of the Falange. There was some resentment that every member of the armed forces on active service was deemed to be a member of the Falange Española Tradicionalista y de las JONS and that, at political functions, the military was obliged to use the fascist salute.[3] These discontents were not consistently translated into hostility against Franco himself but were more often diverted into machinations against his brother-in-law, Ramón Serrano Suñer. Given his concentration of power as both Minister of the Interior, until May 1941, as Foreign Minister from October 1940 and as President of the Junta Política, or executive, of the Falange, the military high command feared that his enthusiasm for the Axis cause would drag Spain into war. At the same time, their resentment of Franco derived from the fact that, not having expected the system of personal power to be eternalized, they felt swindled by his endless postponements of the restoration.

Although many favoured the Axis cause in the war, their monarchist sentiments led to their having more or less clandestine contacts with the British embassy in Madrid and even to their accepting bribes from the British. The sum of $13,000,000 was deposited by the British in a New York bank for this purpose.[4] Their assessments of Spanish military

---

3 *Boletín Oficial del Estado*, 4 August 1937, 17 July 1942.
4 Denis Smyth, *Diplomacy and Strategy of Survival: British Policy and Franco's Spain, 1940–41* (Cambridge, 1986), pp. 35–6; Denis Smyth, '"The Cavalry of St. George": Britain and the Bribery of Spanish Generals, 1940–1942', forthcoming in *Guerres Mondiales et Conflits Contemporains*; Letter of David Eccles to Roger Makins at the Foreign Office, 10 November 1940, in *By Safe Hand: Letters of Sybil & David Eccles 1939–1942* (London, 1983), p. 197.

weakness made them reluctant to see Spain become a belligerent on the Axis side. Contacts with the British, as well as being lucrative, kept the generals' options open. Rather more sporadically, they made tentative overtures to the Germans too about overthrowing Franco in favour of a monarchical restoration. In the main, however, the causes of the Spanish monarchy and of the Western Allies were believed to be linked and shared the added attraction of being opposed to the Falange.

Nevertheless, despite British bribes and monarchist sentiment, only a dozen or so senior officers ever stood up to Franco during the Second World War and then only hesitantly and infrequently. The most prominent were Juan Yagüe, Alfredo Kindelán, José Enrique Varela, Luis Orgaz and Antonio Aranda. Yagüe was closely associated with the Falange. However, his Falangism was austere and radical. He was hostile to Serrano Suñer and somewhat contemptuous of Franco. Kindelán was a conservative monarchist and probably the most consistently irritating thorn in Franco's side. Yet even he was never prepared to go beyond verbal criticism. Varela was a stern reactionary associated with the Carlists but, having been decorated twice with the Gran Cruz Laureada de San Fernando, Spain's highest award for bravery, he enjoyed enormous authority within the army. Orgaz was a staunch Alfonsist monarchist. None of them wanted to overthrow the Franco regime but rather to diminish the power of the Falange within it and to have Spain declared, if only in theory, a monarchy.

Aranda was the most energetic and the most vocal. As military governor of Valencia, he had come to resent the police corruption, the repression and the uncontrolled activities of Falangist *arrivistes* in the Ministry of the Interior. He was also, along with Kindelán, one of the first to perceive that an Axis victory in the war was not a foregone conclusion.[5] Notoriously indiscreet, he was known by Franco to be in touch with the British, as indeed he was with the Germans.[6] He was considered to be a Republican by sentiment and made no secret of his contacts with the real, left-wing, anti-Franco opposition. Although he consistently claimed to his British and left-wing interlocutors that an anti-Franco coup was imminent, his main activity was talk. The British came to regard him as 'a weathercock', 'unreliable and illogical'.[7]

---

5 On Aranda, see Antonio Marquina Barrio, 'Conspiración contra Franco: El Ejército y la injerencia extranjera en España: el papel de Aranda, 1939–1945', *Historia 16*, no. 72, April 1982, pp. 21–30. Ramón Serrano Suñer, *Entre el silencio y la propaganda, la Historia como fue, Memorias* (Barcelona, 1977), pp. 288, 329.

6 Klaus-Jörg Ruhl, *Franco, Falange y III Reich* (Madrid, 1986), p. 68.

7 José María Gil Robles, diary entries for 14 February, 19 December 1943, 31 March, 24 May 1944, *La monarquía por la que yo luché (1941–1954)* (Madrid, 1976), pp. 28, 72, 77, 85; Charles Foltz Jr., *The Masquerade in Spain* (Boston, 1948), pp. 127–9; Smyth, *Diplomacy*, p. 215.

All of them became involved in mutterings against Franco and one by one they ran into problems with him, usually if not always coming off the worst and never seriously threatening him. None the less Franco was obliged to head off their challenges by endless patience, the skilful, if parsimonious, division of the spoils of war in the form of important posts, promotions, pensions, decorations and titles of nobility, and frequent appeals to *esprit de corps* and patriotism. Even so, there was considerable discontent over the slowness of promotions and distribution of medals.[8] In the last resort, however, Franco could always count on the ambition of his military rivals. He was both ruthless and skilled at stringing them along with the carrot of promotions. Aranda, for instance, was led to believe in the summer of 1939 and again in early 1941 that he was about to be made Minister of Defence. During the same period Rafael García Valiño, one of the youngest and most able of Franco's generals and later to become an active critic, was confident of being given the Moroccan army. They both confided their hopes to a Colonel Krahmer of the German general staff.[9] In fact, the Ministry of Defence was abolished in August and the post in Morocco went to the faithful Francoist Carlos Asensio.

The first military crisis faced by the regime was provoked not by a monarchist but certainly by one of the most senior generals in the entire army, Gonzalo Queipo de Llano. He had never made any secret of his low opinion of Franco and of the irregularities surrounding the election of the Generalísimo. At best, he described Franco as '*egoista y mezquino*' (selfish and mean), at worst as '*Paca la culona*' (fatty Francine). There was no shortage of confidants willing to pass his comments on to Franco.[10] Queipo was provoked into a public statement on 18 July 1939 of his outrage that Franco had granted the military decoration of the Cruz Laureada de San Fernando to the city of Valladolid but not to Seville, his own power-base. He not only attributed the central role in the 1936 rising to Seville, but also suggested that, had he been in command in Madrid, the *alzamiento* would have been successful there. Moreover, he implied that Franco's own triumphs with the Army of the Centre were owed to help received from Seville. It was the opportunity that Franco had long sought to get rid of him. The Caudillo regarded Queipo as too powerful and had long

8 Alfredo Kindelán, *La verdad de mis relaciones con Franco*, (Barcelona, 1981), p. 118; Carlos Fernández, *Tensiones militares durante el franquismo* (Barcelona, 1985), p. 12; Gil Robles, diary entry for 15 January 1943, *La monarquía* p. 27; Guillermo Cabanellas, *Cuatro generales*, 2 vols (Barcelona, 1977), Vol. II, p. 440; Jesús Salas Larrazábal, *La guerra de España desde el aire*, 2nd edn (Barcelona, 1972), p. 429

9 Report of Colonel Kramer, 5 June 1939, *Documents secrets du Ministère des Affaires Étrangères d'Allemagne*, 3 vols (Paris, 1946), Vol. III *Espagne*, pp. 61–8; Marquina, 'Aranda', p. 23

10 Francisco Franco Salgado Araujo, *Mis conversaciones privadas con Franco* (Barcelona, 1976), p. 327; Serrano Suñer, *Memorias*, pp. 215–16; Cabanellas, *Cuatro generales*, pp. 439, 443; Pedro Sainz Rodríguez, *Testimonio y Recuerdos* (Barcelona, 1978), pp. 272–4.

resented perceived insults from the days when Queipo had been more senior than he in the Moroccan army. When the German Condor Legion had returned to Germany, Queipo, without Franco's permission and to his chagrin, was there to greet them. By an act of subterfuge, Franco got him away from Seville, sacked him as effective viceroy of Andalusia on 27 July 1939, confined him in a Burgos hotel and then sent him to Italy as head of a military mission.[11]

Queipo's verbal rebellion turned out to be a damp squib. No other general was prepared to side with him and, once Franco reacted as decisively as he did, it went no further. Potentially more dangerous was the simmering opposition of an equally important wartime collaborator of Franco, General Yagüe. One of the more decisive nationalist generals during the Civil War, Yagüe was well-known for his Falangist sympathies and hardly less so for his criticisms of Franco's dilatory military style. He had ended the war as head of the Spanish Moroccan army. Given his talent and his charisma, and his popularity within both the Falange and the army, he was a possible rival to Franco. Fully aware of this, the Caudillo, with typical cunning, made Yagüe Minister for the Air Force in the cabinet changes of 9 August 1939. This apparent promotion was Franco's way of getting him away from a dangerous operational command in Morocco. At the same time, with war imminent, the appointment of an enthusiast for the Axis like Yagüe might well be considered by the Germans to be a significant gesture. As a minister, Yagüe worked hard, albeit in vain, for the rebuilding of the Spanish air force with German help in order for it to be able to take part in the war. He even planned the creation of a large-scale Spanish aviation industry which would have the capacity to supply German air units stationed in Spain. His plans were undermined by the limited possibilities for German assistance consequent upon the necessarily higher priority given to demands upon the war industries of the Third Reich by less ambiguous allies than Spain.[12] As his frustration intensified, he became more explicit in his criticisms of Serrano Suñer and of Franco and in his extreme Falangism. He became involved, as did General Agustín Muñoz Grandes rather more circumspectly, in a plot to remove Franco from power.

With German encouragement, a number of Falangist dissidents had created a clandestine leadership or 'Junta Nacional' whose objective was to carry out the 'Falangist revolution'. Exposed by the regime's intelligence

---

11 Cabanellas, *Cuatro generales*, pp. 438–9; Malcolm Muggeridge (ed.), *Ciano's Diary 1939–1945* (London, 1947), pp. 117, 119, 294–5; Javier Tusell and Genoveva García Queipo de Llano, *Franco y Mussolini: la política española durante la segunda guerra mundial* (Barcelona, 1985), pp. 41–2; Ramón Garriga, *La España de Franco: las relaciones secretas con Hitler*, 2nd edn (Puebla, Mexico, 1970), pp. 64–5; Ian Gibson, *Queipo de Llano: Sevilla, verano de 1936* (Barcelona, 1986) pp. 124–5.
12 *DGFP*, Series D, vol. IX, (London, 1956), pp. 240–3.

services, Yagüe had a tense and emotional meeting with Franco on 27 June 1940, after which he was sacked from his ministerial post. He told the German ambassador Dr Eberhard von Stohrer that he had clashed irreparably with Franco after asking him to sack Serrano Suñer and to reorganize the Falange in such a way as to allow 'a unified party to develop truly in accordance with its principles'. The official pretext used for the sacking was the fact that he had told the British ambassador, Sir Samuel Hoare, at a reception that England was defeated and deserved to be. Since there was already considerable friction with the British ambassador over incursions into Spain of armoured units of the recently arrived German troops, who were mounting semi-official victory parades in the Basque country, Yagüe's remarks were hardly opportune. However, it is more likely that he was sacked for his anti-Franco machinations rather than for his offensive comments to Hoare on the balance of power. He was exiled for twenty-nine months to the village of his birth, San Leonardo in Soria.[13] He was subsequently rehabilitated when it suited Franco to have a pro-Falangist with whom he could counter the growing support enjoyed by the monarchy as Axis fortunes wilted.

The opposition to Franco of both Queipo de Llano and Yagüe, if that is not describing too strongly their speeches and machinations, was tinged with both jealousy and a certain professional contempt for the cautious Generalísimo. Other manifestations of dissent came from generals who regarded Franco with more respect but still felt that they were perfectly entitled by their seniority to treat him as no more than their elected leader. The virtual totality of the higher command, with a few exceptions such as Yagüe and Muñoz Grandes, was monarchist. They were all united by resentment of Serrano Suñer. Franco could have satisfied their political preferences by sacking him and simply declaring that Spain was in essence a monarchy although the moment was not yet ripe for the return of a monarch. However, the Caudillo was inhibited by his own self-interested desire to keep his options open with regard to the changing world order. To be able to share in the spoils of an Axis victory, he needed to avoid a return to a traditional past and maintain the trappings of a fascist polity. At the same time, he had to contend with the Falange itself which, although it remained dependent on him, still enjoyed, as it basked in the reflected glory of Axis successes, a certain autonomy. Accordingly, Franco skilfully played off army and Falange. A patriotic resentment of Falangist malpractice in local

---

13   Luis Suárez Fernández, *Francisco Franco y su tiempo*, 8 vols (Madrid, 1984), Vol. III, pp. 144–8; Ramón Garriga, *El general Juan Yagüe* (Barcelona, 1985), pp. 181–4; *DGFP*, Series D, vol. X, Stohrer to Wilhelmstrasse, 2 July 1940, Document no. 87, pp. 97–9; Manuel Espadas Burgos, *Franquismo y política exterior* (Madrid, 1986), pp. 106–7; Sir Samuel Hoare, *Ambassador on Special Mission*, (London, 1946), pp. 52–3; Stanley G. Payne, *Falange: A History of Spanish Fascism* (Stanford, 1961), pp. 213–15; Ruhl, *III Reich* pp. 61, 317; Smyth, *Diplomacy*, pp. 33–6

and central government came to be a constant feature of military rhetoric. Nevertheless, the Caudillo turned a blind eye to Falangist corruption, as he did to the pro-monarchist conspiratorial dabblings of the higher-ranking generals.

Disgust with the Falange and its alleged corruption motivated all the monarchist critics of Franco within the high command. In particular, it was the special bugbear of the most enduring military opponent of Franco. This was the highly conservative General Alfredo Kindelán. Since it was he who perhaps more than anyone else had been Franco's kingmaker in September 1936, and since he enjoyed immense respect among senior generals, the Generalísimo was obliged to tread warily. The fervently monarchist Kindelán had been effective head of the Nationalist air force during the Civil War. He had never hesitated to speak or write to Franco in a forthright manner, on one occasion protesting at the promotion of Franco's brother, the one-time leftist plotter, Ramón.[14] In August 1939 Kindelán was humiliated by the appointment of the Falangist Yagüe as the regime's first Minister of Aviation.[15]

In the highly charged atmosphere of 1939, with the Falange at the apogee of its power, it was hardly likely that Franco would have appointed to his cabinet someone as committed to a monarchist restoration as Kindelán. The appointment of Yagüe had combined Franco's desire to get a potential rival away from his crucial command post in Morocco with the benefit of appointing a pro-Axis figure to a military ministry in preparation for the forthcoming war. Kindelán had been sent to be military commander of the Balearic Islands. However, that personal snub was as nothing compared with Kindelán's disappointment that Franco had not crowned his Civil War victory by handing over power either to the exiled King Alfonso XIII or to his son Don Juan. Like Queipo de Llano, Kindelán was not given to slavish adulation of Franco. Indeed, while he always treated the Generalísimo with respect, Kindelán, a man of great integrity, never thought of him as more than the first among equals. This was not a view shared by the messianic and ever more self-regarding Franco. However, Kindelán remained convinced that the appointment of Franco as Generalísimo in 1936 had been fundamentally correct but that it had been only for the duration of the Civil War.[16]

Kindelán, like other generals, was concerned that Falangist adventurism was taking Spain into the war on the Axis side. In a similar spirit of apprehension, the Minister for the Army, General Varela, began in

---

14 Kindelán, *La verdad*, pp. 90–9.
15 Kindelán's bitterness is quite clear in the notes which he wrote to prompt himself in the meeting at which he asked Franco at least to spare him the indignity of having to serve under Yagüe and also in an undated letter on the subject which he wrote to the Minister for the Army, Varela. See Kindelán, *La verdad*, pp. 116–18.
16 Kindelán, *La verdad*, pp. 30–2.

early 1940 to gather information from the Capitanías Generales on the condition of the army. In March Kindelán submitted to Varela a report on the lamentable state of the Spanish armed forces in the context of the intensifying world war. In it, he pointed out that Spain was totally unprepared for the contingency of war and that her 'frontiers were still undefended'. Varela read the assessment to a meeting of the Consejo Superior del Ejército. It was adopted by the high command and passed on to Franco. In May 1940 the Alto Estado Mayor submitted to Franco a further report drawn up by General Arsenio Martínez Campos on the armed forces' lack of preparedness, which drew special attention to the lack of aircraft and mechanized units. In June and July 1940, unaware of these sombre documents, the Falangist-controlled press was intensifying its advocacy of entry into the war alongside the Axis. This was to provoke numerous letters of protest to Varela from senior generals including Kindelán, who was still commander in the Balearics; General Miguel Ponte, the High Commissioner in Morocco; General Luis Orgaz, Captain-General of Barcelona; General José Monasterio, Captain-General of Zaragoza and General José Solchaga, Captain-General of Valladolid. In the face of such pressure on his Minister of War, Franco restrained his belligerence. On 13 June he told the Italian chargé d'affaires that the state of the Spanish armed forces prevented any more decisive entry into the war than the seizure of Tangiers – which took place on the following day.[17]

A 'top secret' report by the German high command on the Spanish army drawn up in early August 1940 reached similar conclusions to those of Martínez Campos, a reflection in part perhaps of conversations between the Chief of the Spanish General Staff and the Head of German Military Intelligence, Admiral Canaris. The Germans noted the poor quality of officers, 'superannuated in the higher ranks', and the almost complete lack of qualified engineers. Although paying tribute to the courage and toughness of Spanish soldiers, the report described most older officers as lacking enterprise, tenacity and sufficient interest in their profession. The *alféreces provisionales* were regarded as 'capable, well-disciplined and dedicated'. The Spanish high command was deemed to be 'sluggish and doctrinaire' and bogged down in a colonial war mentality inappropriate to a modern European war. In terms of equipment, it was believed that Spanish artillery suffered glaring deficiencies in both numbers of guns and spare parts. Motorized equipment was also limited, with only about two hundred light tanks fit for use albeit lacking spare parts. There was only sufficient ammunition for a few days of hostilities. Arms and ammunition factories were well below wartime requirements. In terms of fortifications, on the Pyrenees, although there were some defence works in the west, in

---

17 See undated letter of Kindelán to Varela, Kindelán, *La verdad*, pp. 118–19; Tusell and García Queipo de Llano, *Franco y Mussolini*, pp. 79, 97–102.

the centre there were few and in the east none at all. On the Portuguese border there were no fortifications. Installations built around Gibraltar were considered 'of little value and essentially represent a waste of material'. The report noted the pro-German sentiment of many of the officer corps but regarded the Spanish army as fit only for 'limited employment in war'.[18]

Members of the Spanish high command were aware of the deficiencies of the armed forces and were therefore inflamed by what they perceived as Serrano Suñer's adventurism. Their grave misgivings about the possibility of a Spanish entry into the war at a time of famine and military unpreparedness were probably decisive in persuading Franco to renege on the promises made to Hitler at Hendaye on 23 October 1940 and subsequently. On 7 December, in the presence of General Vigón, he declined to give his assent to Hitler's request, carried to him by Admiral Canaris, for German troops to cross the Spanish border on 10 January 1941 in order to carry out an attack on Gibraltar.[19] The requests for German aid drawn up by the Spanish general staff were so large as to be seen in Berlin as a deliberate effort to ensure that there could be no question of Spanish entry into the war.[20] The atmosphere among senior generals was illustrated by the fact that, in late 1940, Kindelán had presented to the Consejo Superior del Ejército a statement on the need for Franco to pass his transitory powers (*poderes accidentales*) to the monarchy. The council accepted the report unanimously and it was read to Franco by the Minister of the Army, Varela.[21] Varela was regarded by the Germans as 'probably the only important Spanish general who is to be regarded as our enemy'. The idea that an attack on Gibraltar should be carried out by the Spaniards themselves without German assistance apparently emanated from Varela. It was assumed by the Germans to be a ploy to sabotage German plans.[22]

The discrepancies between the high command and the Caudillo flared up again in mid-January 1941 when Generals Aranda, García Valiño and García Escámez protested to Franco about Falangist corruption. Throughout the first three months of 1941 both the British and German ambassadors thought it likely that there would soon be an ultimatum to Franco from the senior generals insisting that he form a military government without Serrano Suñer. By the middle of April 1941 the resentment of the generals against Serrano Suñer was reaching fever pitch. Aranda went so far as to seek help from the Germans in the power struggle

---

18 Report of German high command, 10 August 1940, *DGFP*, Series D, vol. X (London, 1957), pp. 461–4.

19 *DGFP*, Series D, vol. XI, pp. 824–5.

20 *DGFP* Series D, vol. XII, pp. 51–3, 78–9.

21 Kindelán, *La verdad*, p. 51. Unfortunately, Kindelán does not give a precise date.

22 *DGFP*, Series D, vol. XIII (London, 1964), pp. 441–2

against the Foreign Minister, even suggesting, not altogether truthfully, that the high command now desired Spanish entry into the war by early July.[23] The interventions of his senior colleagues had some impact on the Caudillo. It is possible to discern an anxiety on the part of Franco to meet some of their complaints, in the mini-power struggle which broke out in May 1941. Since 16 October 1940, when Serrano Suñer had replaced Colonel Juan Beigbeder as Minister of Foreign Affairs, the post of Minister of the Interior had been vacant. In theory Franco had assumed the job, although in practice it was carried out on a day-to-day basis by José Lorente Sanz, the Under-Secretary. On 5 May 1941, Franco named Colonel Valentín Galarza, the Secretario de la Presidencia del Gobierno as Minister of the Interior and replaced him in the Presidencia with a naval captain, Luis Carrero Blanco. This led to protests among prominent Falangists and a token resignation by Serrano Suñer. Although his resignation was not accepted and in a cabinet re-shuffle on 19 May additional Falangist ministers were appointed, Serrano Suñer had overreached himself.[24] Henceforth, Franco was to be more receptive to criticisms of his brother-in-law.

However, if Franco's attitude towards Serrano Suñer was markedly cooler, his enthusiasm for the Axis cause was in no way diminished. In the summer of 1941 alarm grew among the senior generals at Franco's partisan response to the German invasion of the Soviet Union on 22 June. They were galvanized into action by the Caudillo's notorious pro-Axis speech of 17 July, and Serrano Suñer's offer to the Germans to send Spanish volunteers to fight on the Russian front. The senior generals were outraged at what they saw as Serrano's irresponsible adventurism and boundless ambition. Among junior officers, there was some enthusiasm and the military elders were unable to prevent the despatch of the Falangist and military volunteers under the command of General Agustín Muñoz Grandes.[25] General Luis Orgaz y Yoldi, who had recently become the High Commissioner in Morocco, was in touch with civilian monarchists in order to talk about a possible rising against Franco. Along with four other key figures from the Consejo Superior del Ejército, he was anxious to ensure that Spain stayed out of the war and to see Serrano Suñer's power diminished.

Those involved were: Kindelán, recently promoted to be Captain-General of the IV Military Region (Barcelona); General Saliquet, Captain-General of the I Region (Madrid); General Solchaga, Captain-General of the VII Region (Valladolid) and General Aranda, Director of the Escuela Superior

---

23 *DGFP*, Series D, vol. XII (London, 1962) pp. 36–7; 613–14. Cf. Ruhl, *III Reich*, p. 66; Marquina, 'Aranda', p. 24..

24 Stanley G. Payne, *The Franco Regime 1936–1975* (Madison, 1987), pp. 286–9; Tusell and García Queipo de Llano, *Franco y Mussolini*, pp. 131–2.

25 Ruhl, *III Reich*, pp. 22–6; Gerald R. Kleinfeld and Lewis A. Tambs, *Hitler's Spanish Legion: The Blue Division in Russia* (Carbondale, 1979), pp. 1–17.

del Ejército. On 1 August Orgaz told Franco on behalf of the five generals that he should refrain from making such extreme pronouncements on issues of foreign policy without first consulting them. He also passed on severe criticisms of Serrano Suñer and intimated that the generals would like to see him dismissed. Franco agreed to the request but prevaricated, pointing out that removing Serrano was more complicated than it appeared and would require time. As was to be expected, he then did nothing. On 12 August, in response to this inaction, they sent General Aranda to reiterate the message in stronger terms. The tone of such messages was always conciliatory since the generals concerned always wanted Franco to be on their side.[26] In early September 1941, the German ambassador passed on to Berlin complaints by Serrano Suñer about efforts being made by Varela to hamper an early declaration of war.[27]

On 10 October 1941 the German ambassador Stohrer reported a considerable intensification of the internal political crisis, which had culminated in 'a very thorough and evidently very agitated' meeting of Franco and Serrano Suñer. The pressure of the high command had finally had its effect. Serrano Suñer complained that his military opponents, particularly Aranda, accused him of doing great damage to Spain by his pro-German policy. The military now believed that Britain and America would win the war and were already taking their economic revenge on Spain. Serrano Suñer told Stohrer about the efforts of Aranda and the other generals to persuade Franco to unseat him.[28]

However, Serrano survived for the moment. With him still in power and the danger of a Spanish commitment to the Axis still acute, the generals concerned remained in touch with civilian monarchists about the possibility of a forced restoration. General Varela, the army minister and General Juan Vigón, the air minister, were also involved, along with General Ponte, who had moved from Morocco to take over as the Captain-General of the II Military Region (Seville) and others; these included General Espinosa de los Monteros, Head of Military Forces in the Balearic Islands and General Heli Rolando Tella, the military governor of Burgos. Believing a German invasion to be on the cards, they had plans for their own evacuation and the setting up of a military command in Morocco and a provisional civilian government with British backing in the Canary Islands. However, by the end of November 1941, as the danger of a German invasion receded, several of those involved began to withdraw. They were prepared reluctantly to plot to keep Spain

26 Despatches of Sir Samuel Hoare, 5, 13 August 1941, PRO FO371 26891/C8744 and 26891/C9154; Kindelán, *La verdad*, p. 51; Gil Robles, diary entry for 10 June 1941, *La monarquía*, p. 17; Hartmut Heine, *La Oposición política al franquismo* (Barcelona, 1983), pp. 253–4; Smyth, *Diplomacy*, p. 210.
27 *DGFP*, Series D, vol. XIII, pp. 441–3.
28 *DGFP*, Series D, vol. XIII, pp. 630–2.

out of the war but not in any circumstances in order to overthrow Franco.[29]

Despite the bedrock of loyalty to Franco, tensions remained high. In the first half of December 1941 the Consejo Superior del Ejército met again to discuss the internal and external political situation. After meetings involving Kindelán, Varela, Orgaz, Ponte, Saliquet and Dávila, a final session on 15 December 1941 was presided over by Franco himself at his El Pardo palace. The Caudillo was still confident of an Axis victory in the war. This was a view not shared by his senior generals, although many of them favoured the Axis cause. At the meeting Kindelán presented a sternly critical account of Spanish politics, denouncing government incompetence and immorality and in particular the ineptitude and venality of the sprawling Falangist bureaucracy. He criticized the use made by Franco of the army and of military justice as the principal instruments of repression. Military tribunals were now responsible for trying political offences under the Ley de Seguridad del Estado, which had been introduced on 29 March 1941. Kindelán was also hostile to the use of military personnel in local administration, on supply commissions, as prosecutors and as tax collectors. He called upon Franco to abandon his links with the Falange and to separate the posts of Head of State and Head of Government. It was an act of considerable courage to criticize the Caudillo and the Falange at a time when both the party and the Axis cause were at such a high point. Franco skilfully weathered the storm. He avoided confrontation and satisfied the assembled top brass with excuses about external dangers, the difficulties of filling important posts after the loss of so many good men in the Civil War, and the material difficulties that Spain was undergoing. Kindelán was not satisfied and, with the assistance of the British embassy, copies of his speech were distributed among monarchists. Indeed, his links with British diplomats led to protests from the German embassy.[30]

Shortly afterwards, Kindelán made these views public in a speech delivered on 26 January 1942 to commemorate the third anniversary of the Nationalist capture of Barcelona. The speech drew attention to the attrition of the regime's prestige and lamented the lack of any proper constitutional mechanisms for Franco's successsion. Kindelán unequivocally called for Franco to restore the monarchy as the only way to achieve the necessary 'conciliation and solidarity among Spaniards'. Committed as he was to his own survival in power, to the perpetuation of the divisive ideology of Civil War hatreds and to an ever more elevated sense of his own mission, Franco was outraged.[31]

---

29 Heine, *La oposición*, pp. 255–6.
30 Kindelán, *La verdad*, pp. 47–9; Ruhl, *III Reich*, p. 95; Suárez Fernández, *Franco*, III, p. 323.
31 For the text of the speech, see Kindelán, *La verdad*, pp. 120–2.

However, in accordance with his characteristic caution, he did not react. He was more decisive in the case of General Eugenio Espinosa de los Monteros. Espinosa had been Spanish ambassador in Berlin in 1940 and bitterly resented Serrano Suñer's criticisms of his closeness to the Germans. He was rumoured in March 1942 to be involved with Kindelán and Orgaz in preparations for an anti-Franco coup. On taking up the post of Captain-General of the VI Military Region (Burgos) in the following month, Espinosa made a speech savagely attacking 'the disloyalty and limitless ambition' of Serrano, whom he had previously accused in private of treason. Franco's reaction was swift and Espinosa was sacked within a matter of days. However, his dismissal was balanced by that of Serrano's political secretary Felipe Ximénez de Sandoval.[32]

There were also efforts by monarchist generals to get German support for a restoration. The German ambassador reported to the Wilhelmstrasse on 8 May 1942 that General Muñoz Grandes, Commander of the División Azul, had been encharged by some of his peers to use his position in order to broach the subject of the Third Reich's acquiescence in the return of the monarchy.[33] In the summer of 1942 General Juan Vigón, who had replaced Yagüe as Minister of Aviation, arranged a trip to Germany to seek support for a restoration under the subterfuge of seeking technical aid for the air force. Franco got wind of the real intention and obliged Vigón to cancel his visit at the very last minute.[34]

The rivalry between the military and the Falange was at the heart of the most serious crisis faced by Franco in the early 1940s. It concerned his Minister of War, General José Enrique Varela. The tension arose as a result of the annual ceremony held at the Santuario de la Virgen de Begoña, near Bilbao, to pray for the souls of the Carlist *requetés* of the Tercio de Nuestra Señora de Begoña, who had fallen during the Civil War. On 16 August 1942 the ceremony was presided over by General Varela. An Anglophile and an anti-fascist, associated with the Carlists, Varela had been prominent in trying to blame Falangists for the ubiquitous black market which was flourishing in Spain and he was also an outspoken opponent of the national-syndicalist revolution. After the service, as Carlists gathered outside the church shouting monarchist slogans and singing anti-Falangist jingles, there was a clash with a group of Falangists. The fact that they were present at all, and carrying weapons including grenades, indicated their prior determination to provoke a disturbance. One of them, Juan Domínguez, the Inspector Nacional of the

---

32 Cf. despatch by Hoare, 20 April 1942, PRO FO371 31235/C4198; Heine, *La oposición*, p. 257; Pedro Sainz Rodríguez, *Un reinado en la sombra* (Barcelona, 1981), p. 147.
33 *Documents secrets*, pp. 96–101.
34 Von Stohrer to Wilhelmstrasse, 29 May, 11 June 1942, *Documents secrets*, pp. 101–3, 105–6.

Sindicato Español Universitario, threw two bombs; one of them exploded and wounded several bystanders.

Varela seized on the incident as an opportunity to damage the Falange in general and Serrano Suñer in particular. He publicly interpreted the incident as a Falangist attack on the army, sent a communiqué to that effect to the captains-general of Spain and organized the court martial of Domínguez. The Minister of the Interior, Colonel Valentín Galarza, sent telegrams to the civil governors of each province containing an account of the incident in which it was alleged that 'agents at the service of a foreign power' had tried to kill the Minister for the Army. Domínguez certainly had contacts among German diplomats in Spain. Nevertheless Franco was furious, having quickly perceived that Varela's indignation cloaked a bid to make capital out of the incident. In a long and tense telephone conversation, Franco defended the Falangists involved and Varela denounced them as murderers.[35] For fear of antagonizing the army, Franco consented to the execution of Domínguez. However, he was outraged that both Varela and Galarza had committed insubordination by publishing their version of events and drumming up anti-Falangism within military circles. Accordingly, he resolved the crisis by sacking Varela and Galarza.

This defeat for the monarchist camp within the Francoist fortress was soon redressed. Franco was persuaded by the Secretario de la Presidencia del Gobierno, Luis Carrero Blanco, that there had to be 'both victors and vanquished' after the crisis. Carrero suggested that the dismissal of the two monarchists made it look as if Serrano Suñer was really in charge of events. He thereby managed to convince Franco that to balance matters he must effect comparable retribution against the Falange. That meant action against Serrano Suñer, who as President of the Junta Política of the Falange was its leading figure. At the end of August, Franco dismissed his brother-in-law as Foreign Minister. General Francisco Gómez Jordana took over the ministry and Franco himself assumed control of the Falange. Although not strictly of their own making, this was a great triumph for the high command, although paradoxically the Germans were delighted too.[36] The strength of feeling against the removal of Varela in the senior ranks was illustrated by the success which the outgoing Minister for the Army

---

35 For more or less Falangist versions of the Begoña affair, see Serrano Suñer, *Memorias* pp. 364–7; Heleno Saña, *El franquismo sin mitos: conversaciones con Serrano Suñer* (Barcelona, 1982), pp. 263–5; Payne, *Falange*, pp. 216, 219–20, 234–6. For a Francoist version laying the blame on the Germans, see José M. Doussinague, *España tenía razón (1939–1945)* (Madrid, 1949). For the transcript of Franco's telephone conversation with Varela, see Laureano López Rodó, *La larga marcha hacia la monarquía* (Barcelona, 1977), pp. 503–7. See also Antonio Marquina Barrio, 'El atentado de Begoña', *Historia 16*, no. 76, August 1982, pp. 11–19.

36 Ruhl, *III Reich*, pp. 118–19.

had in persuading all his fellow lieutenant-generals not to replace him. Franco was forced to go down to the level of divisional general before he could find a new minister in the person of General Carlos Asensio. A faithful Francoist with Falangist sympathies, Asensio at first also refused, presumably to avoid being in conflict with his immediate superiors. Franco overcame this resistance by telling Asensio that if he did not accept then the Caudillo's rule would soon meet a violent end with him leaving his office feet first. Franco also invoked military discipline, ordering Asensio to accept his appointment.[37]

What is perhaps most significant about the Begoña incident is the restraint, not to say pusillanimity, of the anti-Falangist generals. For nearly a year, the Consejo Superior del Ejército had been criticizing Franco's close links with the Falange. The military monarchists were understandably delighted by the snub to the Falange implicit in the execution of Domínguez. Accordingly, when Franco effectively reprimanded the military and favoured the Falange by dismissing Varela and Galarza, the protest of senior anti-Falangist generals might have been expected to go further than the refusal to replace the Minister for the Army. Even Varela's reaction to the Begoña affair remained within the bounds of the Francoist system. He had been pushing to see how far he could go, jockeying for position on behalf of the monarchist *'familia'*. In the last resort, he was subject to the ultimate balance imposed by Franco. Thereafter, his only further protest was to refuse the posts of Ambassador to Brazil or High Commissioner in Morocco to replace Orgaz, who was having problems with the Calif.[38] On the other hand, it was only a matter of days before Franco was persuaded by Carrero Blanco to restore the balance by removing Serrano Suñer. There remains the possibility that that decision was hastened by the military reaction to the dismissal of Varela. Certainly, the delight of the senior generals at the fall of the *cuñadísimo* may be perceived in the fact that, Kindelán aside, they remained dormant for almost a year.

Despite not having joined Varela in trying to exploit the Falange's moment of weakness during the Begoña crisis, changes in the international situation finally impelled Kindelán to be more bold. On 11 November 1942, three days after the Allied landings in North Africa, he travelled to Madrid to discuss the significance of the landings with senior military colleagues and with Franco himself. Kindelán told Franco in unequivocal terms that if he had committed Spain formally to the Axis then he would have to be replaced as Chief of State. In any case, he advised the Caudillo to proclaim Spain a monarchy and declare himself regent. Franco gritted his teeth and responded in a conciliatory manner. With evident duplicity, he denied any

---

37 López Rodó, *La larga marcha*, pp. 28–30; Saña, *El franquismo sin mitos*, pp. 267, 271–3; Serrano Suñer, *Memorias*, pp. 370–2.
38 Gil Robles, diary entry for 1 October 1942, *La monarquía*, p. 19

formal commitment to the Axis, claimed that he had no desire to stay any longer than necessary in a post which he found every day more disagreeable and confided that he wanted Don Juan to be his ultimate successor.

Kindelán expressed forcibly his view that the superior economic and industrial power of the Anglo-Saxon Allies would guarantee their eventual victory and that Spain must therefore remain neutral. He told the Caudillo that the state was in the hands of a corrupt bureaucracy. Even more galling for Franco must have been Kindelán's assertion that it was not acceptable to the army that its commander should also be the head of a party, particularly one whose failure was as ignominious as that of the Falange. Since Kindelán could claim to be speaking for Generals Jordana, Dávila, Aranda, Orgaz, Juan Vigón and Varela, whom he had also seen on his trip, Franco simulated a cordial acceptance of what was said.[39] However, he chose this moment to rehabilitate Yagüe, making him, on 12 November 1942, commander of the Spanish enclave at Melilla. It was a remarkably clever posting from Franco's point of view in terms of countering the pro-monarchist mutterings in which Kindelán was involved. The Caudillo was in any case aware that Yagüe was being courted by the Germans as a possible replacement for him. In the first place, Franco could expect that, since in Melilla, Yagüe would be under the command of the pro-Allies High Commissioner in Morocco, Orgaz, and there was every chance that they would neutralize one another. Secondly, with the Allied landings on his mind, the pro-Axis Yagüe was unlikely to become involved in plots against Franco. In any case, Yagüe was too rigid, insufficiently devious and indeed, too loyal to Franco to play the German game.[40]

Suspecting that Franco had no intention of declaring the monarchy, on his return to Barcelona Kindelán assembled at his home the generals and other senior officers of the Catalan military region. He told them that 'the ship of state is adrift in a sea of total misrule' and spoke of the incompetence and corruption of the bureaucracy. Declaring that the solution was not likely to come from the present regime, he called for a radical change of persons, methods of government and regime. This time, Kindelán's claim that the monarchy was the only viable option led to his being relieved of his post. He was too powerful to be punished more spectacularly. After a short interval, Franco removed him in early 1943 to what was seen as the innocuous post of Director of the Escuela Superior del Ejército, where he would not have direct command of troops. Kindelán himself lamented to a British diplomat that he could hardly organize a *coup d'état* with the attendants and domestic staff of the school.[41]

---

39 Kindelán, *La verdad*, pp. 32–6.
40 Ruhl, *III Reich*, pp. 178–82.
41 Kindelán, *La verdad*, pp. 55–6; Heine, *La Oposición*, p. 262.

As Director of the Staff College, Kindelán spent a lot of time drafting letters to Franco on behalf of the Consejo Superior del Ejército. Since they were discussed by the consejo, there is little doubt that Franco sooner or later saw even the ones which were not sent him. In one, Kindelán said, with reference to the danger of the war ending with Spain's constitutional status still unresolved, 'we should not be applying ointments to the evil but cauterizing it'. In others, he gave Franco unwelcome reminders that he owed his position as Caudillo neither to divine or hereditary rights nor even to universal suffrage but to the army. He even suggested that the Consejo Superior might be obliged to seize the initiative to resolve the succession. He also asserted that the army should never be asked to defend with its bayonets a regime which did not have the acquiescence of the majority of the Spanish people.[42] It would be wrong to see Kindelán's activities as evidence of out-and-out anti-Francoism. Although his tone was often direct, his calls for change were always shot through with respect for the Caudillo and a commitment to the values of the regime. In other words, he was committed not to the restoration of the constitutional monarchy but to the installation (*instauración*), '*por Franco y con Falange*' as he put it, of a Francoist authoritarian monarchy.[43] He wanted the succession to be resolved in order to perpetuate an illiberal regime. In December 1941, for instance, he had written to Don Juan advising him to reject liberal monarchy publically, to express admiration for José Antonio Primo de Rivera, to praise Franco's services to Spain and to be prepared to keep the Falange in existence.[44]

This needs to be kept in mind in examining what has been considered the most serious incident of military opposition to Franco.[45] Unlike the pro-Allied Kindelán, most senior generals favoured the Axis cause in the Second World War even if they were anxious for Spain to stay neutral. They were prepared to see the question of the monarchist succession kept on ice until the result of the war was clear. By the summer of 1943 the collapse of the Afrika Korps and the Allied invasion of Sicily had convinced many of them that the time had come to prepare for the future. Like Kindelán, they believed that if the fruits of Civil War victory were not to be swept away by the Allies turning against a pro-Axis Franco, then steps had to be taken. Even then, their reactions were extremely timid. On 8 September 1943 a letter asking Franco to consider if the time had not come for him to consider a monarchical restoration was signed by eight lieutenant-generals: Kindelán, Varela, Orgaz, Ponte, Dávila, Solchaga,

---

42 Kindelán, *La verdad*, pp. 125–7. Unfortunately, the drafts are undated.
43 See letter of Kindelán to Franco, 25 December 1943, Kindelán, *La verdad*, pp. 58–9.
44 Kindelán, *La verdad*, pp. 50–5.
45 Fernández, *Tensiones militares*, p. 91; La Cierva, *Franquismo*, I, p. 264.

Saliquet and Monasterio. It was handed to the Caudillo by General Varela on 15 September 1943.

Franco was already aware that there were problems in the wind and for some months previously had been taking appropriate action. Since mid-May 1943 Franco's ambassador to the Holy See, Domingo de las Bárcenas, had been sending full reports from Rome about Mussolini's increasingly precarious position.[46] Accordingly, the Caudillo started to consolidate military loyalty. On 5 June he met the 119 surviving fellow graduates of his own period as a student at the military academy. The wisdom of doing so was quickly revealed. In mid-June a group of twenty-seven senior Procuradores from the Francoist Cortes, including several ex-ministers and Generals Galarza and Ponte, wrote a respectful appeal to Franco to settle the constitutional question before the war ended, by re-establishing the traditional Spanish Catholic monarchy. The clear implication was that only the monarchy could plausibly maintain Spain's neutrality and avoid Allied retribution for Franco's pro-Axis flirtation. The Caudillo's response was complex. In the short term, he immediately dismissed all the signatories from their seats in the Cortes. At the same time, he stepped up his efforts to cultivate his senior officers, spending time with them individually. In particular, he put great effort into winning over General Luis Orgaz y Yoldi, the High Commissioner in Morocco. General Jordana, the Minister of Foreign Affairs, wrote that 'taming Orgaz has been one of the Generalísimo's greatest successes'.[47]

However, with the position of the Axis deteriorating daily, Franco was clearly rattled. Fearful of the poison spreading to the armed forces, he drew up with his faithful confidant, Luis Carrero Blanco, an instruction to the nine Capitanías Generales. It was issued on 17 July 1943, the eve of the seventh anniversary of the outbreak of the Civil War. In it, they tried to play on the reflexes of the most senior officers and provoke them into rallying around the regime. The document claimed that an international masonic plot had been uncovered. Its alleged purpose was to exploit the monarchist sentiments of many generals and their anxieties for the future in the context of Axis defeat in North Africa. To counter this imaginary conspiracy to drive a wedge between the army and the Caudillo, the Franco–Carrero Blanco circular denounced the dangers involved in trying to re-establish a liberal monarchy on the grounds that it would in turn be only the first step to a return to pre-Civil War anarchy and communist domination.[48]

On 25 July 1943 Mussolini was replaced by Marshal Badoglio. There was panic in Madrid political circles and Franco himself was seriously

---

46 Suárez Fernández, *Franco*, III, p. 409.
47 López Rodó, *La larga marcha*, pp. 36–8; Suárez Fernández, *Franco*, III, p. 403.
48 López Rodó, *La larga marcha*, pp. 39–41.

worried.[49] One week later, on 2 August 1943, Don Juan telegrammed Franco, reminding him of the Duce's fate and asserting that the only way to avoid a catastrophe in Spain was the immediate restoration of the monarchy. The Pretender was clearly insinuating that, if the Allies won the war and Franco was still in power, then Spain would be punished as if she were one of the defeated Axis powers. Franco replied on 8 August 1943 with a telegram in which cunning and megalomania were equally balanced. Having asserted that Spain could not suffer the fate of Italy, thanks to the regime's success in keeping her out of the war, he went on to beg Don Juan not to make public any statement which might weaken the position of the regime internally or internationally. On 15 August the Traditionalist Communion appealed to Franco to drop the single party and the totalitarian features of his regime and to restore the monarchy in the light of developments in the war.[50]

The buildup of anxiety among his erstwhile supporters can hardly have failed to preoccupy Franco. No doubt galvanized by the recent military developments in North Africa, and perhaps fancying himself as the Spanish Badoglio, General Orgaz took an uncharacteristic risk. He informed the ex-minister and inveterate *Juanista* conspirator, Pedro Sainz Rodríguez, that, by prior agreement with Aranda and other generals, he was ready to rise with one hundred thousand men to restore the monarchy, provided that immediate Allied recognition could be arranged by Don Juan's followers.[51] The Caudillo's anxiety must have been exacerbated when he was informed during his summer holiday at the Pazo de Meiras in La Coruña that his lieutenants-general were meeting in Seville to discuss the situation and had composed a document calling upon him to take action. The seriousness of the situation was reflected in his alleged response: 'Let them come and see me. I will await them with my back to the wall.'[52]

In this context, the delivery of a letter from eight lieutenant-generals was deeply worrying for Franco. However, even before he accepted it, he unsettled its bearer Varela by a severe reprimand for carrying a swagger stick in his presence. In any case, there were a number of things that helped the Generalísimo to remain calm. Apart from an oblique reference to the fact that Franco had remained in power for 'longer than the term originally foreseen', the tone of the letter was itself so respectful that it clearly suggested that the high command of the army was more Francoist than

---

49 Gil Robles, diary entries for 6, 11 August 1943, *La monarquía*, pp. 51, 53.

50 López Rodó, *La larga marcha*, pp. 515–19; Gil Robles' diary entry for 25 August 1943, refers to Franco's 'impertinent refusal', Gil Robles, *La monarquía*, p. 55.

51 Gil Robles, diary entry for 23 August 1943, *La monarquía*, p. 55; Sainz Rodríguez, *Un reinado*, p. 161.

52 It has been claimed that the report was carried to Galicia by the young Catholic monarchist intellectual, Rafael Calvo Serer. Cf. Ricardo de la Cierva, *Historia del franquismo: I orígenes y configuración (1939–1945)* (Barcelona, 1975), pp. 265–70.

monarchist. Indeed, the monarchist politician José María Gil Robles wrote in his diary of its *vil adulación* and of his conviction that Franco would not pay it the slightest attention. Indeed, it did no more than ask Franco 'with loyalty, respect and affection, if he did not agree with them that the time had come to give Spain a monarchy'.[53] Secondly, Franco could take comfort from the fact that, even among the more enthusiastically monarchist of his senior generals, several, including Generals Juan Vigón, Jordana, Muñoz Grandes, Serrador and Moscardó, did not sign.[54] Moreover, he had every reason to be confident of the unconditional loyalty of his middle-rank officers.

It was largely for this reason that General Orgaz soon changed his mind about the possibility of a military action in favour of the monarchy. He informed Gil Robles in late September that any kind of rising was most unlikely given that the younger generals and the entire officer corps from colonel downwards were committed to Franco. Indeed, Gil Robles, who was extraordinarily well-informed, came to believe that the letter had had the effect of persuading other generals to close ranks around Franco.[55] In fact, the letter of the lieutenant-generals itself explicitly stated that it was not written on behalf of the army as a whole and that the lieutenant-generals had not consulted any subordinates for reasons of discipline. Finally, Franco was fully aware that the Allies had no desire to precipitate a change of government in Spain nor to intervene in her internal affairs. He believed himself to be in possession of guarantees from both Churchill and Roosevelt that there would be no invasion of the Iberian peninsula. He was almost certainly unaware of the fact that the Americans were merely keeping their options open.[56]

Nevertheless, Franco reacted coolly, albeit more quickly than was his wont and with more decisive concessions than hitherto. On 1 October 1943 he declared Spanish neutrality in the World War and announced the withdrawal of the Blue Division from Russia. That was a very substantial recognition of the growing strength of the Anglophile monarchist generals. However, it was countered by the announcement on the same day, the *Día del Caudillo*, of the award of thirty-five military crosses and of the promotion of Yagüe to lieutenant-general. Yagüe was given command of the VI Military Region, Burgos, as a counter-balance to the growing

53 For the full text, see López Rodó, *La larga marcha*, pp. 43–4. For Gil Robles' comment, diary entry for 18 September 1943, Gil Robles, *La monarquía*, p. 60.

54 José Fortes and Restituto Valero, *Qué son las Fuerzas Armadas* (Barcelona, 1977), p. 45.

55 Gil Robles, diary entries for 26 September and 31 October 1943, *La monarquía*, pp. 61, 67.

56 Sir Llewellyn Woodward, *British Foreign Policy in the Second World War*, 5 vols (London, 1970–1976), Vol. II, pp. 353–6, Vol. IV, pp. 8–17; Suárez Fernández, *Franco*, III, p. 433; Gil Robles, diary entry for 11 August 1943, *La monarquía*, p. 53.

pro-Allied and pro-monarchist generals in the high command. Franco also began to cultivate younger Falangist-inclined officers. He regarded the letter as an act of indiscipline, but with the Allies closely monitoring the situation, his inclination to exact punishment was held in check. So, he adopted the divide-and-rule tactic of meeting each of the generals in turn and assuring them that he had taken note of their request. He managed to persuade some of them that Hitler's secret weapons, of which he had been informed, could still win the war for the Axis. Kindelán, Orgaz and Ponte stood by what they had written. Others wavered and General Saliquet allegedly told Franco that he had been browbeaten into signing.[57]

Gil Robles was astonished at the fact that the senior generals seemed to expect Franco himself to take the initiative in bringing back the monarchy. He wrote privately in his diary that 'these "fervent monarchists", whose loyalty (to the Pretender) does not prevent them taking full advantage of the Francoist racket (*tinglado*), are the greatest enemy that the monarchy has'. At the end of September he wrote a strong letter to the Minister for the Army, General Carlos Asensio, pointing out that a monarchist restoration granted by Franco would be worthless. It elicited only a polite acknowledgement. Needless to say, Franco was fully apprised of this correspondence, which was circulated among the higher ranks of the army.[58] By mid-October 1943 the storm had passed and Franco was able to begin an anti-monarchist offensive without worrying about opposition from his senior generals.

One way in which Franco kept control over army officers was by turning a blind eye to army corruption. Many officers who had business interests used rank-and-file troops as well as Republican prisoners-of-war as cheap, or cost-free, labour. Others used army vehicles for private purposes. At a lower level, even junior officers used conscripts as domestic servants, handymen, baby-sitters and the like. Franco was fully aware of this and was happy to let it be known that he knew. On only two occasions did he use that knowledge to have a senior officer expelled from the army. One of these officers was General Francisco Borbón y de la Torre who was accused of illegally trafficking in foodstuffs. The other was General Heli Rolando de Tella y Cantos, a prominent *Africanista*, whose meteoric rise in Morocco had been outstripped only by those of Franco and Yagüe.[59] Despite his distinguished record, Tella was stripped of all military honours for 'administrative irregularities' allegedly committed through the use of

57 Suárez Fernández, *Franco*, III, pp. 431–2; Gil Robles, diary entries for 3 October and 17 November 1943, *La monarquía*, pp. 62, 68; Payne, *Politics and the Military*, p. 434; Heine, *La oposición*, p. 261.

58 Gil Robles, diary entries for 25 August and 31 October 1943, and letter to General Asensio, 28 September 1943, Gil Robles, *La monarquía*, pp. 55, 67, 360–6; Suárez Fernández, *Franco*, III, p. 432.

59 Gabriel Cardona, *El Poder militar en la España contemporánea hasta la guerra civil* (Madrid, 1983), p. 32.

military vehicles and personnel, in connection with his flour factory and the rebuilding of his country mansion (*pazo*) during the time that he was military governor of Lugo. On the grounds that corruption was never considered a serious crime in Francoist Spain, Tella was convinced that he had been persecuted because of his pro-monarchist activities. It may be a coincidence, but the names of Generals Tella and de Borbón were the only ones that a Spanish agent could remember of a list of fifty who had allegedly requested Goering to help in a plot to overthrow Franco and replace him with Don Juan.[60]

From early September 1943 Franco had on his desk a report accusing Orgaz of being involved in corrupt business deals in North Africa.[61] It is not totally beyond the bounds of probability that its existence could have accounted for the diminution of Orgaz's readiness to plot in favour of the monarchy. Franco never showed the slightest interest in putting a stop to corruption in itself as opposed to using knowledge of it to increase his power over those involved. Indeed, he often repaid those who informed him of malpractice not by taking action against the guilty but by letting them know who had informed on them.[62]

Franco's assurances to his generals in October 1943 that Hitler's secret weapons would win the war dampened the urgency of their demands for him to resolve the political future. However, within a year, the inevitability of Axis defeat was obvious to all but Franco, Muñoz Grandes and Juan Vigón. The panic began again and there were indications of dissent within the higher reaches of the armed forces. Some, like Generals Kindelán and Aranda, had never ceased working for a restoration. Aranda had been involved in anti-Franco activities since October 1941 and had been in regular touch with both the Don Juan camp through Gil Robles and with the British embassy. In October 1944, however, all thoughts of anti-Francoism were banished in the army, as a consequence of the invasion of the Val d'Aran in the Pyrenees by Spanish Republicans who had fought in the French resistance. In a way, the repulsion of the original incursions and the subsequent guerrilla war came as a godsend to Franco. They made possible the revival of the Civil War mentality, gave the army something to do and generally reunited the officer corps around Franco. The rehabilitation of Yagüe proved to be particularly useful. As Captain-General of Burgos, he played a major role in repelling the guerrilla incursion. Nevertheless, the imminent collapse of the Axis clearly caused Franco profound anxiety.

---

60 Ridruejo, *Escrito en España*, p. 104; Fernández, *Tensiones militares*, pp. 77–85; Enrique Tierno Galván, *Cabos sueltos* (Barcelona, 1981), pp. 106–7. On the generals' plot, see Garriga, *España de Franco*, I, pp. 287–8.

61 Suárez Fernández, *Franco*, III, p. 432.

62 See the comments of his brother-in-law and of his cousin and aide-de-camp, Serrano Suñer, *Memorias*, p. 230; Franco Salgado Araujo, *Mis conversaciones*, pp. 19, 37, 56–8, 83, 178.

He felt seriously threatened when Don Juan, on the advice of General Kindelán and his civilian advisors, issued his Lausanne manifesto on 19 March 1945. In it, the Pretender denounced the totalitarian nature and the Axis connections of the Francoist regime and called upon Franco to make way for a monarchist restoration.[63]

A group of senior monarchists was set up, consisting of the Duke of Alba and Generals Aranda, Alfonso de Orleáns and Kindelán, to oversee the expected transition. They went so far as to draft the text of a decree law announcing the monarchy and composed a provisional government, in which Kindelán would be President, Aranda Minister of National Defence, Varela Minister for the Air Force and General Juan Bautista Sánchez González Minister for the Army.[64] The Lausanne manifesto had been accompanied by an instruction to prominent monarchists to resign from their posts in the regime. The first to do so was General Alfonso de Orleans y Borbón, the representative in Spain of Don Juan, who was effective head of the air force. Franco responded by ordering General Orleans to be confined to his estates near Cádiz.[65] Franco then mounted an operation to neutralize the resurgent monarchist sentiment in the high command that resulted from Don Juan's manifesto. A three-day-long meeting of the Consejo Superior del Ejército was presided over, unusually, by Franco himself. He made an enormous effort to justify himself in their eyes. He pointed out that the original idea of General Mola in 1936 had been to create an authoritarian republic and that it had taken the efforts of Franco himself to put the monarchist restoration on the agenda.[66] The Caudillo was working hard to counteract the effect of the manifesto. Apparently, many of those present were satisfied by what he had to say, but others, including Kindelán were perplexed by Franco's views on the international situation. He assured them that Russia was finished and that the real communist threat in the future would emanate from Britain and France, which were in the grip of freemasons. He was optimistic about the future because he was convinced that the USA was about to adopt Falangist principles.[67]

With rumblings among the senior generals getting louder, Franco announced a number of important postings in March by way of seizing the initiative. Varela became High Commissioner in Morocco, much to the chagrin of his predecessor Orgaz who was made Head of the General Staff. Solchaga became Captain-General of Barcelona, replacing the faithful mediocrity General José Moscardó, who became Franco's confidant as Head

63   López Rodó, *La monarquía*, pp. 48–50; Suárez Fernández, *Franco*, IV, pp. 18–19.
64   Kindelán, *La verdad*, p. 89.
65   Kindelán, *La verdad*, pp. 229–34. For other resignations, *ibid.*, p. 236.
66   Suárez Fernández, *Franco*, IV, pp. 24–5; Ricardo de la Cierva, *Francisco Franco: un siglo de España*, 2 vols (Madrid, 1973), Vol. II, p. 406.
67   Antonio Marquina, 'La permanencia del franquismo después de la segunda guerra mundial', in *El País*, 25 May 1980.

of the Military Household. These were cunning promotions which again enabled Franco to divide and rule. The crucial posting was that of the dourly loyal pro-Falangist General Agustín Muñoz Grandes to be Captain-General of Madrid, the linchpin in terms of the Caudillo's political security.[68] The continuing anxiety for the safety of the regime was further revealed when the Minister for the Army, General Asensio, sent a remarkable letter to General Varela on 25 April 1945. It was an attempt to explain away all of Franco's vacillations about a restoration as evidence of the Caudillo's concern to give the monarchy the greatest solidity. The regime's fears can be discerned in its closing exhortation that 'the army must maintain absolute discipline, keeping out of politics and accepting the most complete obedience to the plans of the Generalísimo'. This was perhaps a reflection of a fear that, on the eve of the final collapse of the Third Reich, the conspiratorial activities, in which Generals Orgaz, Ponte and Kindelán were playing the leading roles, might lead to something.[69] It was a groundless fear.

68 Suárez Fernández, *Franco*, IV, p. 21; La Cierva, *Historia del franquismo*, I, p. 294.
69 For the letter, see López Rodó, *La monarquía*, pp. 51–4; for the generals, Kindelán, *La verdad*, pp. 236–8.

Part III

INSTRUMENTS OF DICTATORSHIP

5

Populism and parasitism: the Falange and the Spanish establishment, 1939–75

Threatened by the reforms of the Second Republic, the Spanish right's instinctive response was obstinate and violent. However, given the initial failure of attempts to destabilize the Republic by violence, sponsored by the patrician right, less rigidly traditional elements confronted the possibility of mobilizing popular support in defence of rightist interests. Alongside the traditional groups of monarchists, Alfonsines and Carlists, there emerged the populist Catholic authoritarian party, the CEDA, and the much smaller and overtly fascist Falange Española.[1] All of these organizations threw in their lot with the army officers who organized the uprising of July 1936. The Falange started out as the weakest of them but the circumstances of the war and the external influence of the Axis powers pushed it to prominence. The mass support of the CEDA and its youth movement, the Juventud de Acción Popular, had already started to flood into the Falange in the spring of 1936. It was further swelled by wartime recruits. For three decades thereafter, even as its own ideological edge was dulled, it was still playing a central role in the regime. Indeed, it was the dictatorship's identity tag in the outside world. That was hardly surprising since it was the agency which organized mass mobilizations and controlled labour relations and was also the source of the regime's lexicon, iconography and ideological paraphernalia.

The relationship of Falange Española to the other components of the Francoist coalition was complex and constantly shifting. Both the aristocratic and the upper-middle-class right saw the primordial task as the destruction of what they perceived as the threat of disorder, anti-clericalism and communism. Ties of family and class made it natural for them to turn

---

1 Paul Preston, *Las derechas españolas en el siglo XX: autoritarismo, fascismo y golpismo* (Madrid, 1986); Martin Blinkhorn, *Carlism and Crisis* (Cambridge, 1975); Ricardo de La Cierva, *La derecha sin remedio* (Barcelona, 1986); Paul Preston, *The Coming of the Spanish Civil War* (London, 1978).

to the army. Thereafter, the military remained the locus of real power. The contribution of the Falange was thus of a different order. With its swaggering mimicry of Axis models and its loud rhetoric of egalitarianism, it was privately regarded with some distaste. It was acceptable largely because of the need for cannon fodder and for the implementation of various unpleasant tasks associated with the war, not least the repression. During the Civil War and the early days of the Second World War, aristocrats and fascists coexisted well enough despite the gulf between their social composition and their ideological priorities. They shared a common ground of what might be termed clerical authoritarianism and a determination to win the war. They all considered themselves part of the *Movimiento*, the vague generic term used to denote the Nationalist cause both during and after the Civil War. After all, in April 1937, they had acquiesced more or less willingly in their unification into the regime's single party, the Falange Española Tradicionalista y de las JONS. The Alfonsine monarchists had agreed to the dissolution of their organization 'with great joy and pride'. The leader of the CEDA, José María Gil Robles, had similarly written to Franco of 'our willing sacrifice'.[2]

Soldiers or civilians, they were nearly all Catholics. The Falangists aside, many were also monarchists of some kind. They certainly continued to perceive themselves as primarily Falangists, Carlists, Christian Democrats or Alfonsine monarchists and to recognize each other as such. The organizations and apparatuses of their parties had gone but the interests and commitments which they represented remained.[3] Whether they defined themselves in terms of ecclesiastical, military, monarchist, Falangist or more generally Francoist loyalties, however, depended upon a constantly changing balance of ideological commitment and sheer opportunism. Accordingly, the power balance within the coalition altered over the course of the years in response to changing domestic and international circumstances.

There were a number of constant features. Military pre-eminence was only gradually diminished, remaining constant in the three service ministries. The Minister of the Interior was always a general until 1969, when the post passed to a military lawyer. Education remained firmly Catholic territory and the Ministry of Justice was a Carlist fiefdom until 1973. Nevertheless, it is possible to distinguish four periods in the evolution of the Spanish right from 1939 to 1977. They correspond broadly to the

---

2 *Sur* (Malaga), 25, 28 April 1937; Maximiano García Venero, *Historia de la Unificación (Falange y Requeté en 1937)/83 (Madrid, 1970), pp. 216–19; Maximiano García Venero, Falange en la guerra de España: la Unificación y Hedilla* (Paris, 1967), pp. 391–427. For a critical account of Falangist dissidence, see the much censored Angel Alcázar de Velasco, *Siete días de Salamanca* (Madrid, 1976).

3 Sheelagh M. Ellwood, *Spanish Fascism in the Franco Era* (London, 1987), pp. 58–9.

so-called 'blue era' of apparent Falangist dominance between 1939 and 1945, to the period of dour Christian Democrat rule between 1946 and 1957, to the burst for economic modernization presided over between 1957 and 1969 by the technocrats associated with Opus Dei, and finally to the break-up of the regime coalition, the factional rivalries and eventual transition to democracy between 1969 and 1977. Periodic adjustments of ministerial personnel were always calculated in terms of a central objective – the survival of the regime. Cabinets might be retuned according to changes in international circumstances, as was the case in 1945. Changes were sometimes Franco's response to especially fierce clashes between the *familias*, or political clans, and illustrated his determination to maintain the overall balance on which the regime's stability was built. Such was the case in 1942 and 1969. Ministerial reshuffles also reflected the regime's awareness of its obligation to remain sensitive to the changing internal dynamics of Spanish capitalism. Thus, economic interest was behind the cabinet changes of 1951 and 1957.

Immediately after the Civil War and during the Second World War, the regime's ideological tone was set by the Falange. That was largely the reflection of the external circumstance of Axis success. It also reflected the fact that the Christian Democrats of the CEDA had still not lived down their original sin, in Francoist eyes, of their 'accidentalist' co-existence with the Second Republic. The Carlists had withdrawn to their Navarrese strongholds, satisfied with their reward of the Ministry of Justice and preferential economic status. The royalists of Acción Española remained on the margins, suspicious of the upstart anti-oligarchical and anti-monarchical rhetoric of the pro-Axis *Movimiento*. Accordingly, in the eyes of the outside world, the Falange and Francoism were consubstantial. This was illusory but understandable. Falange Española de las JONS provided the structure, the name, the vocabulary and the propaganda mechanisms of the single party. However, Falangism was only one strand of the *Movimiento*.

In fact, the power of the Falange was always somewhat flimsy and never equalled that of the NSDAP in Germany or the Fascist Party in Italy. The Falange had not conquered the state as a result of its own efforts but had ridden to power on the back of the military uprising. It had lost any autonomous dynamism when, after the unification, it allowed itself to provide the bureaucratic structure of the new Francoist state. The Falange became the arena for place-seeking, the ever flexible rhetoric of its leaders merely a means of currying favour and gaining promotion. The goal of national-syndicalist revolution was quietly dropped in the quest for the safe billets of state functionaries. Agrarian reform and the nationalization of the banks became part of the 'pending revolution'.[4] As the leaders

---

4 Amando de Miguel, *Sociología del Franquismo: análisis ideológico de los ministros del régimen* (Barcelona, 1976), pp. 43–8.

aged, the party atrophied in the grip of its own 'iron law of oligarchy'. The six-month internal purge of FET y de las JONS which began in November 1941 was a longer and bloodless version of the Night of the Long Knives, whose purpose was merely to reduce competition for well-paid state jobs.[5] Paradoxically, the Falange's 'corruption' helped it survive the defeat of the Axis. FET y de las JONS was buried too deep into the structures of local and central government to be easily rooted out, and had too little autonomy or even ideological bite for a purge to be necessary.[6]

FET y de las JONS fulfilled a series of useful tasks for the generals who were its real godfathers. Its mass mobilizations provided the veneer of popular support. Its bureaucratic structures stifled the aspirations of the workers and peasants. Its ideologues elaborated a Spanish version of the *Führerprinzip*, the *Teoría del Caudillaje*.[7] Ultimately, however, the fact that Franco was the party's supreme chief (*Jefe Nacional*) was a constant reminder of its endless subordination. It attained a degree of political autonomy during the days of Axis success in the Second World War only because Franco's ambition permitted it to do so. In the last resort, it always hastened to adjust to any political shift or change which he inaugurated. Nevertheless, for all its tacking and trimming, it maintained its hold on the instruments of ideological hegemony until 1975 through the *Movimiento* press network, the vertical syndicates, and the sprawling bureaucracy of central and local administration. In addition to labour relations, responsibility for housing and social security also lay with the Falange. Army officers, civil servants and trade unionists were all automatically members of FET y de las JONS.

Beneath the great umbrella of the *Movimiento*, however, real political power was something that in part had to be wheeled and dealed for and in part depended on the Caudillo's view of how best the survival of his power might be secured. After 1946 the burden passed to the Francoist Christian Democrats deriving from the CEDA and associated with the Catholic pressure group, the Asociación Católica Nacional de Propagandistas. Until they were supplanted by the Opus Dei technocrats in 1957 the ACNP Catholics provided the regime's public legitimacy. After 1957 the technocrats presided over a process of economic modernization and worked hard to streamline the political image of the dictatorship. Thereafter, the loss of control by an aging and infirm Caudillo combined with growing pressure from outside to overthrow the delicate balance of regime forces and open the way to a negotiated transition to democracy. Throughout the complex evolution of the regime from 1946 to 1975, the

---

5 Ellwood, *Spanish Fascism*, pp. 69–70
6 Ricardo L. Chueca, 'FET y de las JONS: la paradójica victoria de un fascismo fracasado' in Josep Fontana (ed.), *España bajo el franquismo* (Barcelona, 1986), pp. 60–77.
7 Francisco Javier Conde, *Contribución a la doctrina del Caudillaje* (Madrid, 1942).

Falange remained like a resentful and obstructive octopus, its tentacles everywhere, incapable of preventing change altogether but with its capacity for disruption unimpaired. It would have suited other elements of the Francoist coalition for the Falange to disappear but it had entrenched itself too well in every area of national life, unwilling to let go and too powerful to be pushed.

Accordingly, behind the apparent dominance of the regime by the Falange, there existed a constant jostling for power, restrained always by a deep sense of the common cause. It had been precisely in the cause of eradicating liberalism, socialism and communism from Spain, that many on the right had acquiesced in Franco's Civil War alliances with Hitler and Mussolini, some with enthusiasm, others with a certain repugnance. Many did so with a passionate appetite for the prospect of Spain belonging to the future fascist world order. It was these latter who were to set the early tone of FET y de las JONS. In the main, young men who had joined the party in the first months of the Civil War, they were anxious for Spain to join Hitler's drive for world domination. Immediately after the Civil War was won, they swamped the more conservative elements, who continued to look in vain to the Caudillo to restore the monarchy.

Franco, however, had other priorities, convinced as he was of the imminence of a war to restructure the world in favour of the new dynamic fascist powers. The partisans of the *ancien régime* were out of fashion. Obstacles were put in the way of the restoration of their press networks.[8] Friction between them and the dominant Falangists surfaced frequently; on one occasion in 1942 it led to a challenge to a duel, issued by the Falangist Miguel Primo de Rivera, brother of the party's founder, against the monarchist President of the Royal Academy, the poet José María Pemán.[9] Dissension had surfaced much earlier as a result of Falangist resentment of the role being granted to the church in educational matters by Franco's first education minister, the monarchist intellectual Pedro Sáinz Rodríguez. Repelled by the Falangist campaign against him and by the totalitarian drift of Spanish politics, he requested that he be relieved of his post on 27 April 1939.[10] The trend in favour

---

8 José Ignacio Escobar, *Así empezó...* (Madrid, 1974), pp. 325–30.

9 José María Pemán, *Mis almuerzos con gente importante* (Barcelona, 1970), pp. 239–43. The relatively innocuous published text of his speech, 'Calvo Sotelo, precursor del movimiento nacional', may be seen in *Homenaje de la Real Academia de Jurisprudencia y Legislación a José Calvo Sotelo* (Madrid, 1942), pp. 255–72.

10 Report of German Ambassador, Von Stohrer, to the Wilhelmsstrasse, 19 November 1938, *Documents on German Foreign Policy* Series D, Volume III (London, 1951), p. 797; Xavier Tusell, *La oposición democrática al franquismo* (Barcelona, 1977), p. 34. In his memoirs, Saínz Rodríguez fails to explain his 'resignation', Pedro Saínz Rodríguez, *Testimonio y recuerdos* (Barcelona, 1978), pp. 254–74. He is slightly more explicit in his contribution to Angel Bayod (ed.), *Franco visto por sus ministros* (Barcelona, 1981), pp. 26–8.

of the Falange could also be discerned behind the replacement of the monarchist General Alfredo Kindelán as Head of the Air Force by the Falangist General Juan Yagüe in August 1939.[11]

The Second World War brought to the surface some of the resentment towards Franco felt by the monarchists. They had considered all along that their support was conditional on the restoration of the monarchy. The Caudillo's failure to make way for a Bourbon king inclined them to be for the Allies in the war. This led to incidents such as the attempted murder by Falangists of the Carlist General Varela, Minister of War, at Begoña near Bilbao on 16 August 1942.[12] Gradually, not to say imperceptibly, a minority of supporters of the dictatorship dissociated themselves from Franco while the bulk remained – Alfonsine monarchists and Carlists, Catholics and Falangists, clerics and soldiers – happily embroiled in jockeying for power among themselves. These collaborationists were confident that the regime would preserve the social order for which they had fought the Civil War.

Loyal Francoists, they often called themselves monarchists only to differentiate themselves from what they saw as the lower-middle-class upstarts of the Falange, with their populist rhetoric of spurious egalitarianism. They joined in the scramble for power around Franco not in order to alter the form or content of the regime but rather to have a say in how its benefits would be distributed. The collaborationist monarchists could salve their consciences with the thought that Franco had not yet institutionalized his regime in a way which might prove an obstacle to a restoration. Moreover, they could still deceive themselves that Franco was more monarchist than Francoist. After all, he had owed his rapid promotions in the army to Alfonso XIII's personal intervention. He had been a *gentilhombre de cámera del Rey* and spoke of himself as a monarchist.[13] He had been elected Nationalist Head of State in 1936 by the most monarchist of the army's generals.[14] They could also take heart from the fact that the pretender, Don Juan, keeping all his options open, was in more or less regular contact with Franco through intermediaries.

---

11 Yagüe's promotion was also an attempt to neutralize him by removing him from command of the powerful Foreign Legion, see Ramón Garriga, *El general Juan Yagüe* (Barcelona, 1985), pp. 171–4. Kindelán's dismissal was not unconnected to the involvement of his son Ultano in a plot to bring Don Juan to Spain, Alfredo Kindelán, *La verdad de mis relaciones con Franco* (Barcelona, 1981), pp. 16–17. See above, p. 89.

12 José María Gil Robles, *La monarquía por la que yo luché (1941–1954)*, pp. 20–4; Laureano López Rodó, *La larga marcha hacia la monarquía*, pp. 503–7; Ellwood, *Spanish Fascism*, pp. 84–8.

13 Juan Antonio Ansaldo, *¿Para qué...? De Alfonso XIII a Juan III* (Buenos Aires, 1951), p. 51; López Rodó, *La larga marcha*, pp. 13, 17; Hugh Thomas, *The Spanish Civil War*, 3rd edn (London, 1977), p. 414.

14 Alfredo Kindelán, *Mis cuadernos de guerra* (Barcelona, 1982), pp. 101–11. For a much more critical account, Guillermo Cabanellas, *La guerra de los mil días*, 2 vols (Buenos Aires, 1973), Vol. I, pp. 640–61.

Franco treated with consideration those monarchists who could combine nominal allegiance to the crown with unconditional service to his own *de facto* regency.[15] Those few who actually left the circles of the regime considered themselves to be in opposition, although clearly their position was not the same as that of the defeated Republicans, who were still being shot by the hundreds or else being herded into labour and concentration camps. Similarly, all those who remained were not necessarily fascists. There was wide common ground between the minority of monarchist and Catholic anti-Francoists and the majority of monarchist and Catholic Francoists. They agreed on issues of public order, religion and anti-communism, for instance. However, the aristocrats, intellectuals and royalist army officers who dabbled with opposition believed that Franco had betrayed the monarchy by failing to restore the king after the Civil War. Francoists, in contrast – even proclaimed monarchists – believed that the Bourbon monarchy should not be restored as of right but installed as a new Francoist monarchy, only after the Caudillo had brought about the political changes necessary, and probably only after his death. Nevertheless, Francoists right across the spectrum were always anxious to secure for the dictatorship the legitimizing power of the monarchy. Their aim was thus to preserve links with Don Juan de Borbón and at the same time neutralize him. It was in this sense that the ultra-conservative General Juan Vigón, Yagüe's successor at the head of the air force, told the Pretender to 'trust in Franco like a father' and concentrate on collecting stamps or coins.[16]

Immediately after the Civil War, the most serious rivalry to Falangist hegemony within the *Movimiento* came from ACNP Catholics, led by the ex-Cedista and President of Acción Católica, Alberto Martín Artajo.[17] Relations between church and state were somewhat strained until 1942. The ecclesiastical hierarchy was suspicious of the statist rhetoric of the Falange. The Falangists were jealous of Catholic influence within the press, education and even banking, and the church's political influence. Many *propagandistas* held key posts in banks and the government holding company, INI. Like the Falange, the ACNP also provided a high proportion of provincial civil governors.[18] They controlled seven daily newspapers and established the influential Consejo Superior de Investigaciones Científicas in collusion with the Opus Dei in 1939. It was precisely this influence

---

15 Norman Jones, 'Monarchism in Spain', unpublished MA thesis (University of Reading 1973), p. 7
16 Rafael Calvo Serer, *Franco frente al rey*, (Paris, 1971), p. 21.
17 See the remarks made in 1940 and 1943 by Fernando Martín-Sánchez Juliá in Jesús Ynfante, *La prodigiosa aventura del Opus Dei: Génesis y desarrollo de la santa mafia* (Paris, 1970), pp. 29–30.
18 A. Saez Alba, *La otra 'Cosa Nostra', la Asociación Católica Nacional de Propagandistas y el caso de 'El Correo' de Andalucía* (Paris, 1974), pp. xxxiii-xxxv.

in the interstices of civil society that the Falangists resented. The Consejo Superior de Investigaciones Científicas was ruled over by one of the most reliable of the *Movimiento* Catholics, the ex-Cedista parliamentary deputy for Murcia, José Ibáñez Martín, since 1939 Franco's Minister of Education. Not surprisingly, after the crumbling of all hopes of Axis victory and the consequent decline of Falangist influence, the Catholic presence in the circles of power grew.[19]

By mid-1943, with German reverses on the Russian front becoming increasingly apparent and the Allies beginning their march up the Italian peninsula, many Francoists assumed that the Caudillo would have to abandon power soon. The fall of Mussolini sent panic waves through the Francoist hierarchy. The news was kept out of the press but copies were circulated of a graphic account in a letter from the secretary to the Spanish ambassador in Rome. The ambassador, the Falangist Raimundo Fernández Cuesta, was severely rebuked by Franco for permitting an act of defeatism. The Caudillo vehemently asserted that there was no analogy between what was happening in Italy and conditions in Spain.[20] In the summer twenty-five prominent members of the Cortes, including five ex-ministers, had already petitioned Franco to restore the monarchy. More crucially, a group of senior generals, including most of those who had bestowed power upon him in Salamanca in 1936, called upon him to withdraw. Franco was facing a similar situation to that which preceded the fall of Mussolini. With characteristic astuteness, he spoke to them all separately and led them to believe that he would soon accede to their request.[21] Don Juan stepped up his involvement in Spanish politics. It was hardly surprising that Franco later referred to the period between late 1943 and early 1944, as 'the most grave moments that we suffered in the war'.[22]

Symptomatic of this was the fact that in October 1944 the Minister of Education, José Ibáñez Martín, rejoined the ACNP in an attempt to dissociate himself from his earlier strident fascism, a significant move by a minister who had been in government for five years and was to remain there for another seven. Correspondence between the Caudillo and the Pretender showed their growing distance, although even Don Juan, in order to protect his dynastic interests, could not afford to break entirely with the Franco regime. This inhibition was reflected in his eventual

---

19 Javier Tusell, *Franco y los católicos: la política interior española entre 1945 y 1957* (Madrid, 1984), p. 24.

20 Xavier Tusell and Genoveva García Queipo de Llano, *Franco y Mussolini: la política española durante la segunda guerra mundial* (Barcelona, 1985), pp. 208–9; Raimundo Fernández Cuesta, *Testimonio, recuerdos y reflexiones* (Madrid, 1985), pp. 221–2; Sir Samuel Hoare, *Ambassador on a Special Mission* (London, 1946), pp. 211–12.

21 López Rodó, *Larga marcha*, pp. 36–44; Tusell and García Queipo de Llano, *Franco y Mussolini*, pp. 222–5; Calvo Serer, *Franco frente al rey*, p. 12. See above, pp. 101–4.

22 Tusell, *Oposición*, p. 76.

reluctant decision to have his son Juan Carlos educated in Spain. Although the USA suspended oil exports to Spain in January 1944, and the fragility of the regime was manifest, the monarchist opposition had little power. Monarchist dissidents merely assumed that Franco could be forced by their pressure or, at worst, by foreign intervention to accept the restoration and to abandon power. Neither the monarchists nor the left, however, could ever convince foreign powers that their plans for the succession to the dictator could avoid civil war and protect the West's economic interests. Franco in contrast had both a measure of popular support and control of a powerful state apparatus. These reserves of strength remained even at the Caudillo's moments of supposedly greatest weakness. Out of fear of the return of a vengeful left, all the forces of the right clung to Franco.

The limits of monarchist opposition to the regime were exposed by the publication of Don Juan's address to the nation, the so-called 'Lausanne manifesto' on 19 March 1945. Inspired by the Allies' restoration of the Italian king, it called upon Franco to abandon power. Monarchists sat tight waiting to see if the Caudillo would leave. Franco kept his head, following the advice of his *eminence grise*, Luis Carrero Blanco, 'to hang on for dear life', although he was worried. The ACNP leader, Alberto Martín Artajo commented that 'those of us who play no part in politics are worried about the international offensive against Spain'.[23] In the postwar government reshuffle of 18 July 1945 Franco recognized, as always on the advice of Carrero Blanco, changes in the configuration of both international and domestic forces. Accordingly, he invited Artajo to join the government as Minister of Foreign Affairs. He hoped thereby to present a Christian Democrat image more in tune with developments elsewhere in Europe. Although a monarchist, Martín Artajo was a typically pragmatic accidentalist. He was less concerned with a monarchical restoration than with diminishing the influence of the Falange inside the regime in favour of Catholic interests.[24]

Catholic readiness to move away from fascism represented a desire to cast off the burdens of Falangism while retaining the regime's essential authoritarianism in a more acceptable guise. Again, as was the case with the monarchists, a truly progressive tendency would emerge among the regime Catholics only decades later and after a painful political evolution which would culminate in open opposition to the regime. After 1945 the pragmatic rightists who had been content to be part of the *Movimiento* in its most pro-Axis phase, despite their discomfort at the anti-oligarchical fascist rhetoric of the Falange, began to make distinctions, proclaiming

---

23 *Texto auténtico del manifiesto de S. M. el Rey* (Lausanne, 19 de marzo de 1945); López Rodó, *Larga marcha*, pp. 48–51; Tusell, *Franco y los católicos*, p. 55.
24 Stanley G. Payne, *The Franco Regime* (Madison, 1986), pp. 350–1; Tusell, *Franco y los católicos*, pp. 52–79.

themselves monarchist, Carlist, Christian-Democrat or just Catholic. To their relief, the regime made serious efforts after 1945 to sever its links with a fascist past. A pseudo-constitution was elaborated, in the form of the 1947 'Ley de Sucesión'. Through the device of plebiscites, the dictatorship was dressed up as an 'organic democracy'. The 'fascist' elements were firmly played down and openly embraced only by groups of zealots who kept their opinions discreetly behind the walls of the Falange.[25]

The feeble commitment to change of the ACNP Catholics was illustrated by the fate of Martín Artajo's extremely conservative political plans. These proposed a 'traditional monarchy'; representative bodies of economic and moral interests and a special freedom of expression, limited to 'diffusion of the truth and certainly not of error'. However, at the cabinet meeting at which his ideas were to be discussed, a hostile atmosphere ensured his silence.[26] Franco, however, used this 'progressive' tendency to promote his regime abroad, particularly in Rome. Martín Artajo as Foreign Minister could project a positive image of Francoist Spain. In September 1946 the youthful and urbane Catholic Joaquín Ruiz Giménez was appointed Director of the Instituto de Cultura Hispánica, a post which involved much foreign travel. The 'Catholic' family was indefatigable in its proselytizing for the regime at home and abroad. Their collaboration was to bear eventual fruit in 1953 with the Concordat with the Vatican and the Bases Agreement with the United States.

In fact, the moment of greatest danger for Franco had passed by the end of 1946. Don Juan had to choose. He could emphasize his democratic credentials at the expense of dialogue with the regime, in order to facilitate joint action with the moderate left. Any *rapprochement* with the left, however, carried with it the certainty that, even if Franco were to go, the monarchy would still have to be subjected to a plebiscite. Aware of King Umberto's unpleasant experience in the Italian referendum of June 1946, Don Juan was reluctant to be committed to such an option. Moreover, with the Cold War turning Franco's anti-communism into an asset, he was tempted to maintain good relations with the Caudillo for the short-term benefits which might accrue to his family and supporters. In fact, the tactical indecisiveness of Don Juan at this time was a reflection of his essential political weakness. The introduction of Franco's Ley de Sucesión on 30 March 1947 brutally exposed the Caudillo's perception of the impotence of Don Juan. Inspired by Martín Artajo, it was the apogee of the Catholic attempt to de-Falangize and legitimize the *Movimiento*. It proclaimed Spain to be a kingdom, whose Head of State for life was Francisco Franco. He could nominate to the Cortes at any moment a king or a regent to succeed himself. Don Juan was warned by Carrero

---

25 López Rodó, *Larga marcha*, pp. 75–104.
26 Tusell, *Franco y los católicos*, p. 110.

Blanco of the imminent announcement, but only a few hours before it was announced on Spanish radio.[27] Incensed by this discourtesy and the indefinite postponement of a restoration, he issued the so-called Estoril manifesto on 7 April 1947. It rejected the law as a 'constitutional fiction' contrary to the principles of monarchy.[28] It was an empty gesture. Once the regime's propaganda machinery went into operation, the referendum on the law provided a massive popular endorsement.

The *Juanistas* were in disarray. Collaborationist monarchists, outside the Falange but none the less part of the *Movimiento*, were beginning to prosper and therefore had ever less reason to risk the dangers of opposition. The law gave them the excuse they needed to relinquish even token opposition. *Juanista* opposition was being neutralized and the embarrassment of Falangism shoved into a corner. The Francoist coalition was intact. The church and the Army remained loyal. The hour of the loyalist Catholics had come. Even Falangists hung on docilely, reluctant to relinquish access to the spoils system. The only cloud on the horizon was the regime's inability to resolve the growing economic and social problems that faced it. That would soon oblige Franco to make further changes which would in turn lead eventually to the break-up of his regime. Otherwise, all seemed well.

The United States had already begun the process of bringing Franco's Spain into the Western sphere of influence. Moreover, Don Juan had effectively acknowledged the way things were moving in the Caudillo's favour. While the more anti-Francoist members of his privy council were negotiating with the socialists, the Pretender was holding talks on the dictator's yacht, *Azor*. On 25 August 1948 he agreed to his son Juan Carlos being educated in Spain. He did not want his dynasty to be forever separated from its homeland like some of the forelorn Balkan royalty who frequented the casino at Estoril.[29] Franco had drawn the sting of the monarchist opposition. Inside Spain, however, the collaborationist monarchists and Catholics were delighted. They happily jumped to the fanciful conclusion that Franco had promised an early restoration, which thereby absolved them of any obligation even to toy with opposition.

Don Juan knew that their confidence was baseless. Whatever else he did, he had to counter Falangist pressure on Franco definitively to slam the door on a future restoration. In such an event, it might have been difficult, even after Franco's death, to get the monarchy back on to the political agenda. His caution was justified by the solidity of the Francoist coalition and by Franco's ability to tack to the prevailing winds. Army officers, traditionalists, monarchists, Falangists, and Catholics as loyal to

---

27 López Rodó, *Larga marcha*, pp. 88–9.
28 Gil Robles, *La monarquía*, p. 209; Tusell, *Oposición* pp. 162–9.
29 Gil Robles, *La monarquía*, pp. 267–73.

the Vatican as Martín Artajo and Ruiz Giménez continued to work in harmony with hard-line Francoists such as the ever-present Carrero Blanco or the Minister of Information, Gabriel Arias Salgado. Moreover, there seemed to be movement from the regime side. When the government was exposed as incapable of a creative response to the strike wave of 1951, Franco reshuffled the cabinet. Long-serving ministers associated with the Falange, such as Juan Antonio Suanzes and Ibáñez Martín, were dropped. The Carlist Antonio Iturmendi returned as Minister of Justice and the Conde de Vallellano came in as Minister of Public Works. Joaquín Ruiz Giménez became Minister of Education. With the regime presenting a more acceptable face, the possibility of removing it altogether seemed to be drifting away. The return of ambassadors in 1950, Spanish entry into UNESCO in 1952 and the Concordat with the Vatican and the treaty with the USA in 1953 were harsh blows both to the democratic opposition and to those monarchists who hoped for an early restoration.

By the same token the 1951 reshuffle heralded a major crisis for the Falange. The strengthening of the regime monarchists drove a wedge into the *Movimiento*. Henceforth FET was to be divided between a collaborationist majority which was prepared to swallow the creeping monarchism of the regime and a minority of hard-line purists, committed to a totalitarian republic. The collaborationists were prepared to compromise their ideological principles rather than relinquish the fruits of power. The various liberalizing initiatives of Ruiz Giménez exacerbated tensions within the *Movimiento*. Indeed, at the November 1955 rally in El Escorial to commemorate the anniversary of the death of the Falange's founder, José Antonio Primo de Rivera, Franco was called a traitor.[30]

The regime's Catholic monarchists began to press home their advantage. Rather as Martín Artajo had done in the mid-1940s, they began to seek ways of contributing to the regime's stability by modifying its dictatorial features. A curious amalgam of collaborationist followers of Don Juan and Opus Dei intellectuals emerged, known collectively as the Tercera Fuerza, a third force against the Falange and the conservative Catholics, or self-proclaimed Christian Democrats, of Artajo. Some but not all the leading lights were figures connected with the Opus Dei: Rafael Calvo Serer, Florentino Pérez Embid and Gonzalo Fernández de la Mora. Others, like the industrialist Joaquín Satrústegui, were liberal supporters of Don Juan. They were committed to the eventual restoration of a traditional monarchy under Don Juan, albeit within the context of the ideals of the *Movimiento*. In an article published in Paris in September 1953, and widely circulated within the Francoist establishment, Calvo Serer claimed that the Falangists and the old regime Catholics had lost their way. For

30   Calvo Serer, *Franco frente al rey*, p. 14.

suggesting that only a team from the new group could modernize the regime, liberalize the administration and modernize the economy, Calvo Serer was dismissed from his posts in the Consejo Superior.[31]

The Tercera Fuerza was put to the test in the municipal elections held in Madrid on 25 November 1954, the first since the Civil War. Sponsored by the monarchist newspaper *ABC*, their candidates were subjected to intimidation by Falangist thugs and by the police. Nevertheless, although official results gave a substantial victory to the Falangist candidates, the monarchists claimed to have received over 60 per cent of the vote.[32] Revealingly, Martín Artajo wrote to Franco, 'what is the point of allowing an opposition candidate and an independent candidate? I fear that with this we have fallen into the old game of political parties'.[33] In attempting to curry favour thus, Martín Artajo achieved the near-impossible and made the dictator appear more liberal than his own cabinet. More realistic than his minion, Franco concluded that the strength of a critical right-wing force called for some action. Accordingly, he met Don Juan at the estate of the Conde de Ruiseñada in Extremadura on 30 December 1954. He made no concessions on a restoration, but his gesture momentarily pacified the monarchists. Shortly afterwards, in interviews in *Arriba* on 23 and 27 January 1954, Franco talked of his successor and declared that he had to be someone 'completely identified with the *Movimiento*'. Within six months, Don Juan stated that the monarchy had always been 'in agreement with the spirit of the *Movimiento* and the Falange'.[34]

This apparent *rapprochement* between the dictator and the Pretender caused further disquiet in Falangist circles. Indeed, throughout the Francoist establishment, battle lines were already being drawn up for a future power struggle. Falangists, Francoist Catholics and Tercera Fuerza, realizing that outside the *Movimiento* little could be done, all hoped to mould the *Movimiento* in their own image. Tensions came to a head in early February 1956. There were violent incidents between Falangists, progressive Catholics and left-wingers in the law faculty of the University of Madrid. In a typical judgement of Solomon, Franco sacked both Ruiz Giménez and the most senior Falangist in his cabinet, Raimundo Fernández Cuesta. As Minister Secretary General of the *Movimiento*, Fernández Cuesta had been unrestrained in his criticism of the Tercera Fuerza. He was replaced by José Luis de Arrese.[35] Throughout 1956 serious efforts were to be made by Arrese to alter the fundamental laws in order to give the

---

31 Calvo Serer, *Franco frente al rey*, pp. 29–30.
32 Calvo Serer, *Franco frente al rey*, pp. 31–2.
33 Tusell, *Franco y los católicos*, p. 294.
34 Tusell, *Oposición* pp. 235–7.
35 For a dense and elliptical account of the intra-regime tensions accompanying the university disturbances, see Ricardo de la Cierva, *Historia del franquismo: aislamiento, transformación, agonía (1945–1975)* (Barcelona, 1978), pp. 136–43.

National Council of the *Movimiento* the ultimate right to dismiss Franco's successor and thereby perpetuate the Falange's pre-eminence. Arrese's scheme so resembled the pseudo-constitutions of the Soviet bloc that regime monarchists, Carlists and the church joined in opposing it.[36] The balance of power was tipping ever further away from the Falange. Some of its brighter young stars in the Frente de Juventudes and the Sindicato Español Universitario, such as Rodolfo Martín Villa and Juan José Rosón, were already coming to terms with this and turning themselves into 'apolitical' administrators deeply entrenched in the regime's structures. Other slightly more senior figures were working on creating an altogether more anodyne and 'progressive' variant of developmental Falangism. Two such figures were Manuel Fraga Iribarne, who became Director of the Instituto de Estudios Políticos and Torcuato Fernández Miranda who was made Director General of Universities.[37] These *Movimiento* apparatchiks, and others like them, would eventually play a crucial role in the transition away from dictatorship after 1975.

Franco, however, still faced the problems of tension between Falangists and monarchists and of the growing stagnation of the the Spanish economy. After lengthy consultations with Carrero Blanco, he turned in February 1957 to the so-called 'technocrats'. A thorough-going remodelling of the cabinet brought in the experts who were to control the levers of economic power. Alberto Ullastres was made Minister of Commerce and Mariano Navarro Rubio Minister of Finance. In various ministries, technocrats such as Gregorio López Bravo, José María López de Letona and José Luis Villar Pallasí became under-secretaries and departmental heads (*directores generales*). Laureano López Rodó was given overall responsibility for major administrative reform as Secretario General Técnico de la Presidencia del Gobierno (the cabinet office). The Falangists who remained in the cabinet were of the domesticated variety: Arias Salgado, Arrese, and José Solís Ruiz. Like the Tercera Fuerza group, the technocrats were closely associated with the Opus Dei but were keener on modernizing than on liberalizing the regime. They were neo-Francoists, concerned only with their own survival and that of the regime. In that sense, the technocrats became accomplices to Franco's immobilism by providing the means to close the door on political reform and substituting economic and administrative reform.[38] They were monarchists but were not *Juanistas*. They believed, under the influence of

---

36 José Luis de Arrese, *Un etapa constituyente* (Barcelona, 1982), *passim*; Fernández Cuesta, *Testimonio*, pp. 243–5; Ellwood, *Spanish Fascism*, pp. 118–21.

37 Manuel Fraga Iribarne, *Memoria breve de una vida pública* (Barcelona, 1980), pp. 25–6; Manuel Durán, *Martín Villa* (San Sebastián, 1979), pp. 39–55; Pablo Lizcano, *La generación del 56: la universidad contra Franco* (Barcelona, 1981), pp. 231–4.

38 Luis Suárez Fernández, *Francisco Franco y su tiempo*, 8 vols (Madrid, 1984), Vol. V, pp. 320–6; Calvo Serer, *Franco frente al rey*, pp. 14–15.

Carrero Blanco, that the future lay with a Francoist monarchy under Juan Carlos resting on the authoritarian foundations of the dictatorship.[39]

To a certain extent, the rise of the technocrats signified Franco's acceptance of a muted Tercera Fuerza option. However, it did mean that the hopes of the genuinely liberal supporters of Don Juan were dashed and they were forced into a form of internal opposition. The monarchists were divided between those who were still committed to a constitutional monarchy under Don Juan and those within the regime who had become identified with the plans of Carrero Blanco for a Francoist monarchy under Juan Carlos. Increasingly, the more perspicacious elements in the regime came to recognize a need to create a broad extra-Francoist platform, in readiness for the eventual demise of the Caudillo and of the Falange. Admittedly, at the end of the 1950s, the regime was gradually starting to solve its economic problems without political reform, as it had its diplomatic ones in the 1940s. Nevertheless, Spanish liberals of right and left had reason to feel that the tide was turning. They hoped that Kennedy, the new American president, would reverse Eisenhower's pro-Franco policies and that Spain's need to enter the EEC could only favour their cause. The focusing of attention on Europe proved especially beneficial for the opposition, given the regime's growing interest in international acceptance and, in particular, its petition to join the European Community on 9 February 1962. The European activities of the opposition and their good reception stood in stark contrast to the outright rejection of the regime's abortive overtures to the European Community. Indeed, the appeal of Europe was broad enough to provide a meeting ground for the tolerated conservative opposition of the interior and the exiled opposition. Monarchists, Catholics and renegade Falangists met socialists and Basque and Catalan nationalists in Munich at the Fourth Congress of the European Movement from 5 to 8 June 1962.

The reaction of the Francoist press was hysterical. This was understandable. As a result of the strike wave in the spring of 1962, the first signs of conflict with the Catholic Church were becoming visible. There was suddenly a plausibility about the communists' claims that their policy of national reconciliation was about to bear fruit in a wide front of anti-Franco forces. Respectable Catholics and monarchists had consorted with exiled democrats. The signs that the Francoist coalition was breaking up were immensely disturbing. Many of the Spanish delegates were arrested and sent into exile for their part in what came to be known as the 'filthy Munich plot'.[40] Significantly, on 10 July, Franco introduced

---

39 López Rodó, *Larga marcha*, pp. 136 ff.
40 Dionisio Ridruejo, *Ibérica*, July 1962, quoted in Dionisio Ridruejo, *Casi unas memorias* (Barcelona, 1976), pp. 391–2; Paul Preston, *Salvador de Madariaga and the Quest for Liberty in Spain* (Oxford, 1987), pp. 28–9.

more 'progressive' Opus Dei elements such as Gregorio López Bravo, as Minister of Industry, and Manuel Lora Tamayo, as Minister of Education, into his cabinet. The energetic Manuel Fraga came to greater prominence as Minister of Information. The regime was being forced to change. When that change was eventually exposed as inadequate, a gradual process would begin whereby its more far-sighted servants would embark on the slow path to the democratic opposition. The democratic right-wingers at Munich had provided them with a bridge of respectability. The Munich Congress revealed the growing strength of non-Francoist groups in the interior and their greater willingness to act in public and in unison. The false European pretensions of the regime had been exposed in international terms. More important, there had emerged publicly a moderate democratic right, to which the left could relate and with which it could establish a dialogue. Munich had underlined a moment of crisis and it had shown a way out without bloodshed.

Inevitably then, from the mid-1960s, concern over the future dominated the attitude of the right both inside and outside the regime. It was this preoccupation which largely underlay a resurgence of interest in the monarchy. Now, however, the monarchists' options were widened by the presence of Juan Carlos in Spain, and his apparently close relationship with the Caudillo. The more sophisticated Francoist politicians placed themselves squarely in the Juan Carlos camp. They saw this as the most plausible way to ensure a continuation of the regime after Franco's death. These *continuistas* embarked upon *operación príncipe* to get him named Franco's successor. This goal was pursued with especial enthusiasm by the Opus Dei and was brought to a successful conclusion in 1969.[41] The Francoist advocates of Juan Carlos hoped that he would preside over a limited reform. They had little idea that he would, however, turn out to be the paladin of full-scale democratic change.

The Falangists hoped to perpetuate a *Movimiento* in which they would continue to control the great institutions, the vertical syndicates, the social security system and local administration. The non-Falangist elements, however, while paying lip-service to the idea and the ideals of the *Movimiento* preferred to see it as a great ideological umbrella over all loyal Francoists. This broad interpretation of the *Movimiento* tended to gain ever greater sway as Franco himself came to acknowledge that his regime had to adjust to the changing circumstances of the world in the 1960s. The rise of Luis Carrero Blanco, Laureano López Rodó and the Opus Dei technocrats symbolized that. The job of modernizing the *Movimiento* was entrusted to the least dogmatic of the senior Falangists, José Solís Ruiz, a political conjuror.[42] Together, they spread the rhetoric

---

41 Payne, *Franco Regime*, pp. 536–42; López Rodó, *La larga marcha*, pp. 222–386.
42 Ellwood, *Spanish Fascism*, pp. 121–6.

of 'political development', 'liberalization' and 'modernization'. They did so with an air of desperation, after the rejection of the regime's application for membership of the EEC in February 1962. While the technocrats tried to gain democratic credibility for the regime, both the EEC and the Munich meeting effectively denied it. However, the desperate efforts of the technocrats were to open cracks within the Francoist establishment from which would eventually sprout some democratic growths.

There was talk of setting up political associations, limited of course to those who were unequivocally committed to the principles of Francoism and to their survival. Associations would effectively systematize what had previously been random jockeying for power between informal pressure groups, in a way which would allow the regime to derive some moral legitimacy. The idea was never fully implemented until 1974. However, together with the Press Law introduced in 1966 by Manuel Fraga, the idea exposed some of the divisions within the Francoist élite. The Press Law was cautious and restrictive yet it did allow limited debate at the moment when preparations for the future were on the agenda of both some regime elements and the opposition.[43] Three broad tendencies could be discerned within the regime. On the far right were those Falangists committed to what was known as *inmovilismo*; in the centre were the so-called *continuistas*, led by Carrero Blanco, who hoped to perpetuate the regime under a closely invigilated monarchy of Juan Carlos; and on the left were the so-called *aperturistas*, who hoped for a limited democratic solution under Don Juan. This latter group straddled the regime and the opposition. Out of its ability to maintain dialogue both with the genuinely democratic left and with the *continuistas* was eventually to emerge the negotiated and bloodless transition to democracy between 1975 and 1977.

Anxiety about the future also played a large part in the development of non-Francoist conservatism. There was an awareness that the right as a whole was in serious danger of being inextricably linked with the regime in the popular mind. There were fears of a total conservative eclipse in a post-dictatorial regime that might be created under the aegis of democratic forces dominated by the communists or socialists. Accordingly, there was a general agreement that the non-Francoist right should aim to be a source of dialogue and gradual change and that this set it apart from the other increasingly confrontational opposition forces. This underlined the ambivalence in the conservative ranks throughout the Franco period. Christian Democracy, as had been the case previously with *Juanista* monarchism, tended to become a political refuge for those conservatives

---

43 A fascinating account of this period from inside the regime is provided by Rafael Calvo Serer, *La dictadura de los franquistas 1 El 'affaire' del 'Madrid' y el futuro político* (Paris, 1973), *passim*.

who, having benefited from, and tacitly approved of, Francoism, now saw that political change was on the horizon.[44] This was to be increasingly the case as the regime began to disintegrate in the late 1960s and particularly as the church evolved into a stern critic of the dictatorship.

Carrero Blanco assumed the vice-presidency in July 1967 with the express intention of preparing the ground for a Francoist monarchy in the person of Juan Carlos. Such a monarchy was to be irrevocably committed to the continued exclusion from Spain of communists, socialists and liberals. The irrelevance of such a project was starkly exposed by the fact that, until his assassination in 1973, Carrero's governments reeled under the combined assaults of working-class unrest, student dissent and Basque terrorism. That in itself made many erstwhile Francoists reconsider their futures. What tipped the balance for many was the fact that, under threat, the regime *continuistas* were forced to resort to unrestrained brutality against their opponents. Moreover, they found themselves increasingly in alliance with the *inmovilistas*, who came to be known as the 'bunker'.[45] Its starkest manifestion consisted of ultra-rightist terror squads which subjected left-wing students and professors, clandestine union leaders and liberal priests to sporadic violence.

They were merely the most visible symptom of Falangist anxieties about Franco's increasing frailty and the dangers of the succession of Juan Carlos. Disturbed by the increasing scale of working-class and student unrest and by the emergence of ETA, an organization capable of undermining the regime's image of invulnerability, the Falangist right of the regime felt itself to be under siege. The slogans, pamphlets and wall-daubings of their young activists used a nostalgic Civil War rhetoric which reflected their feelings that history was turning against them. The Falange had adapted to disagreeable change for over thirty years in order to enjoy the fruits of the Civil War victory. That the party seemed to be over was reflected in Hitlerian talk of withdrawing to a bunker and fighting in the rubble of the Chancellery. At best, neo-Nazi groups played a useful role in the tactics of beleagured Francoism, terrorizing the opposition without stigma for the regime. More sophisticated was the propaganda effect of blurring the government's adoption of an increasingly hard line against all forms of dissent, because the invention of a fanatical extreme right put the regime as if by magic in a centre position. Yet even in June 1973, when Carrero Blanco became head of government it was already too late. He was the only plausible guarantor of a Francoist monarchy, and within six months he would be dead.

---

44 Fernando Alvárez de Miranda, *Del 'contubernio' al consenso* (Barcelona, 1985), pp. 88–9; Paul Preston, *The Triumph of Democracy* (London, 1986), pp. 8–30.
45 Preston, *Las derechas españolas*, pp. 135–42; Luis Ramírez, 'Morir en el búnker', in *Horizonte español 1972*, 3 vols (Paris, 1972), pp. 3–20. See Chapter 7 below.

The more the ultra-right lashed out at the enemies of the regime, the more the church tended to identify itself with regional and working-class protest. At first implicitly and later explicitly, the church withdrew its stamp of moral legitimacy from the regime.[46] At the same time, the regime was revealing its incapacity to respond to the social discontent consequent upon economic development. That led many in the business community to hanker after a more modern political context for their activities. The technocrats' scenario had assumed that rises in per capita income would obviate the need for political change. The wave of strikes, demonstrations and terrorist attacks which marked the period between 1969 and 1973 undermined that assumption. Hard-line Francoists in the army and the Falange muttered that development had been a mistake and that survival demanded a return to the ethos of 1939. With Franco increasingly senile and closeted with an ultra-rightist clique in his El Pardo residence, these were the regime forces most likely to influence him.[47] Even one-time collaborationist monarchists and Catholics were forced to the conclusion that a democratic *apertura* (opening) was necessary to avoid the entire edifice being swept away. Their attitude was revealed in the increasingly critical line adopted by the principal monarchist and Catholic newspapers, *ABC* and *Ya*. In consequence, many young and perceptive Francoist functionaries began to toy with the idea of a dialogue with the opposition and their natural interlocutors were the monarchists of Satrústegui and Areilza and the left Christian Democrats of Gil Robles and Ruiz Giménez.

In Catalonia, Madrid and Seville, liberal *Juanista* monarchists began to join wide opposition fronts with socialists, communists and other leftists. The most influential conservatives, like Gil Robles, Satrústegui and Areilza, hoped for some kind of bloodless transition to a democratic monarchy under Don Juan. However, with the regime increasingly in the hands of those prepared to go down fighting, the progressive right was concerned by the left-wing opposition's belief that mass pressure would overthrow the dictatorship. A search began for a middle way. Monarchist thinkers and academic theorists began to comb the pseudo-democratic rhetoric of the Francoist constitution to see if it could be exploited to permit real democratization. At the same time, many liberal *Juanistas* came to the conclusion that to have any opportunity of bringing about a 'legal' evolution to democracy, they must re-capture Juan Carlos from

---

46   Norman B. Cooper, *Catholicism and the Franco Regime* (Beverly Hills, 1975), pp. 37–43; José Chao Rego, *La Iglesia en al franquismo* (Madrid, 1976), pp. 150–231; Guy Hermet, *Les Catholiques dans l'Espagne Franquiste*, 2 vols (Paris, 1981), Vol. II, pp. 398–421; Rafael Díaz Salazar, *Iglesia, dictadura y democracia* (Madrid, 1981), pp. 227–83.

47   Preston, *The Triumph of Democracy*, pp. 36, 51, 63; Antonio Izquierdo, *Yo, testigo de cargo* (Barcelona, 1981), p. 37; Vicente Gil, *Cuarenta años junto a Franco* (Barcelona, 1981), pp. 139–202.

the technocrats. Given that the prince was not as committed to the perpetuation of Franco as the regime's propaganda had made out, that was to be easier than they expected. The legalist and evolutionary project was to come into its own in 1976.

Conservatives and 'apolitical' *Movimiento* functionaries played a significant role in the peaceful transition to democracy after Franco's death. Their willingness to accept and participate in the process of change undermined the diehard reactionaries of the regime. A forum for debate was established involving both right and left, based on a mutual acceptance of the need for democracy. The fact that the progressive right was able to recognize the need for pragmatism and flexibility in the face of the changed social and economic structure of Spain was a considerable contribution to the bloodless nature of the transition. The appearance of a recognizable contemporary Spanish conservatism was not, however, the culmination of a gradual and inexorable political development. It owed more to the peculiarities of the Franco regime and its incompatibility with the demands of a modern industrialized nation. The monarchists and the Falangist zealots of the 1940s bore little resemblance to the conservatives and *Movimiento* apparatchiks of the mid-1970s. The latter's capacity to evolve was greater than that of a regime that had lost its main asset, its pragmatism. The activities of the ultra-rightist bunker had the inadvertent effect of advertising the fact that the regime's obsolescence would admit of no further tinkering. The patricians in whose interests the Civil War had been fought were not threatened by the change. The only victim of the transition was the Falange, and it had been paid well over forty years for the services it rendered.

6

Destiny and dictatorship: the Spanish army and the Franco regime, 1939–75

Between 1814 and 1981 there were more than fifty *pronunciamientos*, or military coups in Spain. That crude statistic provides a graphic indication of the divorce between soldiers and civilians. In fact, in the first third of the nineteenth century, those *pronunciamientos* were liberal in their political intent. Thereafter, a tradition of mutual misunderstanding and mistrust between the army and civil society developed to a point at which soldiers considered themselves more Spanish than civilians. By the early twentieth century, officers were ripe for persuasion by those on the extreme right that it was their right and duty to interfere in politics in order to 'save Spain'. Unfortunately, that noble objective tended to mean the defence of the interests and privileges of relatively small segments of society. Accordingly, from the civilian point of view, popular hostility to the armed forces derived fundamentally from the fact that deep-rooted social conflicts, at a time of imperial decline and military defeat, were repressed by the army. Military resentments of politicians in general and of the left and the labour movement in particular were the other side of the same coin.

Within this broad context, the army developed internally in a way which made the underlying hostility between soldiers and civilians virtually irremediable. Three deep-rooted and inextricably inter-linked problems were to constitute a near insuperable obstacle to the integration of the military and society. The first was the exaggerated rhetorical patriotism of the officer corps. This was a compensation for the fact that, from the Peninsular War until the present day, the Spanish army did not win decisively any war against foreign enemies. The second was an acute sensitivity to civilian criticism. Inevitably, given the poor external performance of the army, which was a consequence of inadequate financial provision, education and training, and its use to repress social discontent, such criticism was intense. Its most visible manifestation was popular hostility to conscription, fomented without exception by left-wing parties and unions. The third was the excessive, indeed macrocephalic, size of the officer corps in relation both to the numbers of rank-and-file troops and to Spain's realistic military needs and capacity. That was a consequence of the fact that, after each civil war of the nineteenth century, the peace settlement tended to involve the incorporation into the senior ranks of the officers of the defeated side – a tradition broken in 1939 by General Franco. That was to lead to blockages of channels for advancement and the drying up of initiative. In consequence, there was an increasing resort to the most rigid system of promotion, one by the strictest seniority only. Political efforts to deal with this problem created difficulties for such diverse political regimes as the Primo de Rivera dictatorship, the Second Republic and the post-Franco democracy.[1]

These three central problems were fused after the final loss of empire in 1898. The 'disaster' was blamed on the army, which in turn felt that it had had its hands tied by political corruption and incapacity. As the bulk of the population was determined that Spain should never again go to war, embattled army officers came to believe that they held the monopoly on patriotism and were the executors of a 'national truth' which they could impose on the rest of the nation whenever the need arose. That was reflected by successful efforts to impose military jurisdiction over a range of civilian offences. After the Cuban disaster, the army was inefficient, overburdened by bureaucracy and ill-equipped – with fewer artillery pieces per 1,000 men than even the armies of Romania, Montenegro and Portugal.[2] Difficulties with the army's African enterprises intensified military/civilian tensions. While working-class conscripts became militant pacifists in response to the appalling conditions in North Africa, there emerged within the military an élite corps of tough, brutal professional officers, the *Africanistas*. This inevitably exacerbated the military sense of apartness from a society which officers increasingly felt had betrayed them. The consequent resentment, fuelled by an arrogant confidence in the army's right to dictate the political direction of the nation, was to lead to the 1923 coup of General Primo de Rivera and the subsequent dictatorship. Inevitably, it would also guarantee the army's determination to destroy the Second Republic.

---

1 On the growth of civilian/military tensions, see Stanley G. Payne, *Politics and the Military in Modern Spain* (Stanford, 1967); Carlos Seco Serrano, *Militarismo y civilismo en la España contemporánea* (Madrid, 1984); Alberto Gil Novales (ed.), *Ejército, Pueblo y Constitución. Siglos XIX y XX: Homenage al General Rafael del Riego* (Madrid, 1988); Daniel R. Headrick, *Ejército y política en España (1866–1898)* (Madrid, 1981); Jorge Cachinero, 'Intervencionismo y reformas militares en España a comienzos del siglo XX', *Zona Abierta* (Madrid), nos 39–40, pp. 115–48.
2 Fernando Reinlein García-Miranda, 'Del siglo XIX a la guerra civil', in Colectivo Democracia, *Los Ejércitos... más allá del golpe* (Barcelona, 1981), pp. 13–33.

At the beginning of the Spanish Civil War, the director of the military conspiracy against the Republic, the *Africanista* General Mola stated that 'the reconstruction of Spain on a new basis is the exclusive task of the military, a task which corresponds to us by right, because it is the desire of the nation and because we have an exact concept of our power to do so'.[3] Mola's brutal statement could not have more clearly revealed the arrogance typical of certain parts of the military establishment. The idea that the nation's political destiny lay in the hands of soldiers was a commonplace of military ideology. Moreover, it was a belief readily accepted by the beleagured upper and middle classes. They turned to the army in 1936 precisely because of their confidence that the military conception of the national destiny was such as to guarantee the defence of oligarchical privileges and middle-class social, economic and religious interests.

Mola would no doubt have been surprised had he been present thirty-three years later when General Narciso Ariza, Director of the Escuela de Estado Mayor, made a speech on 4 May 1970 about the lamentable condition of the armed forces as regards equipment, resources and salaries. Claiming that the rapid economic development of the 1960s had passed the military by, Ariza described the armed forces as the 'poor relation of the boom' (*pariente pobre del desarrollo*). He was dismissed from his post. However, the fact that Ariza had been prepared to take the risk was a clear indication of the resentment felt among the high command about the fortunes being made elsewhere in the Francoist élite during the boom.[4] Mola would have been even more surprised to discover that in the 1970s Spanish society would increasingly reject the political destiny mapped out for it in 1939. The journey from swaggering arrogance in the 1940s to political isolation and technical decay in the 1970s reflected the use to which General Franco had put the army since the Civil War. The sense of near omnipotence discernible in Mola's remarks was born of the fact that the Spanish armed forces, despite their lack of external success, were used to fighting, and winning, against the civilian population. The despair of General Ariza reflected a sense of impotence born of the fact that, under Franco, Spain effectively lacked any kind of defence policy. With colonial wars fresh in the memory, Spanish army officers had still been able to feel a degree of professional pride in 1936. However, at the end of the 1960s, having just lost Ifni and Guinea, the remnants of Spanish Africa, those elements of the military with a developed sense of professionalism were appalled at the state of the armed forces.

---

3 Julio Gonzalo Soto, *Esbozo de una síntesis del ideario de Mola* (Burgos, 1937), p. 53 (quoted by Josep Fontana, 'Reflexiones sobre la naturaleza y las consecuencias del franquismo' in *España bajo el franquismo* (Barcelona, 1986), p. 13.
4 *Le Monde*, 12 May 1970.

A similar, and more ironic, reversal was evident in the relationship between the military and the Falange. In 1936, convinced of their role as the arbiters of the national destiny, senior army officers looked down on the Falangists as an unpleasant necessity, a rabble who provided some of the cannon fodder of the war effort. Forty years later, that situation had been dramatically reversed. The Falangist old guard (known as the 'bunker' because of its readiness to defend the dictatorship from the rubble), was confident of the support of the generation of ultra hard-line Francoist generals who now dominated the high command. Many of them had joined the army as extreme rightist volunteers during the Civil War, and became acting second lieutenants or *alféreces provisionales*. They had stayed on and, by the late 1960s and early 1970s, held posts of crucial importance in the military hierarchy. This military bunker joined its civilian counterparts in vain efforts to use the army to block popular demands for democracy.

The tension between professional disquiet and political arrogance was constant in the military during the period 1939–77. Reminders of victory in the Civil War and of the army's role as the guardian of national destiny and as the bulwark against communism, freemasonry and godlessness were used to build an exaggerated sense of pride, which in turn was used to compensate the army for its real professional decay. When divisions emerged, they usually had at their core unease at the political role assigned to the army by Franco. At one level, the military could hardly have been surprised by the turn of events. In 1936, important sectors of the officer corps had acquiesced in defending conservative interests rather than the nation as a whole. On the other hand, few officers could have foreseen the extent to which the army would be reduced to becoming an inert barrier against social and political progress. Other forces of the Francoist coalition evolved during the years of the dictatorship in response to social and economic change. The army in contrast simply became more alienated from society.

That was the inevitable consequence of its explicit political commitment to Franco. Moreover, it was conditioned by a military education system based on the inculcation of Civil War values, to the defence of what by the 1960s were increasingly anachronistic political structures. Divorced from civilian society by the fact of ruling over it through the system of military justice, the army became more like the foreign occupation force which its deployment around the major industrial towns inclined it to be. Military tribunals were responsible for the trial of offences committed by the regime's political and labour opponents, deemed to be 'military rebellion'. Effectively, from 1939 to 1975, Spain was under martial law, although the wartime emergency powers of the army were officially relinquished in 1948. For thirty-two and a half of the thirty-six years of the regime, the Ministry of the Interior was in the hands of soldiers.[5]

The fact that Franco put his own immediate political requirements before Spain's need for coherent military plans or defence policy could be seen in the overall organizational structure which he adopted. On January 1938 he had created the Ministerio de Defensa Nacional which, had it been maintained, would have permitted the co-ordination of the armed forces, unity of command, combined purchasing and economies of scale. However, by a law of 8 August 1939, the Ministry was re-divided into three separate army, navy and air force ministries. The only co-ordination between them was henceforth provided by a joint general staff and a National Defence Junta. Neither was much more than an advisory body to Franco himself. Lacking any military rationale, this was largely an exercise in divide and rule, which also significantly increased the preferment at Franco's disposal. It prevented the emergence of a powerful Minister of Defence capable of challenging Franco's own pre-eminence or even of merely being able to see and express the professional discontents of the three services. Franco himself was supreme commander, the *Generalísimo de los Ejércitos* and the three military ministers were merely administrators. A similar divide-and-rule rationale may be perceived behind the decision to revive the eighteenth-century institution whereby the army was distributed geographically and administratively into nine *Capitanías Generales*, or military regions.[6] The historical origins and the operational irrelevance of the post of Captain-General was indicated by the fact that three out of the nine were in Castilla. The post provided another level of seniority to complicate lines of command. The same was true of the reintroduction of the rank of lieutenant-general, which had been abolished by the Republic. It created a greater sense of hierarchy and increased competition for Franco's favour within the senior ranks. The consequent conflict of authorities did nothing for efficiency but, since they all ultimately depended on Franco, they enhanced the capacity of the Caudillo to play them off against each other.

The territorial deployment of the army's best-equipped units was not related to any possible international conflict but followed pre-Civil War dispositions. In consequence, it was dictated by the needs of controlling

---

5 For a thorough account of a system in which the army was both protagonist and judge in public order cases, see Manuel Balbé, *Orden público y militarismo en la España constitucional 1812–1983* (Madrid, 1983), pp. 402–49; Pierre Celhay, *Consejos de guerra en España* (Paris, 1976), pp. 64–88; Dionisio Ridruejo, *Escrito en España*, 2nd edn (Buenos Aires, 1964), p. 284; José Fortes and Restituto Valero, *Qué son las Fuerzas Armadas* (Barcelona, 1977), p. 13; Jesús Ynfante, *El Ejército de Franco y de Juan Carlos* (Paris, 1976), pp. 95–9.

6 Francisco Javier Mariñas, *General Varela: de soldado a general* (Barcelona, 1956), pp. 237–9; Julio Busquets and Gabriel Cardona, 'Unas Fuerzas Armadas para el Movimiento', in Justino Sinova (ed.), *Historia del franquismo*, 2 vols (Madrid, 1985), Vol. I, pp. 168–9.

the industrial working class and to a lesser extent the North African colonies. Otherwise, the post-1939 armed forces in Spain were a ramshackle affair. They possessed large quantities of equipment acquired before and during the Civil War whose heterogeneity was an obstacle to efficiency. Moreover, already worn out by use in the war, it was soon rendered entirely obsolete by the vertiginous technological advances of the Second World War.[7] Captured Russian equipment was still in use in the Spanish army at the beginning of the 1950s. The decision to maintain a large force meant that an absurdly high proportion of the total military budget was absorbed by salary costs. Once normal administration and running costs were added, this left very little for manoeuvres, exercises or new equipment, let alone for the thoroughgoing rearmament that was required. The basic infantry rifle was either the 1893 Mauser first issued during the Cuban War, or the 1916 Mauser, or else one of eight different foreign rifles or carbines. There were ten different types of machine-gun in service and four types of hand grenades. The mortars, cannons and armoured cars were museum pieces. At the outbreak of the Second World War, the Spanish army moved on foot, wore second-hand uniforms and rope sandals (*alpargatas de esparto*), carried its equipment on the backs of mules or on horse-drawn carts and lived in poor conditions on execrable rations. Moreover, at a time when the techniques of war were changing dramatically, of 22,100 officers, only 94 were trained in the command of tank and armoured car units, only 377 had taken radio transmission courses and only 104 were skilled in topography.[8]

Penury might have been expected to be the seedbed of future military discontent. However, despite the deficiencies of its equipment and the fact that salary levels were relatively low, the morale of the Spanish armed forces was extremely buoyant. Spirits were high because of the recent victory in a war in which their cause had been legitimized by the church as being for the defence of Christian civilization. Moreover, the fact that the German and Italian allies in the Civil War were expecting a forthcoming war to redistribute the political geography of Europe contributed briefly to a sense of bellicose expectation. In any case, there were numerous economic supplements for low salaries, if hardly for deficient equipment. In a period of acute hunger for the civilian population, with diseases such as tuberculosis, typhoid and rickets rampant, special military foodstores (*economatos*) and pharmacies were well stocked with food

---

7 Fortes and Valero, *Fuerzas Armadas*, pp. 42–3.

8 Busquets and Cardona, 'Fuerzas Armadas', pp. 170–1; Cf. a report by General Arsenio Martínez Campos written for the Alto Estado Mayor in May 1940, quoted by Javier Tusell and Genoveva García Queipo de Llano, *Franco y Mussolini: la política española durante la segunda guerra mundial* (Barcelona, 1985), p. 98.

and medicines at subsidized prices, and there was an exclusive medical service at the disposal of military personnel. Access to supplies provided obvious opportunities for participation in the black market, which were taken by some officers. There were other additional benefits such as housing facilities and widespread educational provision for the children of officers. These paternalist measures had the side-effect of intensifying the isolation of the military from civilian society.[9] In addition, wartime salaries were increased considerably on 1 July 1940, albeit on an extremely low base.[10]

Senior officers also had the additional reward of posts and sinecures in the civilian administration. Between 1936 and 1945, 31.3 per cent of senior posts in the civil service were held by army, navy or air force officers. Posts of subsecretarios and Director General in ministries, in local administration and in the military justice system abounded. Of the *procuradores* in the pseudo-parliament, the Cortes, 12.3 per cent were officers nominated by Franco. Ministry men held 34 per cent of senior posts in the *Movimiento*. The biggest presence in any department other than the specifically military ministries was in the Presidencia del Gobierno, Franco's cabinet office, in which military men held 26 senior posts, 89.6 per cent of the total. In the Ministry of the Interior, officers held 32 senior posts, 49 per cent of the total. In the Subsecretaría de Orden Pública within the Ministry of the Interior, 70 per cent of senior posts were held by officers. In the regime's first ten years of existence, 106 army officers held the job of civil governor of a province. Between 1938 and 1945, that constituted 38 per cent of the total of civil governors. From 1945 to 1960, officers made up a steady 22 per cent of the total.[11] There can be no doubt that such a prominent role in the civilian state apparatus not only handsomely supplemented the income of the officers concerned but also greatly augmented their self-esteem and professional pride.

However, if Franco still had any worries about military discontent, the spirit of unity and messianic anti-communism generated by the recent war and also the generational structure of the armed forces would have reassured him. The greatest source of dissent was found among the Caudillo's peers, the high command. It was dominated by *Africanista* generals and senior colonels who had risen to prominence during the

---

9 Julio Busquets, *El militar de carrera en España*, 3rd edn (Barcelona, 1984), p. 214.

10 The increase for colonels was by 15 per cent, for captains by 26 per cent, for first lieutenants by 40 per cent; Payne, *Politics and the Military*, p. 527; Coronel Jesús Pérez Salas, *Guerra en España (1936–1939)* (México D.F., 1947), pp. 88–9.

11 Carlos Viver Pi Sunyer, *El personal político de Franco (1936–1945)* (Barcelona, 1978), pp. 70–2; Miguel Jerez Mir, *Élites políticas y centros de extracción en España 1938–1957* (Madrid, 1982), pp. 228–39.

Moroccan wars, had been behind the 1936 military rising and had voted to make Franco supreme commander, Generalísimo and Head of State on 28 September 1936. None had done so in order to make Franco *de facto* regent for life and most were anxious to see an early monarchical restoration. However, of those who had started out in the war, many were already dead – Sanjurjo, Mola, Fanjul, Goded, Cabanellas – some in suspicious circumstances.[12] Others – Queipo de Llano, Yagüe, Kindelán, Aranda, Varela, Orgaz, García Valiño – mounted some timid opposition to Franco in the 1940s. Their dissidence consisted largely of muted attempts to oblige Franco to keep Spain out of the Second World War and, as it became clearer that an Axis defeat was likely, to make provision for a monarchist restoration. However, their remonstrations aside, Franco had relatively little to worry about. As a caste, the *Africanistas* had reached a level of seniority when the risks of conspiracy were no longer worth taking. Moreover, they also had their ambitions and Franco was supremely skilful in maintaining their loyalty by the cunning distribution of post, promotions, decorations, pensions and even titles of nobility.[13]

Below the most senior generals, the Caudillo had even less to worry about. The ranks which in many armies often produce dangerous machinations were, for different reasons, of proven loyalty to Franco. Many colonels, majors and captains were of the generation educated at the Academia General Militar de Zaragoza in its so-called second epoch between 1927 and 1931, under the direction of General Franco himself.[14] In the period in which Franco had been able to impose his views on the academy, the level of technical education had been lamentable and stress laid on anti-democratic indoctrination. The teaching body had been dominated by *Africanista* friends of Franco, noted more for their ideological rigidity than for their intellectual attainments and brutalized by their experiences in a minor but cruel colonial war. They included Emilio Esteban Infantes, soon to be involved in the attempted Sanjurjo coup of 1932, Bartolomé Barba Hernández, who was to be, on the eve of the Civil War, leader of the conspiratorial organization Unión Militar Española, and Franco's close friend Camilo Alonso Vega, later to be a dour Minister of the Interior. Virtually without exception, the academy's teachers were to play prominent roles in the military uprising of 1936. With such men on the staff, the AGM had concentrated on inculcating the ruthless arrogance of the Foreign Legion, the idea that the army was the

---

12 Paul Preston, 'Franco and the Hand of Providence', in John M. Merriman, (ed.), *For Want of a Horse: Choice and Chance in History* (Lexington, Mass, 1985).

13 Alfredo Kindelán, *La verdad de mis relaciones con Franco* (Barcelona, 1981), p. 118; José María Gil Robles, diary entry for 15 January 1943, *La monarquía por la que yo luché (1941–1954)* (Madrid, 1976), p. 27.

14 Mariano Aguilar Olivencia, *El Ejército español durante la segunda República* (Madrid, 1986), pp. 119–29.

supreme arbiter of the nation's political destiny, and a sense of discipline and blind obedience. Franco's brother Ramón wrote to him to complain of the 'troglodytic education' imparted at the Academia General Militar. A high proportion of the officers who passed through the AGM were later to be involved in the Falange.[15]

The lieutenants and junior captains were dominated by the so-called *alféreces provisionales*. Largely Falangist, but including some Carlist, volunteers, these 'acting second-lieutenants' had swelled the ranks of the army in the early days of the Civil War. Many stayed on after 1939. After a period of eight months' study in the specially created Academias de Transformación, 10,709 were incorporated into the regular army as lieutenants, between 1939 and 1946. That was the equivalent of fifty years of graduates from the military academies.[16] The glut of *alféreces provisionales*, in a system based on promotion only by strict seniority, soon choked promotion channels. Even where preference was not given to *alféreces provisionales*, their mere presence blocked or slowed down the promotion of better-trained officers from the academies. This undermined morale and devalued initiative. The solution adopted, of occasional block promotions, did little to resolve the congestion and stagnation in the middle ranks.[17] However, from Franco's point of view, the political loyalty of the *alféreces provisionales* outweighed their military deficiencies. Their ideological commitment ensured that they would be a loyal counterbalance to monarchist conspiracies against the Caudillo. In 1939 their loyalty to Franco was assured because he was the victorious Generalísimo, the *Jefe Nacional* of the Falange, and the man most likely to ensure that Spain would benefit from the forthcoming war for a new fascist world order. As the years passed, that loyalty was consolidated by habit and by the 1970s the one-time *alféreces provisionales* were the fiercest defenders of the regime in its dying agony.

Problems with even younger generations would come later as they reached more senior ranks. In the 1950s and 1960s it was the officers produced by the revived AGM who rankled at the inefficiency of an under-resourced army. Despite a transitory boost to military morale provided by the guerrilla war of 1945–7, the unchanging penury of the armed forces continued to take its toll in the early 1950s. There was the minimum of professional activity, extremely poor equipment and limited career prospects.[18] Spain's lamentable economic situation did not permit any significant renovation of equipment. Nevertheless, the

---

15   Guillermo Cabanellas, *Cuatro generales* (Barcelona, 1977), pp. 140, 142; Pérez Salas, *Guerra*, pp. 85–7; Antonio Cordón, *Trayectoria (recuerdos de un artillero)* (Paris, 1971), pp. 192–4; Busquets, *El militar*, pp. 117–39.
16   Carlos Iniesta Cano, *Memorias y recuerdos* (Barcelona, 1984), pp. 141–2; Busquets, *El militar*, pp. 107–8, 263, gives slightly contradictory figures.
17   Balbé, *Orden público*, p. 437; Busquets, *El militar*, pp. 109–14.
18   Manuel Gutiérrez Mellado, *Un soldado de España* (Barcelona, 1983), pp. 55–6.

military budget itself remained high because of the still inflated officer corps. Equipment was delapidated when not technologically obsolete and often out of use for lack of spare parts. There were insufficient funds for petrol and ammunition for exercises and manouevres, other than drilling on open spaces near bases. The exceptions were the units based in Spanish Africa and the air force. Even the latter was humiliated by being equipped with German-designed aircraft of Second World War vintage: Messerschmidt 109, Heinkel He 111 and Junkers Ju 52, built under licence. To prevent discontent reaching boiling point, substantial pay rises of 40 per cent were decreed across the board in 1949, the first since 1940.[19]

Two other things helped keep dissent under control: the international situation and a general slide into resigned cynicism about the deterioration of military standards. The ongoing action against the communist guerrillas, and the sense of beleaguerment drummed up by the regime in response to the international ostracism to which Spain was subject at this time helped unite the armed forces around the Caudillo. He was helped by the outbreak of the Korean War in June 1950. The generalized fear of world war had the effect within the Spanish forces of intensifying awareness of poor equipment but banishing any thoughts of dissent. Franco for his part made a major effort to rekindle the military spirit of anti-communism. At the same time, he made a successful bid to ingratiate himself with the Western Allies by an offer at the end of July to send Spanish troops to fight in Korea. Convinced also that, in the event of war with the Eastern bloc, and if Europe fell, the USA would need a base on which to land men and material, Franco offered Spain as a last redoubt. This was to help dramatically in his quest for international recognition despite being a meaningless offer, given the technological backwardness of his armed forces and the lamentably antiquated condition of Spain's road, rail and port infrastructure. Franco himself admitted to the American Admiral Forrest P. Sherman that the Spanish armed forces had no radar and were short of aircraft, heavy tanks, anti-aircraft and anti-tank equipment.[20]

Franco's grandiose offers meant little within his own armed forces in terms of budget, equipment or operational efficiency. Accordingly, as pay levels drifted along behind inflation, increasing numbers of officers began to take civilian jobs in addition to their commissions. The sense of professional shame engendered by this necessity was counterbalanced by an increased stress on the special mission of the army and its 'apartness'

---

19 Payne, *Politics and the Military*, p. 532.
20 Angel Viñas, *Los pactos secretos de Franco con Estados Unidos* (Barcelona, 1981), pp. 88–9, 99; Ricardo de la Cierva, *Historia del franquismo*, Vol. II, *Aislamiento, transformación y agonía (1945-1975)* (Barcelona, 1978), pp. 92–3; Juan Antonio Ansaldo, *¿Para qué. . .? de Alfonso XIII a Juan III* (Buenos Aires, 1951), pp. 523–5.

from civil society. An intensification of the rhetoric of the Civil War filled the gap in professional pride for the majority. However, it was not accepted by all officers.[21] For instance, in 1948, in a small academy for preparing entrants into the military profession under the direction of Captain Luis Pinilla, a group of Catholic cadets, known as *Forja* ('Forge') developed a considerable sense of professional pride. As they joined the official academies, they proselytized the idea of *Forja* and in 1951, in Segovia, sixty-six of them met to create a secret society of the same name. Its members thereafter were prominent in creating and running military journals and they produced regular circulars on professional and political subjects. Although it was not subversive, it constituted the nucleus of a body of critical opinion within the army. Accordingly, at the end of the 1950s, it was forcibly dissolved by the government. The ideas of *Forja* continued to be cherished by its members and fifteen years later a handful of them were to form the basis of the Unión Militar Democrática, an organization devoted to ensuring that the army would not be an obstacle to the democratic transformation of the country.[22]

Curiously, the disquiet being felt among the more professionally committed officers was expressed by the hard-line Civil War veteran, General Juan Yagüe, Captain-General of the VI Military Region (Burgos). Hardly a liberal critic of the regime in any sense, Yagüe's outburst came in a speech made in March 1950. Its publication outside Burgos itself was banned by the authorities. In it, he expressed the long-standing praetorian contempt for Falangist parasitism – his own Falangism being of a more radical and purist kind – and also the first indication of a military feeling of being left behind by a society which was moving away from the values of the 'crusade'. Yagüe complained about

the ignorant and the uneducated, with no more baggage than their knack of buying off consciences, who enrich themselves rapidly and are even proud of their shamelessness; others are given distinguished posts without anyone knowing whose is the black hand which elevates them and maintains them; others without any merits of any kind occupy posts for which they have no qualifications. . . We ask ourselves just how long can our patience last, just how long does God want us to go on suffering these individuals.[23]

---

21 A sense of the lack of direction felt by many officers can be gleaned from one of the more fortunate generals, Franco's cousin, in command of a relatively well-equipped unit stationed just outside Madrid, Francisco Franco Salgado Araujo, *Mi vida junto a Franco* (Barcelona, 1977), pp. 328–9.

22 Julio Busquets, *Pronunciamientos y golpes de Estado en España* (Barcelona, 1982), pp. 142–5

23 Indalecio Prieto, *Convulsiones de España: pequeños detalles de grandes sucesos*, 3 vols (México D.F., 1967–9), Vol. I, pp. 307–8.

Yagüe was not the only one to feel that things were going wrong. There began to emerge a substantial minority of professionals concerned with the decline of the Spanish armed forces. Although not in any sense organized, they looked to the leadership of General Juan Bautista Sánchez González, who since 1949 had been Captain-General of Barcelona. Like several others, Bautista Sánchez believed that it was wrong for the army to be an instrument of repression. There has been speculation that, during the March 1951 strike of tramway users which paralysed Barcelona, he was instrumental in preventing troops being used and therefore prevented large-scale bloodshed. The much-disliked Civil Governor of Barcelona, the Falangist Eduardo Baeza Alegría, requested troops when some cars and buses were overturned. However, Bautista Sánchez remained calm and kept the garrison confined to barracks. Baeza was dismissed and replaced by the hard-line General Felipe Acedo Colunga.[24] In this period, most of the generals sufficiently senior to be able to show dissent to Franco died, including Orgaz (1946), Queipo de Llano, Varela (both in 1951), Yagüe, Monasterio, Ponte (all in 1952) and Solchaga (1953).

The Minister for the Army in the 1951 cabinet changes was Agustín Muñoz Grandes, who had commanded the División Azul of Falangist volunteers for Hitler on the Russian front, his service there constituting a major asset in the Cold War ambience. Not an especially good administrator, he was none the less loyal to Franco. He began the thankless task of trying to reduce numbers and render the Spanish army more efficient. In 1952 the retirement age was reduced by two years. On 17 July 1953 the much-belated first postwar reserve law was introduced. It offered immensely generous conditions for those who left the active list. They retired on almost full pay linked to the subsequent pay rises of those who remained, together with full social and medical insurance. Most of the wartime *alféreces provisionales* were now in their middle to late thirties and were not receptive to the idea of starting an entirely new career. Accordingly, the law managed to secure the voluntary retirement of only 2,000 captains, majors and lieutenant-colonels.[25] It was a not inconsiderable achievement but the office corps remained over-blown in relation to Spain's military needs and economic capacity.

In consequence, morale continued to plummet. As it reached its lowest ebb, the situation was saved by the signing on 26 September 1953 of the defence pacts with the USA. The mutual defence pact brought massive economic, military and technological assistance from the USA. In return, Franco permitted the establishment on Spanish soil of American air bases at Torrejón near Madrid, Zaragoza and Morón, and a naval base at Rota in

---

24 Félix Fanés, *La vaga de tramvies del 1951* (Barcelona, 1977), pp. 137–41; Franco Salgado Araujo, *Mi vida*, pp. 329–30; La Cierva, *Historia del franquismo*, Vol. II, pp. 96–7.
25 Payne, *Politics and the Military*, p. 439; Busquets, *El militar*, p. 127.

Cádiz, as well as an enormous range of smaller installations. The benefits for the regime were the integration of Spain into the Western system, the transfer of the bulk of military expenses out of the general budget and the neutralization of military discontent over resources. The acquisition of more modern equipment than hitherto available and training in its use had obvious attractions for most, albeit not all, officers. The newly arrived armoured cars and tanks were refused by certain cavalry regiments whose generals reaffirmed the values of horsemanship.[26] However, improved technical preparation was welcomed by the more professionally aware officers; but it was weighed against the diminution of national sovereignty and the fact that the majority of the equipment was second-hand. The tanks and the destroyers acquired had seen service in the Second World War and the jet planes and the more powerful artillery in Korea. A minority of officers felt that, if US aid was to justify the mortgaging of national territory, control of its content should remain in Spanish hands. They were aware that US aid combined with a reduction in the size of the army's personnel and the adoption of a coherent defence policy could have led finally to the redemption of the Spanish armed forces.[27] As it was, what they got was second-rate and the techological dependence of Spain's defence industries was confirmed. The failure to move to a thoroughgoing reform of military administration via the creation of a Ministry of Defence meant that the ludicrous system was perpetuated whereby the three military ministries made unnecessary repeat purchases of equipment and technical licences.

From Franco's point of view, the treaty with the USA was an excellent device to head off the discontent; but it surfaced in 1956 when unexpectedly, and contrary also to Franco's own predictions, Spain was obliged to give up her Moroccan colony. With the immediate complaints about equipment muted by the arrivals of American cast-offs, military tensions in this period sprang, as so often before, from the rivalry between military advocates of a monarchical restoration and the Falangist efforts to perpetuate Francoism. Morocco, however, was also of primordial importance to military honour. However, the lamentable condition of the Spanish army was hardly such as to allow it to fight a major colonial war with any hope of success. The French empire was crumbling in both the Arab world and in the Far East, so Spain could not hope to fare better. Moreover, the rise of Nasser had encouraged militant Arab nationalism. At best, Franco could hope to derive benefit from his own weakness and from French discomfort. By allowing his High Commissioner in Morocco, the ambitious General Rafael García Valiño, to encourage local aspirations, the Caudillo thought to ingratiate himself with the

---

26 Busquets, *El militar*, p. 253.
27 Gutiérrez Mellado, *Un soldado*, p. 56.

Arab world and perhaps secure Arab votes in the United Nations for Spanish membership.[28]

Subsequently, Franco was to maintain that García Valiño had been out of control and acting on his own initiative. This was simply not true.[29] In overall strategic terms, the Caudillo had fully endorsed García Valiño's policy. Throughout 1954, as the French repression intensified, García Valiño encouraged the anti-French liberation movement in Morocco. In August 1955, under pressure in both Vietnam and Algeria, the French began to cut their losses in Morocco, lifting martial law. In November the sultan was brought back. Both García Valiño and the Caudillo seemed to believe that the deterioration of the French position had no relevance for the Spanish zone. With a sort of blind and patronizing racism, they were confident that the Moroccans loved their Spanish rulers.

There were token references to future independence but, on 30 November 1955, Franco with equal short-sightedness confidently predicted that the Moroccans would not be ready for twenty-five years. With the French beginning to talk seriously to the Moroccans, at the beginning of 1956, Madrid issued vague statements about future independence. The local nationalists reacted to the implicit procrastination by using the same violent methods which had been successful against the French. García Valiño was forced to denounce his erstwhile nationalist friends as communist subversives, closing down their newspapers and arresting prominent militants. When, in March 1956, the French announced independence for Morocco, the Caudillo was left stranded. He was obliged on 15 March to free all political prisoners in the zone and to announce that Spain would relinquish its own protectorate. The declaration of independence was signed on 7 April 1956.[30] In the aftermath of its loss, there were rumblings of discontent within the Spanish officer corps but no replica of the rebellion in the French army. In the garrisons of Madrid, Barcelona, Seville, Valladolid and Valencia, semi-clandestine Juntas de Acción Política were created. Beyond resentful mutterings, they came to nothing.[31] García Valiño was punished by being deprived of a senior post for eighteen months, until on 18 October 1958 he was made Director de la Escuela Superior del Ejército. A combination of inertia, cynicism and fear of playing into the hands of the regime's left-wing enemies inhibited even the most disgruntled. The year 1956

. 28 Miguel Martín, *El colonialismo español en Marruecos (1860–1956)* (Paris, 1973), pp. 219–23.

29 Luis Suárez Fernández, *Francisco Franco y su tiempo*, 8 vols (Madrid, 1984), Vol. V, pp. 176–80, 183–5, 192–207; Franco Salgado Araujo, diary entries for 17 March 1956 and 27 December 1957, *Mis conversaciones privadas con Franco* (Barcelona, 1976), pp. 168, 223.

30 Martín, *El colonialismo*, pp. 227–39; Arthur P. Whitaker, *Spain and Defense of the West: Ally and Liability* (New York, 1961), pp. 328–9; La Cierva, *Historia del franquismo*, II, pp. 138, 146.

31 Payne, *Politics and the Military*, pp. 443–4.

was after all the one in which major opposition had surfaced again and embraced Catholics and students as well as the clandestine trade unions. Franco himself recognized that the loss of Morocco removed the last excuse for not reducing the size of the officer corps. Addressing the assembled officers of the II Military Region in Seville on 29 April 1956, he declared that fire power was more important than numbers and that the army must be reduced in size.[32]

Symptomatic of the rising tide of opposition were the notorious clashes between left-wing students and Falangists in the University of Madrid in 1956. In an unexpected way they were to involve the army, revealing that the identification between the Falange and the high command which was to overshadow Spanish politics in the 1970s was still a thing of the future. In the mid-1950s at least, with the regime confident of its survival, the arrogant contempt felt by the military for the Falange remained as potent as it had been in the 1940s. After a Falangist was seriously hurt in the student disturbances of February 1956, there were indications that the Falange was planning a 'Night of the Long Knives' both for immediate revenge and also to reassert its political position. It was reported' that on 10 February General Agustín Muñoz Grandes, the Minister for the Army, General Miguel Rodrigo Martínez, the Captain-General of Madrid and General Arsenio Martínez Campos, the private tutor to Prince Juan Carlos, all visited Franco to ask, in the name of the army, what he planned to do to control the Falange. With his customary ambiguity, the Caudillo replied that he thought that the threats would come to nothing. They told him that if there were any victims of the Falange, then the army would take over Madrid. Franco allegedly responded by ordering the arrest of the Falangist conspirators.[33] It is certainly the case that, with the agreement of Muñoz Grandes, the energetic Rodrigo Martínez warned senior Falangists not to permit any disturbances. He ordered Falangist centres searched and arms found there seized. He was reported as saying that 'without my permission, no one moves a muscle' (*no se mueve ni Dios*).[34]

In the meanwhile, perhaps because of the Moroccan débâcle, complaints over pay and conditions were beginning to surface again. Morocco was one of the few places where officers could live on their salaries and promotions could come rapidly. Officers stationed there would now have

---

32   Francisco Franco, *Discursos y mensajes del Jefe del Estado (1955–1959)* (Madrid, 1960), pp. 172–7.

33   Payne, *Politics and the Military*, p. 443. Cf. Suárez Fernández, *Franco*, V, p. 256, who doubts that the three generals visited Franco on the grounds that Muñoz Grandes was hunting. In fact, Muñoz Grandes and Franco did go hunting together on 11 February, that is, after the alleged interview. Cf. Franco Salgado Araujo, diary entry for 11 February 1956, *Mis conversaciones*, p. 164.

34   Franco Salgado Araujo, diary entry for 10 February 1956, *Mis conversaciones*, p. 163; Pedro Laín Entralgo, *Descargo de conciencia* (Barcelona, 1976), pp. 422–3; Pablo Lizcano, *La universidad contra Franco* (Barcelona, 1981), p. 142.

to join the long queues for promotion in the Peninsula. With the main colonial possession lost, chances to see action were reduced to a minimum. There remained only garrison duties in Spain itself. Morale was already low because of an awareness that huge amounts were being paid to, or obtained by, Falangists in the administration while officers were forced to take other jobs merely to make ends meet.[35] These complaints were taken up by General Juan Bautista Sánchez González. The Captain-General of Barcelona was the most respected professional and the most eminent monarchist in the armed forces in the 1950s. Bautista Sánchez made no secret of his royalist sentiments and from 1945 had figured in several lists of provisional governments drawn up by monarchist opponents of the regime.[36] In the 1950s his personal austerity led him to be increasingly critical of the regime and especially of the corruption associated with the Falange. He had been in touch since 1950 with Juan Claudio Güell (the Conde de Ruiseñada), Don Juan's representative inside Spain, whom he met regularly.

In 1956 Ruiseñada co-ordinated royalist efforts to frustrate the plans by the Minister–Secretary General of the Falange, José Luis de Arrese, to block a monarchist restoration and perpetuate the Falangist domination of the regime. Bautista Sánchez mobilized the support of the other Captains-General against Arrese's scheme.[37] Although they were personal friends, the activities of Bautista Sánchez provoked a certain tension between him and the Minister for the Army, the ascetic pro-Falangist General Agustín Muñoz Grandes. Muñoz Grandes still proudly declared his admiration for Hitler and entertained his own plans to be Caudillo in a Falangist regime.[38] In the spring of 1956 Ruiseñada had handed over to Bautista Sánchez a plan for the restoration of the monarchy together with a request that he circulate it among other monarchist generals. The plan was for Franco to be obliged to withdraw from active politics to the position of regent. The day-to-day running of the government would be assumed by Bautista Sánchez until the king was restored. As much as anything, it was aimed at the Falange. In this context, on 1 July 1956, General Antonio Barroso y Sánchez Guerra, Director de la Escuela Superior del Ejército and soon to become Head of the Caudillo's Military Household, protested to Franco about the Arrese plan. Along with other monarchist generals, he is alleged to have talked to the Caudillo about the possibility of a military directory taking over

---

35 Franco Salgado Araujo, diary entries for 19 February, 3 August 1955, *Mis conversaciones*, pp. 83, 128.

36 Kindelán, *La verdad*, pp. 82, 89.

37 Pedro Sainz Rodríguez, *Un reinado en la sombra* (Barcelona, 1981), p. 163; Suárez Fernández, *Franco*, V, pp. 153, 266.

38 Franco Salgado Araujo, diary entries for 4 February and 3 August 1955, *Mis conversaciones*, pp. 77, 128. For a favourable character sketch of Muñoz Grandes, see Benjamin Welles, *Spain: The Gentle Anarchy* (London, 1965), pp. 57–61.

and holding a plebiscite on the issue of monarchy or republic, in the confident expectation that such a plebiscite would produce support for the monarchy. While Franco did not, as was to have been expected, agree to that suggestion, he was quick to decree significant pay rises for the officer corps on 1 June 1956, the first since 1949. The salaries of majors and lieutenant-colonels were increased by 104 per cent, of first lieutenants by 81 per cent and of lieutenant-generals by 62 per cent.[39]

In mid-August 1956, when Barroso replaced Franco Salgado-Araujo as Head of the Caudillo's Military Household, he confided a number of worries to his predecessor. He had come to the conclusion that Franco was losing touch with the military hierarchy. Even Franco Salgado-Araujo shared the view that the increasing ostentation of the Franco family was creating tension with the generally austere high command. Since the marriage of their daughter to the playboy Cristobal Martínez de Bordiu, the dictator's wife had plunged into high society and given free rein to her penchant for jewellery. More pressingly, Barroso was worried that if Franco died, the succession problem would simply be resolved by the decisive action of the most daring, probably García Valiño or Muñoz Grandes.[40] Like many generals, Barroso was deeply alarmed that Franco, no doubt aware of the monarchist conspiracy taking place, had made a speech on 1 May 1956 in Seville, in which he had declared that 'the monarchy cannot live without the Falange, but the Falange can live without the monarchy'.[41]

Barroso, despite his unconcealed monarchist sympathies, was renowned for his personal loyalty to Franco. Bautista Sánchez, however, was being watched by the intelligence services. Moreover, according to the inveterate monarchist conspirator Pedro Sainz Rodríguez, Muñoz Grandes, who regularly visited Bautista Sánchez in Barcelona, simulated support for his plans. It seems likely that Muñoz Grandes was actually working to delay Bautista Sánchez taking any serious steps. The Caudillo, who was extremely close to Muñoz Grandes, was fully apprised of Bautista Sánchez's activities and had begun to criticize him within his own inner circle. In December 1956 a meeting of those military and civilian monarchists involved was planned under the cover of a hunting party at the estate of Ruiseñada. Bautista Sánchez was prevented from attending by the specific order of Muñoz Grandes, who informed him that he must attend a meeting of the Cortes.[42] Things reached a head in mid-January 1957, when another transport users' strike broke out in Barcelona. While it was not as dramatic nor conflictive

---

39 Payne, *Military*, pp. 443, 534; Whitaker, *Spain*, pp. 141–2.
40 Franco Salgado-Araujo, diary entries for 11, 16 and 18 August 1956, *Mis conversaciones*, pp. 175, 178–9.
41 Franco, *Discursos 1955–1959*, pp. 181–90.
42 Rafael Calvo Serer, *Franco frente al Rey* (Paris, 1972), p. 36; Sainz Rodríguez, *Un reinado*, p. 164; Laureano López Rodó, *La larga marcha hacia la monarquía* (Barcelona, 1977), pp. 123–4; Suárez Fernández, *Franco*, V, pp. 319–20.

as that of 1951, it was linked with disturbances in the university. The Civil Governor, General Felipe Acedo Colunga, used considerable violence in evacuating the university and stopping demonstrations in favour of the strikers. Bautista Sánchez was critical of Acedo Colunga's harsh methods, counselled caution and was therefore considered in some circles to have given moral support to the strikers.[43] Franco was displeased by the Captain-General's failure to help Acedo.

There were rumours flying around in Madrid that Bautista Sánchez was planning a coup. Franco himself seems to have believed that the Captain-General was fostering the strike in order to provide the excuse for a monarchist *pronunciamiento*. It is difficult to ascertain what if any foundation there was to Franco's fears. There can be little doubt about the plan hatched with Ruiseñada, which would have been more than enough to rouse the ire of the Caudillo. However, as far as military action is concerned, it is likely that the rumours were based at least in part on the wishful thinking of prominent monarchists. The conversations of royalist plotters with the Pretender's household in Portugal were being tapped by the security services. The Caudillo, ever cautious, reacted as if the rumours merited some anxiety.[44]

To be on the safe side, Franco sent two regiments of the Spanish Foreign Legion to join in manoeuvres being supervised by Bautista Sánchez in Catalonia. The lieutenant-colonel commanding the regiments actually informed Bautista Sánchez that he would follow only the direct orders of Franco himself.[45] Muñoz Grandes also appeared in the course of the manoeuvres and had a tense interview with Bautista Sánchez, in which he apparently informed him that he was being relieved of the command of the Capitanía General de Barcelona. On the following day, 29 January 1957, Bautista Sánchez was found dead in his room in a hotel in Puigcerdá. The most dramatic and bizarre rumours that he had been murdered quickly ran around Spain.[46] What is most likely is that, having long suffered poor health,[47] Bautista Sánchez had died of a heart attack after the shock of his painful interview with Muñoz Grandes. The large numbers of mourners

---

43   Luis Ramírez, *Nuestros primeros veinticinco años* (Paris, 1964), pp. 111–12; Franco Salgado-Araujo, diary entry for 4 February 1957, *Mis conversaciones*, p. 200; Jaume Fabre, Josep M. Huertas and Antoni Ribas, *Vint anys de resistència catalana (1939–1959)* (Barcelona, 1978), pp. 208–11.

44   Franco Salgado Araujo, diary entries for 12 August 1956, 30 January 1957, *Mis conversaciones*, pp. 176, 195–8; Suárez Fernández, *Franco*, V, pp. 269, 319; López Rodó, *La larga marcha*, p. 124; Sainz Rodríguez, *Un reinado*, p. 166.

45   Calvo Serer, *Franco*, p. 37; La Cierva, *Franquismo*, II, p. 155, who quotes, without naming him, a minister.

46   Franco Salgado Araujo, diary entry for 6 April 1957, *Mis conversaciones*, p. 209 comments on the rumours having been picked up by the Cuban press. For the more outlandish versions of what happened, see Ramírez, *25 años*, p. 117 and Busquets, *Pronunciamientos*, pp. 140–1; cf. Serrano Suñer, *Memorias*, p. 238.

47   Franco Salgado Araujo, diary entry for 17 May 1955, *Mis conversaciones*, pp. 107–10.

at his funeral were testimony to the hopes that had been placed in him. Shortly after his death, two colonels closely linked to him were stripped of their rank.[48]

There is little doubt that, after the death of Bautista Sánchez, Franco felt the need to meet military complaints; this he did, as far as the high command was concerned, through the medium of a major cabinet re-shuffle on 25 February 1957. Muñoz Grandes, perhaps because of his involvement with Bautista Sánchez, was removed as Minister for the Army. He was compensated by a purely symbolic promotion to the rank of Captain-General. This rank, as opposed to the post of head of a military region which also carried the title of Captain-General, had previously been held only by Franco himself and the late General Moscardó, and then only after his retirement. General Barroso, whom Franco was said to distrust as a liberal and a monarchist, became Minister for the Army. This was almost certainly a sop to monarchist sentiment in the high command. The task he was given ensured that he would not be able to make the position a power-base for monarchist conspiracy. He was burdened with the difficult and highly sensitive job of reducing the size, and modernizing the structure and equipment, of the army in the wake of the agreement with the USA and the loss of Morocco. He was supposed to do this 'without suppressing posts and without prejudice to the staff'.[49] The February 1957 cabinet included the 'technocrats' encharged with the modernization of the economy. Accordingly, to guarantee public order during a period of economic upheaval, the Caudillo's close collaborator, the bluff General Camilo Alonso Vega, became Minister of the Interior. In 1962, after suffering a shooting accident, Franco reintroduced Muñoz Grandes into the cabinet as vice-president of the government. The purpose was threefold. The promotion was a sensible precaution in the light of the intimations of mortality provided by the accident; it diverted Muñoz Grandes from any preparations he might be making to supersede the Caudillo; and it was a sop to the Falangists who were jealous of the pre-eminence of the Opus Dei technocrats.

However, the entry of seven military ministers into the cabinet did not resolve the continuing discontent over pay and conditions. The Spanish army remained a generation behind the world's major fighting forces. General Barroso's efforts to carry out a reduction of the officers corps by 25 per cent were extremely slow and provoked the private criticisms of Franco, although he took no action. Some reductions were carried out between 1958 and 1961 but not on a scale which could resolve the fundamental problem of macrocephalia. On 17 July 1958 those who agreed

---

48 Busquets, *Pronunciamientos*, p. 141.
49 Franco Salgado-Araujo, diary entries for 23 February, 15 July 1957, *Mis conversaciones*, pp. 201, 246–7.

to leave the active list were offered posts of equivalent seniority in civilian ministries. They retired from the army on almost full pay and received in addition their full civilian salaries. However, very few accepted these generous terms since many of the *alféreces provisionales* were now in their forties and even less open to the notion of looking for a new career.[50]

Moreover, there were divisions coming to the surface between two conceptions of the role and function of the army. The long-term competition between monarchist and Falangist officers was complicated as the end of the dictatorship loomed inexorably on the horizon. The senior monarchist generals hoped eventually for the possibility of some controlled transition to the monarchy and were content, in the meanwhile, to look to their technical concerns. They constituted the 'liberals' in the army. Somewhat to their left stood, at the junior level, the enthusiastically professional officers, many of them university educated, among whom those associated with the *Forja* group were prominent. These groups considered that the army should not dictate the political complexion of Spain. On the other hand, there were those who were preoccupied with ensuring that the power of the army would be put at the service of a particular political option within Francoism. In 1958 the Hermandad de Alféreces Provisionales had been founded as a pressure group aimed at maintaining the spirit of the Falange and the Civil War within the officer corps. Its purpose was not simply to be a society for ex-combatants but was rather to manipulate a powerful group of increasingly senior officers in a given direction. In the late 1950s and early 1960s, with the stability of the regime as yet unquestioned and, after the demise of Bautista Sánchez, with no officers prepared to stand up to Franco, internal conflict within the army was virtually indiscernible. That situation was to change dramatically by the mid-1960s. The fact that important elements of the officer corps soon became engaged in a deadly struggle over the survival of Francoism after Franco is an indication of the extent to which strictly military and defence policy preoccupations were not the first priority in the Caudillo's army.

The 1960s witnessed vertiginous social and economic change in Spain. Such changes dwarfed the feeble continuing efforts to make the armed forces more efficient by initiatives to shift the budgetary burden from pay to equipment. Since Draconian measures to reduce the size of the officer corps were out of the question, the drive consisted largely of attractive early retirement schemes. In 1968, 80 per cent of the total military budget still went on pay and the Spanish army had 804 generals, enough for a force of several million men.[51] General Pablo Martín Alonso replaced Antonio Barroso as Minister of War in the cabinet changes of July 1962.

---

50   Busquets, *El militar*, pp. 127–8; Franco Salgado-Araujo, diary entry for 21 February 1957, *Mis conversaciones*, pp. 256–7.
51   Ynfante, *El Ejército*, p. 12.

Until his death on 11 February 1964, Martín Alonso was active in drawing up plans to improve the army's efficiency. In particular, the deployment of the army came under his scrutiny and he was instrumental in originating what, when it was introduced in 1965 by his successor, General Camilo Menéndez Tolosa, was known as the *plan a largo plazo* or the 'long-term plan'. This divided the army into two operational groupings, the Fuerzas de Intervención Inmediata and the Fuerzas de Defensa Operativa del Territorio. The FII, consisting of three infantry divisions – the armoured, the mechanized and the motorized – and three brigades – the parachute, the airborne and the armoured cavalry/artillery – was officially concerned with defence against external enemies, but was none the less deployed around the big cities. The FDOT, consisting of two mountain divisions, eleven infantry brigades and two artillery brigades was intended to play a more openly anti-subversive role against both political demonstrations and guerrilla activity.[52] The reorganization did constitute a modernization, albeit one which improved the army's domestic repressive function rather than its external defensive role.

Early retirements and organizational changes aside, this was above all a period marked by growing unease for those officers who gave thought to politics and to the future. Student and labour unrest were on the increase and they would soon be augmented by opposition to the regime from the church and the regions. For some, a growing awareness of the army's inadequacy as a national defence force and of its social isolation were causes of deep disquiet. Others simply accepted that the job of the army was to protect the regime. This was reflected in the fact that the Ley Orgánica del Estado introduced in 1966 contained the explicit statement that the task of the armed forces was 'to guarantee the unity and independence of the fatherland, the integrity of its territories and national security and the defence of the institutional order'. The blatant stress on the repressive function of the military was repeated by Admiral Carrero Blanco in a speech to the Escuela de Estado Mayor (General Staff College) on 24 April 1968. In it he underlined publicly what had hitherto been the unspoken premise of the Francoist army, that national defence took a back seat to political repression.[53]

For some senior officers, the conflict between the army's military and political roles caused more distress than for others. García Valiño, who had succeeded General Rodrigo Martínez as Captain-General of Madrid on 12 January 1962, was particularly struck by the implications of military

52 Alfonso Armada, *Al servicio de la Corona* (Barcelona, 1983), pp. 74–5; Carlos Ruiz Ocaña, *Los ejércitos españoles: las fuerzas armadas en la defensa nacional* (Madrid, 1980) pp. 282–7.
53 Almirante Carrero Blanco, *Discursos y escritos 1943–1973* (Madrid, 1974), pp. 212–15.

involvement in the trial and execution of the communist Julián Grimau.[54] As Captain-General, he had to ratify the sentence of death passed on 18 April 1963 and give the orders for the execution. His disquiet made him the object of flattery by monarchists who saw him as a possible successor to Kindelán and Bautista Sánchez as the senior military proponent of a monarchical restoration.[55] He became increasingly involved in political contacts and conversations which, when duly reported by the intelligence services, preoccupied Franco himself.

There was even a suspicion that García Valiño was conspiring with Muñoz Grandes for the post-Franco future. Perhaps for that reason, although he was the logical choice to be Minister for the Army on the death of General Pablo Martín Alonso in February 1964, García Valiño was overlooked in favour of the doggedly faithful Head of Franco's Military Household, General Camilo Menéndez Tolosa. García Valiño himself was furious and there was much comment in the higher ranks of the army.[56] Thereafter, García Valiño's hostility to Franco knew no bounds and he made little secret of it, calling him a 'hypocrite' and complaining of his meanness in the presence of ministers. In any case, he was already under suspicion. In order to monitor his contacts with the monarchist camp, he was being followed and his telephone was being tapped by the intelligence services.[57]

From 1963, the Dirección General de Seguridad was reporting regularly to Franco on García Valiño's connections with Muñoz Grandes. It seems that they were involved in tentative discussion of plans to force Franco to withdraw at least as executive president of the government, if not as Head of State, and for the vice-president to take over as regent. Their conversations were discovered by military intelligence.[58] Muñoz Grandes was eventually removed from the cabinet, but not until the summer of the following year. His notorious ill health provided a reasonable excuse for a decision made public on 22 July 1967.[59] No longer enjoying the support

---

54 The trial of Grimau was marked by a serious legal lapse within the Code of Military Justice, as a result of one of the army's juridical officers having falsified his legal qualifications, Balbé, *Orden público*, p. 425; Armada, *Al servicio* pp. 72–3, 76–7.

55 Suárez Fernández, *Franco*, VII, pp. 90–1.

56 Franco Salgado Araujo, diary entries for 24 July 1963, 17 February, 2 March and 13 June 1964, *Mis conversaciones*, pp. 389, 413, 416, 473; Manuel Fraga Iribarne, diary entries for 21 February, 17 April 1964, *Memoria breve de una vida pública* (Barcelona, 1980), pp. 103, 107; Armada, *Al servicio*, p. 75; Rafael Calvo Serer, *La dictadura de los franquistas: el 'affaire' del 'Madrid' y el futuro* (Paris, 1973) pp. 92, 382.

57 Fraga, diary entry for 6 July 1966, *Memoria*, p. 175; Sainz Rodríguez, *Un reinado*, pp. 415–16; Suárez Fernández, *Franco*, VII, p. 319.

58 Carlos Fernández, *Tensiones militares durante el franquismo* (Barcelona, 1985), p. 168; López Rodó, *La larga marcha*, p. 238.

59 López Rodó, *La larga marcha*, pp. 263–4; La Cierva, *Historia del franquismo*, II, pp. 250–1. Cf. the curious view of Manuel Fraga who claims that Muñoz Grandes effectively resigned by insistently pressing Franco to drop him from the cabinet, Fraga, diary entries for 11 and 21 July 1967, *Memoria*, pp. 205–6. Suárez Fernández, *Franco*, VII, pp. 390–7, is

of Muñoz Grandes, García Valiño's opposition to Franco faded into merely verbal disgruntlement as he approached retirement age.

. The machinations of García Valiño and Muñoz Grandes were the last of their kind. They were after all the final survivors of Franco's own generation and no other generals felt that they had the right to displace Franco. Indeed, while some elements within the Francoist hierarchy began to plan for their own post-Franco future, the *azules* in the army clung ever more desperately to the Caudillo. Concerns about the political future were the divisive obsession of both civilian and military Francoists throughout the 1960s. Within the armed forces, there was to be a growing division between various conceptions of that future. Fundamentally, the fault lines ran between those who were happy with a conception of the army as an instrument of political repression and therefore as the praetorian guard of an increasingly beleaguered regime, and those who were not. By the late 1960s, the so-called *generales azules*, such as Alfonso Pérez Viñeta, Tomás García Rebull, Carlos Iniesta Cano, Angel Campano López, some, if not all, of whom had been *alféreces provisionales*, were reaching key operational positions. From 1970 onwards, in collaboration with the civilian bunker, they would use their political influence to block reform from within the system and their repressive apparatus to smash opposition from outside. The military bunker was countered by those with a more professional view who were, by comparison, liberal. In the navy and the air force, the primacy of technocracy over politics was increasingly the norm. Within the army, however, the 'liberals', like Generals Manuel Diez Alegría, Manuel Gutiérrez Mellado and Jesús Vega Rodríguez, were a minority within the high command albeit not throughout the officer corps as a whole.

Significantly perhaps, in the cabinet changes of 29 October 1969 that followed the Matesa affair, Franco chose as Minister of War, not an *azul* but a technocrat, General Juan Castañón de Mena. Like his predecessor, Menéndez Tolosa, Castañón had spent the previous three years as Head of Franco's Military Household. He was regarded as being particularly close to both the Caudillo and Prince Juan Carlos and was an important link between El Pardo and the Zarzuela Palace. He was also a sympathizer of the Opus Dei and party to Carrero Blanco's schemes for a modified Francoist monarchy.[60]

The repressive function of the army had already caused considerable internal disquiet, as a consequence of the execution of the communist Julián Grimau in April 1963. The army was losing what popular affection

strangely taciturn on the reasons for Muñoz Grandes' dismissal, merely commenting that he was 'finished' (*acabado*).

60 *ABC*, 29 October 1969. See the profile of Castañón in Equipo Mundo, *Los 90 Ministros de Franco* (Barcelona, 1970), pp. 431–4; Calvo Serer, *La dictadura*, pp. 166, 168; Armada, *Al servicio*, pp. 68, 72, 78, 93–4, 100–1, 119, 121, 135; José Ignacio San Martín, *Servicio especial* (Barcelona, 1983), pp. 198, 253; López Rodó, *La larga marcha*, p. 200.

it might have enjoyed. In late 1967 press coverage of the personal use of official cars being made by senior officers had led to the vehicles of several generals being attacked by gangs of youths.[61] It is difficult to know precisely how much effect the Grimau affair had had in producing popular opprobrium. However, there can be little doubt that the fact that the army was responsible for the trial and punishment of many political and labour infractions divorced it from civil society. The repressive function of the army had relaxed somewhat in the 1950s and it was to do so again in the mid-1960s. However, in the last stages of the regime's decomposition after 1969, there was a return to a hard line which exacerbated the divisions within the army.

Doubts about the wisdom of permitting the military to have the role of political oppressor deepened over the trials at Burgos in December 1970 of militants of the Basque revolutionary separatist organization ETA. On 1 December, García Valiño, now in retirement, wrote to General Tomás García Rebull, Captain-General of the VI Military Region (Burgos), warning him not to let the army be used in a way that would estrange it from the people. He saw this danger in the use of military justice in the trial of actions for which a state should have its own proper instruments. Just as he had had to ratify the death sentence on Grimau, García Rebull would be called upon to sign the sentences passed on the young Etarras. Referring to the trial of Grimau, García Valiño wrote

> I had occasion to appreciate the extent to which the execution of a death sentence could create a rarified atmosphere in the country and, what is more, an atmosphere hostile to the Army. The shock affected even the garrisons where, in the final stage, some highly disagreeable discussions took place as to which body of troops would have to carry out the sentence.[62]

However, with the gradual break-up of the regime discernible, the *azules* were willing accomplices in an operation to block change. There was festering resentment among the *azules* of the rising tide of student, ecclesiastical, regional and labour discontent and of the failure of the civilian apparatus to stem it. They believed that the state was simply not doing its job and that politicians were too busy lining their pockets. The Burgos trials were taking place, after all, only seven months after General Narciso Ariza had been dismissed from the post of Director of the General Staff College for his complaints about the poverty of

---

61 Franco Salgado Araujo, diary entry for 4 December 1967, *Mis conversaciones*, pp. 511–12.
62 *Le Monde*, 11 December 1970; Suárez Fernández, *Franco*, VIII, pp. 218–19; Edouard de Blaye, *Franco and the Politics of Spain* (Harmondsworth, 1976), pp. 302–3.

the armed forces. Throughout the 1970s, the *azules* used their extreme version of the values of the Civil War in order to consolidate their influence within the immediate entourage of the Caudillo. They could thus scupper attempts at reform from within the system, by mobilizing the Caudillo against them. Franco's progressive senility in the 1970s made it easier for them to manipulate him. In the meanwhile, however, some just got on with the job of repressing what they saw as subversion. In particular, General Pérez Viñeta, as Captain-General of Barcelona, stimulated Franco's enthusiasm by the energy with which he acted against the left-wing and liberal activities of priests and university students.[63] On the last day of the Burgos trials, 9 December 1970, Pérez Viñeta declared at a military ceremony in Mérida, 'The Army is not in the least disposed to permit a return of the disorder and indiscipline which have once already imperilled our country. If necessary, a new crusade will be launched to rid Spain of men who acknowledge neither God nor law'.[64]

Pérez Viñeta was not alone in his belief that civilian politicians were incapable of maintaining order. There were rumours of secret associations of over 5,000 junior officers, mostly captains and majors, who since August 1970 had been meeting to discuss what they discerned as a deterioration of the political situation. With their slow promotions and poor pay, they were resentful of the fortunes being made in the economic boom. They were especially outraged by the Matesa affair. The Burgos trials and the anti-military propaganda provoked by them were the most obvious symptom of a deteriorating order, although there were also minor incidents of officers being insulted in the streets.[65] In response to international and timid domestic criticism of the trials, a bilious resentment fermented among *ultra* officers and was expressed in terms of contempt for the technocrats. In the Madrid military region, officers from key units, including the División Acorazada and the BRIPAC, or parachute brigade, the two crucial operational units for the control of the capital, began to meet to voice their complaints.[66] On 14 December 1970 the Captain-General of Madrid, General Joaquín Fernández de Córdoba, called a meeting of twenty-odd generals and colonels to discuss the implications of the Burgos trials. They concluded that the opposition had been allowed to go too far and they produced a manifesto calling for more energetic government. A delegation consisting of Fernández de Córdoba, García Rebull, Pérez Viñeta and the Captain-General of Sevilla, Manuel Chamorro, visited Franco to inform him of their deliberations. The Caudillo held an emergency cabinet meeting at

---

63 *Le Monde*, 14 March 1969; Franco Salgado Araujo, diary entries for 30 January, 1 March and 14 April 1969, *Mis conversaciones*, pp. 540, 541, 547.
64 Blaye, *Franco* p. 304.
65 *Le Monde*, 29 December 1970.
66 San Martín, *Servicio especial*, pp. 168–9.

which the Minister of the Interior, General Tomás Garicano Goñi, and the three military ministers called for the suspension of *habeas corpus*. Franco went along with them.[67]

The atmosphere was screwed even tighter on 16 December by a demonstration outside military headquarters in Burgos by army officers and Falangists. They were addressed by García Rebull. Not a sophisticated man, he was devoted to Francoism and was a willing collaborator of those Falangists who were seeking military support to prevent change after the death of Franco. On the following day many army officers joined in the massive demonstration outside the Palacio de Oriente.[68] The army wanted the strongest sentences against those on trial. When García Rebull hesitated to confirm the death sentences for the reasons indicated to him in García Valiño's letter, he was subjected to pressure for a hard line by delegations of officers from all over Spain. Some called for the executions to be by garrot instead of by firing squad. Pérez Viñeta called García Rebull a 'softie' (*blando*).[69]

Although the army was united in wanting to see the defendants given death sentences, the more liberal elements were open to the idea of a pardon. Castañón and the other two military ministers recommended mercy at the cabinet meeting called on 29 December 1970. However, despite the fact that Franco subsequently pardoned the defendants, the army was left feeling, as García Valiño had predicted, that it had somehow been besmirched.[70] There were liberals who drew the conclusion that the army should distance itself from a regime in decomposition. A substantial group, however, believed that, now more than ever, the army should be defending the regime. Pérez Viñeta addressed a demonstration outside the headquarters of the VI Military Region and spoke again of the need for another crusade.[71] His words were a barely veiled criticism of the Opus Dei technocrats who ruled Spain's political destinies. Because of Pérez Viñeta's closeness to Franco and the fact that his retirement was imminent his indiscretion went unpunished.

Nevertheless, the military bunker's vision of the future was severely at odds with that of Carrero Blanco and the Opus Dei, who were planning a modified Francoism under Juan Carlos. Accordingly, when General Fernando Rodrigo Cifuentes, Captain-General of Granada, emulated Pérez Viñeta, he was punished. An energetic opponent of left-wing and liberal priests, students and workers, he was none the less sacked on 8 January 1971 and placed under house arrest, as a result of a speech made on the

67 *Le Monde*, 16, 18 December 1970.
68 Blaye, *Franco*, pp. 304–10; Vicente Gil, *Cuarenta años junto a Franco* (Barcelona, 1981), p. 140.
69 *Le Monde*, 29 December 1970; *L'Express*, 4 January 1971.
70 Suárez Fernández, *Franco*, VIII, p. 221; *The Times*, 11 October 1971.
71 *Le Monde*, 30 December 1970.

occasion of the Pascua Militar. His offence was not his call for a harder line but rather his criticism of Carrero Blanco and the technocrats. In the aftermath of the Matesa affair, the term technocrat had come to be synonymous in ultra-rightist circles with civilian weakness. Rodrigo's speech, with its remarks about 'white freemasons' struck a chord in the hearts of many soldiers who were unhappy about the conduct of the Burgos trials and their outcome. He was inundated with telegrams of support, although he did nothing to encourage hopes that he might lead a military faction to reimpose 'authority'. Within a few weeks a similar incident occurred, when the Captain-General of Zaragoza, Gonzalo Fernández de Córdoba made a similar speech and was transferred to the general staff.[72]

Less vocal hard-liners, however, were rewarded for their loyalty to the regime during the Burgos crisis. García Rebull, a close friend of the Falangist ultra, José Antonio Girón de Velasco, was promoted to be Captain-General of the I Military Region, Madrid. Another crony of Girón, Carlos Iniesta Cano, was made Director General of the Civil Guard. These promotions reflected the extent to which Franco himself, or those in his immediate entourage, realized that the resurgence of opposition, increasingly placed upon the army the onus for the defence of the regime against change. One of the key tasks would be the control of Madrid. The military governor of the capital, General Angel Campano López, had nailed his colours firmly to the mast during the Burgos trials with the widely publicized remark that what was needed was to impose martial law for a week and to shoot a thousand leftists.[73]

Through the Hermandad de Alféreces Provisionales and the ultra-rightist press, a major effort was being made to attract support within the army for the so-called *inmovilista* option. The same Falangists who had seen themselves defeated politically by the Opus Dei in the course of the 1960s were happy to generate military criticism of corrupt technocrats. Ultra officers effectively banned legally published journals and magazines from barracks and virtually imposed the reading of the publications of the extreme right such as *Fuerza Nueva*.[74] The ultras had two centres of power within the army. On the one hand, the generation of *azules* dominated the senior ranks and were consistently given the crucial posts in the key units in terms of the regime's political security – the armoured division at Brunete and the parachute brigade outside Madrid, as well as the Military Governorship of Madrid, the Captaincy-General of the I Military Region and

---

72 Calvo Serer, *La dictadura*, p. 236; San Martín, *Servicio especial*, p. 268; Blaye, *Franco*, pp. 324–5.
73 *Mundo Obrero*, 22 January; *Le Monde Diplomatique*, January 1971.
74 *Le Monde*, 19 December 1970; José Fortes and Luis Otero, *Proceso a nueve militares demócratas: las Fuerzas Armadas y la UMD* (Barcelona, 1983), p. 22.

the Directorship of the Civil Guard. On the other hand, less senior ultras held the important command positions within the intelligence services. Some, but not all, of the ultras were *alféreces provisionales*. In 1974, 328 full colonels, 956 lieutenant-colonels and 792 majors currently on active service had been *alféreces provisionales*.[75]

One of them, General Campano, who had been decorated twice with the Iron Cross during his service in the División Azul on the Russian front, held the key posts in quick succession. Having commanded the División Acorazada, the armoured division which dominated Madrid, in the late 1950s, by the end of the 1960s he was military governor of Madrid, by 1972 Captain-General of Burgos, by February of 1973 Captain-General of Madrid, and was Director-General of the Civil Guard six weeks before the death of Franco. Others had been *Africanistas*, often Falangists and had fought in the División Azul. García Rebull, who had joined the Falange in 1934, had also been decorated with the Iron Cross in Russia. Prior to being Captain-General of Burgos, he had also commanded the División Acorazada and often tested his men in manouevres to seize Madrid. After his retirement in February 1973, when he passed command of the I Military Region to General Campano, García Rebull devoted himself to his role as Jefe Nacional del Servicio de Asociaciones de Antiguos Combatientes.[76]

Every bit as important as the dominance of the senior ranks and command of the most important posts, was the *azules'* control of the ever-proliferating military intelligence services. With parallel and often over-lapping concerns in the universities, the labour movement and the church, there were a dozen intelligence services of which the most potent were Army Intelligence (SIBE or Servicio de Información del Ejército de Tierra, Segunda Bis); the special service for the General Staff, set up by Muñoz Grandes in 1968; and the Servicio de Documentación de la Presidencia de Gobierno, set up by Carrero Blanco in the early 1970s under Colonel José Ignacio San Martín and Colonel Federico Quintero, both of whom were to be involved in the attempted military coup of 23 February 1981.[77]

The rhetoric of apoliticism used by the *azules* permitted them to describe the military as 'above politics', at the service of permanent or eternal national values, which for them meant the *Cruzada* (the nationalist war effort between 1936 and 1939) and the Franco regime. The army was therefore free to intervene against anyone who opposed the survival of the dictatorship. In the final crisis-ridden years of Francoism, the *azules* made

---

75   'Reflexión crítica sobre el Cuerpo de Oficiales' (a clandestine document drawn up by young Academy-trained officers) in Ynfante, *Ejército*, pp. 69–74.

76   Pierre Celhay, *Consejos de guerra en España* (Paris, 1976), pp. 106, 109–10.

77   San Martín, *Servicio especial*, pp. 21–45; José Luis Morales y Juan Celada, *La alternativa militar* (Madrid, 1981), pp. 67–78; Ynfante, *Ejército*, pp. 24–9; Balbé, *Orden público*, pp. 447–9; Colectivo Democracia, *Los Ejércitos... más allá del golpe* (Barcelona, 1981), pp. 52–3.

no secret of their partisanship. Clearly riddled with an element of panic, their views were expressed in numerous public political statements. In late August 1972 General Carlos Iniesta Cano, Director General of the Civil Guard and a *Procurador* in the Cortes, made a speech in El Ferrol. Using the rhetoric of the Falange, he declared that

> Francoism can never disappear, because God does not want it to come to an end in Spain and, after Franco, Francoism will continue and there will be Francoism for centuries because Spain which is eternal and which has an eternal destiny in the universal scheme needs Francoism.

Shortly afterwards, General José María Pérez de Luna, Captain-General of the Canary Islands, affirmed, in a speech on 24 October 1972, that 'the mission of the Army is political in so far as it is encharged with defending the fatherland against the exterior and against the internal enemy'.[78]

The 'liberal' generals, such as the Chief of the General Staff, Manuel Díez Alegría, were committed to the army remaining neutral.[79] The difficulties which he faced were illustrated by the fact that when he tried to introduce a single Ministry of Defence, he was vilified by the ultra press and eventually hounded out of his post.[80] However, younger liberal officers were working actively to prevent the *inmovilistas* blocking change altogether. In 1973, a group of junior and middle-rank officers issued an appeal to the officer corps expressing their concern that, in the political disintegration of the dictatorship, one faction, the ultras, were working to use the army for their own purposes. The assassination by ETA of prime minister Admiral Carrero Blanco on 20 December 1973 provided a brief glimpse of the tensions simmering within the officer corps. At this point, the Director-General of the Civil Guard, Carlos Iniesta Cano, issued an order for his men to repress subversives and demonstrators energetically 'without restricting in any way the use of firearms'. He explicitly ordered them to go beyond their rural jurisdiction and keep order in urban centres. It was a gross abuse of his authority. However cooler heads prevailed. After taking advice from the Chief of the General Staff, Manuel Díez Alegría, a triumvirate consisting of the Minister of the Interior, Carlos Arias Navarro, the senior military minister, Admiral Gabriel Pita de Veiga, and the interim prime minister, Torcuato Fernández Miranda, acted to prevent a bloodbath. Within less than an hour, Iniesta was obliged to withdraw his telegram.[81]

---

78   Celhay, *Consejos de guerra*, pp. 112, 118.

79   *L'Express*, 14 December 1970.

80   Ynfante, *Ejército*, p. 77. See p. 184 below.

81   *Pueblo*, 22 December 1973; Iniesta Cano, *Memorias*, (Barcelona, 1984), pp. 218–22; San Martín, *Servicio especial*, pp. 90–114; Joaquín Bardavio, *La crisis: historia de quince días* (Madrid, 1974), pp. 111–16; *El País* Equipo de Investigación, *Golpe mortal: asesinato*

Much more dramatic than the assassination of Carrero Blanco in intensifying divisions within the officer corps was the fall of the dictatorship in Portugal. Apart from disagreements over the wisdom of unleashing a Night of the Long Knives against the left, the armed forces had been united in outrage at the murder of the prime minister. Now, the Portuguese revolution of 25 April 1974 polarized the ultras and liberals within the officer corps. Both events could only intensify fears for the future but the two major factions reacted differently, the liberals being prepared to consider change and adjustment before it was too late, the ultras being ready to prepare the last-ditch defence of the regime. Innumerable empty declarations were made, vainly dismissing the events in Portugal as irrelevant to the Spanish situation. General Jesús González del Yerro, an increasingly influential hard-liner and Director of the Escuela del Estado Mayor del Ejército, told the press that 'the Spanish Army does not have rifles in order to decorate them with carnations and carnations do not bloom in the barrel of a gun'.[82] Despite such ultra optimism, liberal junior officers were soon busy working to create the Unión Militar Democrática. In response to that disturbing development, the military right resorted to its secret weapon, the intelligence services.

The military intelligence services made strenuous efforts to root out any Portuguese-style leftism within the armed forces. At the same time, the senior *azules*, both military and civilian, were distressed by the public, albeit intensely feeble, commitment to political reform of the prime minister Carlos Arias Navarro. On 28 April 1974, merely three days after the cataclysm in Portugal, José Antonio Girón launched the broadside against Arias known as the *Gironazo*. As part of the same operation, the military bunker set about blocking any slide to liberalism in the armed forces. A powerful group formed, including the retired García Rebull, the Captains-General of the VII Military Region, Valladolid (Pedro Merry Gordón), and of the I Military Region, Campano, and the Director General of the Civil Guard, Iniesta Cano. It plotted to establish and maintain total control of the crucial sectors of the army. While Girón and other civilian ultras attacked the regime, García Rebull declared that he regarded political parties as 'the opium of the people' and politicians as 'vampires'. The parallel military scheme was for Iniesta to side-step his own imminent retirement and to replace the liberal Manuel Díez Alegría as Chief of the General Staff. Campano would take over as Director-General of the Civil Guard and there was to be a purge of officers suspected of liberalism. The scheme enjoyed the support of Franco's personal entourage although the

---

de Carrero y agonía del franquismo (Madrid, 1983), pp. 184–7. The Communists claimed to have been in contact with Díez Alegría, but he denied this. Conversation of the author with Santiago Carrillo. See *Golpe mortal*, pp. 211–12.
82   Morales and Celada, *Alternativa*, p. 26.

failing Caudillo was not kept informed. In fact, apart from that part of the plan concerning Iniesta, it was eventually, if not immediately, successful. The Minister for the Army, General Francisco Coloma Gallegos, was not sympathetic to Iniesta's plan to beat retirement and forced him to retire on schedule on 12 May 1974. However, Díez Alegría was removed from his post after a trip to Romania for medical treatment during which he met President Ceaucescu. He was replaced by the hard-line Captain General of the VIII Military Region, La Coruña, Carlos Fernández Vallespín. The removal of Díez Alegría was an enormous triumph for the ultras and greatly facilitated their efforts to put the army at the service of the civilian bunker. In parallel with the activities of Iniesta, the civilian extreme right was also mobilizing and Girón's Asociación Nacional de Ex-Combatientes changed its name to the Asociación Nacional de Combatientes.[83]

The most senior military ultras were closing ranks with the civilian bunker to prepare the last-ditch defence of the regime. In addition to undermining the efforts of civilian politicians to open up the system, they found themselves faced with the need to eliminate an enemy within. A small but influential grouping of liberal middle-rank and junior officers were attempting through the Unión Militar Democrática to ensure that the army would be fully apolitical during the post-Franco period. They were eventually arrested, subjected to a humiliating show trial, imprisoned and hounded out of the army. In that particular task, the *azules* were to be successful. In their wider ambitions, they were not. After the death of Franco on 20 November 1975, the dictatorship would disintegrate rapidly and its military defenders would find themselves increasingly isolated from the huge political consensus in favour of democratization. That would not, of course, inhibit them from endeavouring to impose their view of what Spain's political destiny should be.

In the last resort, the military right would fail in its attempt to dictate the nation's future. Nevertheless, the triumph of *azules* over the democrats of the UMD was to endure throughout the democratic transition. It was a symbol of the strength of the military right, although an altogether more graphic illustration could be seen in the kid-glove treatment given to the army by successive governments.[84] Ultras continued to gather in key units like the División Acorazada and the BRIPAC, which they hoped to use for decisive interventions in military coups. The Minister for Defence Affairs, General Gutiérrez Mellado, was insulted and humiliated. *Golpismo* was permitted to flourish without punishment. There were serious attempts at coups in November 1978 and January 1980 before the fatal weakness of

---

83 *Le Monde*, 15 May 1974; *Financial Times*, 29 May 1974; Gutiérrez Mellado, *Un soldado*, pp. 47–9; Paul Preston, *The Triumph of Democracy in Spain* (London, 1986), pp. 60–2.
84 See Chapter 8, 'Francoism's last stand: the military campaign against democracy 1973–82'.

such a tolerant policy were brutally exposed by Colonel Tejero's seizure of the parliament on 23 February 1981.

Despite the apparent escalation of its activities, the military bunker was already on the defensive. In fact, the activities of the military bunker were almost always defensive. With the disappearance of the Caudillo, they had lost their trump card. Thereafter, they were steadily losing ground – with the appointment of Adolfo Suárez as prime minister and of Gutiérrez Mellado as vice-president of the cabinet with responsibility for Defence Affairs, with the success of Suárez's political reform, the legalization of the Communist Party and the first democratic elections in June 1977. *Golpismo* was given a spurious relevance by the terrorism born of the failure of the government to resolve the Basque problem, by the post-1977 economic recession, and by the political lethargy of Suárez's UCD after 1980. Ultimately, *golpismo* was the fruit of the way in which an army which had been deprived by Franco of professional pride took refuge in the timeless notion that above and beyond all other considerations lay its duty as guardian of Spain's political destiny.

Franco's defence policy was based on the calculated risk that nothing in the way of external aggression would happen. He permitted the Spanish armed forces to fall into a state of considerable professional and technical decay. The technological poverty of the Spanish army, the apathy of the many officers who gave top priority to their civilian jobs, its division along political lines and the determination of its most influential sectors to thwart the national will were all part of the poisoned military legacy of General Franco. The army was used as an inert barrier against social change. This confirmed an existing tendency for it to be alienated from civil society and to function as if it were a foreign army of occupation. In the course of the forty years of Francoism, society evolved slowly and inexorably. The Spain which, in the eyes of the right, justified the military rising of 1936 and the violence of the Civil War, simply did not exist by 1975. However, the army was committed legally and institutionally to defending the basic premises of Francoism. It was also in technical terms not suited to any other more difficult task. Other elements associated with Francoism, the church, the banks, political groups of monarchists and Catholics, managed to evolve and distance themselves from the regime. Only the Falange and the army failed to do so.

Part IV

RESURRECTING THE PAST

7

Into the bunker:
the extreme right and the struggle
against democracy, 1967–77

The maintenance of public order and domestic tranquillity always had the highest priority within the Franco dictatorship. The regime's primordial objectives of eliminating the class struggle and silencing left-wing and trade union protest could, in the eyes of its supporters at least, be measured in terms of quiet, trouble-free streets in the major cities. In addition, the external publicity value of an apparently soporific public order under Franco was enormous. It was relentlessly contrasted by the regime's propaganda apparatus with the alleged disorder both of the Republic which had gone before and of the decadent democracies. Franco's peace of course meant little for his opponents. In the factories and the universities, it had been established at the cost of considerable and continued violence. For Francoists, however, it was in fact a reality. It was based in the short term on the weight and efficiency of the virtually unaccountable forces of order. The armed police in the cities and the Civil Guard in the smaller towns and the countryside were well-armed, well-resourced and virtually unrestrained. Moreover, they had to deal with a population which had learnt the hard way that public political protest was an unaffordable luxury, that day-to-day survival lay in political apathy. The post-Civil War repression, the overcrowded prisons, the labour camps, the tortures and executions, policemen trained by Gestapo advisers and a range of secret police organizations active in the factories and the universities all played their part in establishing and safeguarding '*la paz de Franco*'.[1]

---

1 There exists no satisfactory survey of the Francoist repression in Spain as a whole, although there have been excellent local studies, and there has been virtually no historical work on the Policía Armada or the Civil Guard in this period. However, it is worth consulting the provocative essays by Alberto Reig Tapia, *Ideología e historia: sobre la represión franquista y la guerra civil* (Madrid, 1984) and Diego López Garrido, *El aparato policial en España* (Barcelona, 1987). See also Juan Martínez Alier, *La estabilidad del latifundismo* (Paris, 1968), pp. 131–47.

There was an element therefore of theatrical unreality, when in September 1973, a loyal Francoist *procurador*, or parliamentary deputy, rose in the Cortes to question the apparent impotence of the police to deal with a wave of political violence which had been growing steadily since the end of the 1960s. The intriguing issue was not just to do with apparent police impotence but also concerned the fact that the press had been permitted to report the violence and to do so in a way which, in some cases at least, condemned those responsible. This was unusual since, under Franco, such criticism was normally reserved for common criminals and the left-wing, liberal or Catholic opponents of the regime. As the police knew well enough, the culprits were neo-fascist groups carrying out a systematic campaign of what the conservative Catholic newspaper *Ya* denounced as cultural terrorism.

There had always been an extreme right within Francoism which believed that the dictator and his regime had betrayed the fascist purity of the Falange.[2] However, for the first three decades of Franco's rule, with the Falange playing a dominant role in the dictatorship's syndical and propaganda apparatuses, they had little reason or opportunity to move beyond embittered talk, slogans on walls and the occasionally shouted insult against the Caudillo during Francoist ceremonies.[3] In the 1960s, for several reasons, things began to change in such a way as to force the ultra right on to the offensive. The Opus Dei was apparently emerging ever more victorious from the power struggle with the Falange. In consequence, the prospects seemed more likely of there being a monarchist succession to the Caudillo. There were even signs of some erstwhile Francoists and percipient state functionaries following the path of the more far-sighted businessmen and preparing themselves for a limited opening towards some kind of political reform.

The first signs that there was a fascist right ready to use violence outside the usual channels of the institutions of repression had been seen in the universities in 1963. In response to the growth of leftist student groups, there emerged Defensa Universitaria, whose activists were mainly Falangists, together with a few Carlists and extreme right-wing Catholics. They acted both as police spies, informing on leftist militants and as terror squads breaking up anti-regime meetings, beating up individuals, intimidating female leftists.[4] Six years later, the general political situation of hard-line Francoism had worsened and Defensa Universitaria was

---

2 Sheelagh M. Ellwood, *Spanish Fascism in the Franco Era* (London, 1987), pp 134–75.

3 For the most notorious of such incidents, see Daniel Sueiro, *El Valle de los Caídos: Los secretos de la cripta franquista*, 2nd edn (Barcelona, 1983), pp. 220–30; Francisco Franco Salgado-Araujo, *Mis conversaciones privadas con Franco* (Barcelona, 1976), pp. 302–3.

4 This short account is based on personal knowledge. I am also indebted to Isabel Cardona de los Ríos and Elías Díaz for their recollections of that period.

reorganized as Los Guerrilleros de Cristo Rey (the guerrillas of Christ the King) and strengthened by the addition of paid thugs, a process probably masterminded by Admiral Carrero Blanco's more or less private intelligence service, the Servicio de Documentación de la Presidencia del Gobierno.[5] Led in the streets by a fanatical Falangist activist, Mariano Sánchez Covisa, the *Guerrilleros* were linked by many commentators to the neo-fascist political association Fuerza Nueva and its journal of the same name.[6] *Fuerza Nueva*'s editor, the notary Blas Piñar, was the intellectual dynamo of Spain's ultra-right and an influential member of the Francoist establishment, sitting on the National Council of the *Movimiento*.

The *Guerrilleros* were not the only such group. The openly Neo-Nazi organization, Círculo Español de Amigos de Europa (Spanish Circle of Friends of Europe), known as CEDADE, was organized in Barcelona by a sinister figure of the international ultra-right, Jorge Mota. Straddling both Madrid and Barcelona was the equally pro-Nazi Partido Español Nacional Socialista. Extreme rightist activities varied from the celebration of masses for Hitler and Mussolini, lamented as 'defenders of European civilization', to brutal physical attacks on workers and priests.[7] These loose organizations were not in any sense political parties, seeing themselves as more or less freelance patriots acting as flying squads wherever the essences of Francoism were in danger. They operated in an *ad hoc* fashion under many names, which they changed according to their location and targets. For all their alleged patriotism, they were closely linked to international right-wing terrorist networks and in contact with exiled rightists such as Léon Degrelle and, even possibly trained by, Otto Skorzeny.[8]

In 1971, they mounted a spring offensive against 'left-wing' bookshops, that is to say those specializing in legally authorized books on sociology and politics. In night raids carried out by the *Guerrilleros*, some of whose leaflets left at the scenes of their attacks also used the name Comandos de Lucha Antimarxista (Commandos of the Anti-Marxist Struggle), windows and doors were smashed, stock destroyed, red paint smeared and threatening pamphlets scattered about. The tone of the leaflets was revealing: 'like filthy rats, you should be kept apart from the national community; the only place that you should be permitted to inhabit is the sewers where you were thrown after your parents and your evil ideology were

---

5 This is impossible to prove although it was widely believed to be the case among Spanish journalists at the time. For some intriguing hints, see the memoirs of the officer in charge of the SDPG, José Ignacio San Martín, *Servicio especial: A las órdenes de Carrero Blanco* (Barcelona, 1983), pp. 23–42.

6 Luis Ramírez, 'Morir en el bunker', in *Horizonte español 1972*, 3 vols, (Paris, 1972); Martín Prieto, 'El discreto encanto de la ultra derecha', in *Gentleman*, no. 15, July 1974.

7 *Informaciones*, 30 April 1973.

8 Stuart Christie, *Stefano delle Chiaie: Portrait of a Black Terrorist* (London, 1984), pp. 71–4; Magnus Linklater, Isabel Hilton and Neal Ascherson, *The Fourth Reich: Klaus Barbie and the Neo Nazi Connection* (London, 1984), pp. 203–11.

defeated'. In each case, the bookshop owners complained to the police who told them that nothing could be done. One bookseller claimed that the officer who took his statement admitted to having been a member of the *Guerrilleros*.[9] The attacks were crude and noisy, yet the police were unable to intervene in time in any case. Not surprisingly, there grew a belief on the Spanish left that these groups enjoyed official connivance.

The subsequent autumn campaign of 1971 took the *Guerrilleros* into the headlines of the world's press. Three bookshops displaying Picasso prints were smashed in November that year. An acid attack destroyed twenty-four Picasso engravings in the Theo gallery of Madrid and Picasso's first studio in Barcelona was blown up with Molotov cocktails.[10] The 'commandos' responsible justified their acts by claiming that Picasso subsidized the Communist Party. Blas Piñar denied any connection with the commandos but he did proclaim his sympathy with their action. He declared 'I neither know, nor direct, and therefore nor do I have any relationship with the so-called "Guerrilleros de Cristo Rey".' Blas Piñar asserted that the works by Picasso which he had seen were 'in the worst taste, obscene and gravely offensive to the Chief of the Spanish State and Head of the *Movimiento Nacional*' and that he could understood why the young men in question found themselves 'carried away by their patriotism and by their fervent and enthusiastic loyalty to Francisco Franco'.[11]

World publicity caused something finally to be done. Eight of those responsible for the Madrid incident were arrested. Opposition sources claimed that three of them were police employees and that one worked in Blas Piñar's office. In its first number of 1972, *Fuerza Nueva* praised the destruction of 'these pseudo-artistic daubings' and denounced Picasso's work as 'no more than a joke on the Western world, unmitigated obscenity and pornography with which communism hopes to demoralize Christian culture, corrupting it and destroying it'.[12] Given the power of the censorship at the time, the publication of such remarks only intensified speculation about possible official complicity. Suspicion was increased further by the circulation in Madrid opposition circles of a photocopy of a letter from a former under-secretary of commerce to various industrialists, asking for cash to create bands of 'determined young men to defend patriotic values'.

Throughout 1972 the main field of ultra-rightist operations passed to Barcelona and Valencia, with liberal bookshops and journals the prime targets.[13] Pamphlets that were found after raids similar to those in Madrid

---

9 In an interview with the author.
10 *Informaciones*, 6 November; *Madrid*, 6, 23 November; *ABC*, 7 November 1971.
11 *Madrid*, 23 November 1971.
12 *Fuerza Nueva*, 1 January 1972.
13 *Informaciones*, 17, 26 April 1972.

in 1971, proclaimed a determination to defend the values of the Nationalist victory in the Civil War against the 'pseudo-liberals clinging on to power'. The atmosphere of terror being created in Barcelona was clearly revealed on 6 March 1972. An explosion in the apartment of an alleged neo-fascist sympathizer wrecked the building and killed eight people. It was popularly supposed that what had exploded was an arms dump and not a gas fitting as the authorities claimed. In 1973 the rhythm of operations quickened. Six thousand people in the Barcelona booktrade received anonymous threats. Two prominent liberal Catholic journals, *El Ciervo* and *Agermanament*, the publishing house Nova Terra linked to the Catholic Workers' Association, the Hermandad Obrera de Acción Católica, and a great symbol of Catalan cultural vitality, the Gran Enciclopedia Catalana all had their offices attacked by the PENS. Journals in Madrid were also threatened and the self-styled Fifth Adolf Hitler Commando of the PENS commited acts of violence against lawyers who defended workers' cases.[14]

The targets of the neo-Nazis pointed clearly at their function within the crisis of late Francoism. They also explain why the state was ready to turn a blind eye. The ultras frequently did work which a state hovering on the fringe of the EEC would find embarrassing to undertake itself. In the universities, Defensa Universitaria continued to subject left-wing students and professors to sporadic terror. Equally significant were the forays into working-class districts. Since the meetings of the clandestine trade unions were prohibited, progressive clergymen offered their churches for the purpose. It was virtually impossible, if the Concordat was observed, for the police to prevent this. Accordingly, the church was one of the main victims of ultra violence. Groups of *Guerrilleros* frequently entered churches and attacked both clergy and congregation. Various raids in 1973 created considerable scandal. One in particular, attributed to a group calling itself 'Cruz Ibérica' (Iberian Cross), on the Opus Dei-controlled Banco Atlántico in Madrid, a blow against the relatively more progressive regime forces, suggested that the ultra groups were pawns in an intra-regime power struggle. After the Banco Atlántico incident and the attack on the Gran Enciclopedia Catalana, questions were raised in the press and *Ya* commented on the ultra's audacity and success in avoiding capture.[15]

Unlike comparable terrorist groups in Italy or Chile which worked to overthrow democratic regimes, the Spanish ultras were positively enthusiastic about the regime under which they functioned. Their aim was rather one of repairing leaks in the dam of Francoism. Attacks on workers and students were attacks on the regime's enemies, but the assault on the Banco Atlántico was a direct attack against the progressive bourgeoisie, the patrons of economic development, and therefore by implication of

---

14 *Informaciones*, 6 August; *Pueblo*, 7 August 1973.
15 *Ya*, 8 August 1973; *Sábado Gráfico*, 16 February 1974.

eventual liberalization. Similarly, the enmity against the church expressed by the ultras betrayed a frustration against a force which once sustained the regime and was moving ever faster into the ranks of the democratic opposition.

Blas Piñar was reported to have cordial relations with Admiral Carrero Blanco.[16] Under the dry-land admiral, the regime did not tolerate opposition yet it acquiesced in the existence of neo-Nazism. The only logical explanation was to be found in a split between the regime families. The tepid liberalization expected from Carrero Blanco's Opus Dei-dominated 1969 cabinet was being abandoned. That was made clear by the cabinet changes of mid-1973. Economic liberalization, grudgingly tolerated by sectors of the old guard and most grudgingly of all by the immediate entourage of the Caudillo at El Pardo, had done little to curtail growing worker and student opposition. General strikes in Granada in 1970, in El Ferrol in 1972 and in Pamplona in 1973 were put down only with considerable difficulty. The universities were more militant than ever. In January 1972 a thousand students battled with the police permanently stationed at the Universidad Complutense. Colegios de Abogados (bar associations) and Colegios de Médicos (medical associations) were beginning to show their discontent. The church was openly criticizing the regime with the result that bishops were attacked by the Guerrilleros de Cristo Rey, and ultra-rightist gatherings were raucously punctuated by demands for the execution of Cardinal Enrique y Tarancón, the Archbishop of Madrid, president of the Episcopal Congress and the most visible leader of the dominant liberal wing of the church.

The growth of the neo-Nazi groups was therefore clearly connected with the crisis through which the regime was passing. The function of the black terrorist squads was to resolve the contradiction inherent in the Opus Dei attempt to modernize a political system whose proudest boast had always been that it had eliminated the Enlightenment. Economic modernization, intended to guarantee the survival of the regime, had meant the emergence of a new working class with new demands, and a new student body to meet the need for trained personnel. Continued progress had also required that some of the heavy-handed control of the unions and universities be relaxed. Appetites were whetted and the extreme right concluded simplistically that modernization was responsible for the crisis that it was intended to solve. Aware that Franco was failing, paranoically anxious about the political implications of a succession to Juan Carlos, disturbed by the scale of working-class and student unrest and by the emergence of an organization capable of penetrating the regime's image of invulnerability, ETA, the extreme right of the regime was on the verge of panic. Indeed,

16 Ricardo de la Cierva, *La Derecha sin remedio (1801–1987)* (Barcelona, 1987), pp. 324–5.

for the first time, there was talk in Hitlerian terms of withdrawing to a bunker and fighting in the rubble of the Chancellery. Neo-Nazi groups played a useful role in the tactics of beleaguered Francoism, terrorizing the opposition without stigma for the regime. More sophisticated was the propaganda effect of encouraging the ultra right. It effectively blurred the government's adoption of an increasingly hard line against all forms of dissent, because the invention of a fanatical extreme right placed the regime as if by magic in a centre position.

The function of the ultra right was starkly illustrated in the summer of 1973. During the May Day demonstrations, a member of the secret police was stabbed to death. There were hundreds of arrests and reports of torture. More immediately significant were the mass protests organized by the ultra right. The way in which they were orchestrated indicated the extent to which the regime's rightists felt themselves to be under siege. Government ministries, army barracks and syndical offices were inundated with leaflets whose nostalgic use of Civil War rhetoric gave some sense of their feelings that history was turning against them. One was headed 'The Civil War has begun again' and warned that 'with the blood shed by the Marxists on 1 May, stabbing to death the young policeman Juan Antonio Fernández, the war which ended on 1 April 1939 has started again. This time, the war will be short'. Several made appeals to the armed forces. Another took the form of a warning – 'Warning to Traitors' and continued:

to those who once wore the blue shirt of the Falange and today are ashamed of having worn it; to those who once wore the red beret of the Carlist movement and have since thrown it on to the rubbish heap; to those who do not wish to sing the Falangist anthem *Cara al Sol* nor raise their arm in the fascist salute; to those who condemn as ultras and right-wing extremists those Spaniards who reply with their fists against those who insult the Fatherland, religion or justice. Just because you commit such apostasy, the Marxists will not spare you your lives. If you give up the chance to be heroes or martyrs you will be vile victims.

A rally was held at Madrid Cathedral, San Francisco el Grande, on 7 May. Policemen publicly demanded repressive measures. About 3,000 Civil War veterans called for satisfaction. The demands on their placards were similar to those of the neo-Nazi groups in that they attacked all forms of liberalism. 'Red Bishops to the Firing-Squad' was a typical slogan. Leaflets were distributed praising the activities of the extreme right.[17] The very fact that the regime tolerated what was effectively a police

---

17 *Informaciones*, 7 May 1973. The quotations come from leaflets collected by the author at the time.

mutiny suggested that the demonstrators' aims had found sympathy in high circles. A month later, the ministers who were accused of weakness and liberalism were dropped. The cabinet sworn in on 12 June 1973 was a defensive one. The technocrats were on the run and those who managed to stay did so only at the cost of their liberalism. The formal handing over of executive power to Carrero Blanco indicated the preparation of a holding operation to cover the succession to Franco. An increase of activities by the *Guerrilleros*, PENS, CEDADE and company suggested that they would be snipers in that operation. Carrero Blanco's final cabinet consisted of a team fitted to crush opposition and stifle reform. It was a return to the past and a rejection of the present. The ruling clique, aware that it had been too long aboard ship could think of no better tactic than to put on diving suits.

Yet even in mid-1973 it was already too late. By the end of the year Carrero Blanco would be assassinated by ETA. Despite the enormity of that crime, to the amazement of the ultras, there was no battening down of the Francoist hatches. Civilian and military extreme rightists alike were foiled in their hopes for a bloody Night of the Long Knives against the left. They managed only to win a small victory in the question of Carrero's successor. They were able to ensure that the dour Carlos Arias Navarro would be chosen rather than the sinuously intelligent Torcuato Fernández Miranda, Carrero's vice-president and the logical choice. Fernández Miranda was considered by the ultras to be dangerously close to Prince Juan Carlos, who as Franco's designated successor was considered at that time to represent the Opus Dei option of a modified Francoism. They were right to block Fernández Miranda; indeed righter than they knew at the time since he was to play a key role as adviser to the king during the transition to democracy.[18] However, when even Arias was forced to attempt some form of change, announcing his limited commitment to reform on 12 February 1974, the ultras became more desperate and more daring. As the centre of gravity moved away from Francoism and towards some sort of democratic evolution, they were forced to direct their attacks ever closer to home.

The Portuguese revolution of 25 April 1974 added even greater urgency to the need to ensure that there would be Francoism after Franco. Merely three days later, they launched what came to be known as the *Gironazo*. On 28 April 1974 the wealthy ex-Minister of Labour, José Antonio Girón de Velasco, courtier of Franco and head of the organization of Nationalist Civil War veterans, the Confederación Nacional de Ex-Combatientes, launched a savage public attack on Arias and the relatively progressive civil servants

---

18 On Fernández Miranda, see José Luis Alcocer, *Fernández-Miranda: agonía de un Estado* (Barcelona, 1986) and Paul Preston, *The Triumph of Democracy in Spain* (London, 1986), pp. 50–1, 79–80, 92.

who were helping plan his democratic reform. It was the beginning of a major political offensive, also involving Blas Piñar, and enjoying the support of key figures of the *Movimiento* press. The *Gironazo* was also linked to efforts by the military bunker to secure key operational posts to enable them to be ready to seize power in the immediate post-Franco struggle.[19] The publicity campaign, aimed not so much at ultra-rightist public opinion as at Franco himself and the high command of the army, finally bore fruit with the sacking of Arias's relatively progressive Minister of Information, Pío Cabanillas, on 29 October 1974. That was followed by a chain of dramatic resignations, including those of the relatively liberal Minister of Finance, Antonio Barrera de Irimo, of the director of the massive government holding corporation, Francisco Fernández Ordóñez, of the Director-General of Spanish Television, Juan José Rosón, and of a significant number of highly influential civil servants, known as the *Tácito* group.

The ultra-rightists were delighted at their apparent success but, as a plummeting stock market quickly showed, all they had achieved was to accelerate the same crisis of Francoism which they were trying to halt. In fact, it would appear that just as the ultras had passed from the use of sporadic low-level terrorism and the use of thugs to intimidate opponents, to efforts to influence the Caudillo himself, they now began to hatch rather more dangerous and grandiose schemes involving the military. Veterans such as Girón and José Utrera Molina, a close friend of Franco and, until March 1975, Minister Secretary-General of the *Movimiento*, had mobilized the dictator in October 1974 to help block the 'spirit of 12 February' as Arias's feeble commitment to political reform was known. However, with the Caudillo increasingly moribund, that was not a tactic that could be used with any frequency. Moreover, the ironic consequence of ultra-rightist actions, whether violence committed by their young men or the manipulation of Franco, was merely to convince many percipient and influential Francoists within both the banking and business community and the government apparatus that the time had come to open negotiations with the opposition.

Indeed, both at the time and subsequently, the activities of the bunker were, in its own terms, counter-productive. A desperate attempt to block the rapid progress towards democratization in late 1976 and early 1977 by means of an Italian-style strategy of tension resulted in the murder of five people, on 24 January 1977 at a law office in the Atocha district of Madrid. The victims included four communist labour lawyers. The effect was to dissipate public hostility to the eventual legalization of the Communist Party.[20] Thereafter, ultra activity was concentrated on encouraging army

---

19 See the following chapter pp. 183–4.
20 Preston, *Triumph*, pp. 107–8.

officers to rise against the democratic regime. Falangism had come full circle. Unable to make its own fascist revolution in 1936, either by the ballot box or the violent seizure of power, the Falange had been a parasitical observer of the military rebellion. Even more impotent in the late 1970s, the divided remnants of Falangism tried to do the same as their predecessors in the 1930s. When the military failed, however, the civilian ultra-right also found itself electorally rejected by the Spain which they had claimed that they were going to save.

8

Francoism's last stand: the military campaign against democracy, 1973–82

At 6.30 p.m. on 23 February 1981 Lieutenant-Colonel Antonio Tejero Molina, at the head of 200 Civil Guards, entered the Spanish parliament buildings in Madrid. The Cortes was in full session, in order to vote on the investiture of Leopoldo Calvo Sotelo as president of the government. The aim of Tejero and his fellow-conspirators was to sequestrate the entire political élite in order to create the political vacuum which would in turn justify the imposition of military rule. At approximately the same time, other participants in the plot were occupying the headquarters of Radio-Televisión Española at Prado del Rey outside Madrid. Further plans envisaged the occupation of key strategic points of the capital by units of the crack Brunete armoured division. Meanwhile, the Captain-General of Valencia, the third of Spain's nine military regions, Jaime Milans del Bosch, was moving tanks into the streets there and declaring that the grave events taking place in Madrid necessitated such a take-over. In the event, the coup failed. In retrospect, it may be seen as the high point in the efforts of ultra-reactionary elements in the Spanish army to overturn the transition to democracy. From the early 1970s, when the prospect of democratic change after the dictatorship became an increasingly palpable threat, military hard-liners had been struggling both to stamp out liberalism within their own ranks and to use their power to block civilian efforts to bring about a transition.

Within twenty months of the failed Tejero coup, the Socialist Party would be in power. There would be other despairing efforts at coups, but they would fail as the socialists embarked on a massive programme of military modernization, consolidating Spain's membership of NATO and replacing the Spanish army's obsession with domestic politics by a concern for international strategic issues. At the time of the Tejero coup, however, that outcome was anything but clear. The nervous media, hoping to diminish the enormity of what was happening, stressed Tejero's track record as the prime mover behind the abortive 'Galaxia' coup of 1978, and tried to write off the attempt as the work of an isolated madman. Moreover, a number of technical failures perhaps made the coup attempt seem more ramshackle than in fact it was. Certain important radio transmitters were not occupied as planned. The cavalry regiment which had seized RTVE at 7 p.m. was persuaded to leave two hours later by the officer in charge of the king's military household. The ramifications of the coup were deeper than its defective execution implied and were obscured only by wavering loyalties and hesitations on the night. For instance, the general in command of the Brunete armoured division, José Juste Fernández, played a crucially ambiguous role. Probably aware that the coup was being prepared, yet anxious not to be implicated, he had been on his way to inspect some units in Zaragoza. In the course of his journey to Aragón, he had been informed that something was afoot and had returned to Brunete. Once there, realizing that the king opposed the coup, Juste eventually reimposed his command and prevented the mobilization of units which were to occupy Madrid.[1]

Neither the technical hitches nor the fact that only thirty conspirators were eventually tried justified atttempts to play down the coup's importance. To begin with, Tejero was merely the battering ram of much more deeply laid plots, whose lack of unanimity was to be their weakness. Tejero was to be the trigger for a Turkish- or Chilean-style *coup de main* plotted by General Milans del Bosch and involving key figures from military intelligence, such as Colonel José Ignacio San Martín. Their Pinochet-style *coup* was to be followed by a Draconian repression of the left and a 'dirty war' to wipe out ETA.[2] In contrast, General Alfonso Armada Comyn envisaged a de Gaulle-style take-over and had even approached a number of politicians with the idea during the previous months.[3] Armada had been for many years one of Juan Carlos's tutors and Secretary-General of the Royal Military Household. He had been sacked from that position in October 1977, allegedly for mis-using royal notepaper on behalf of the parliamentary candidacy of his son for the right-wing political party Alianza Popular. Nevertheless, he had managed to become second-in-command of the general staff at the beginning of 1981. The two plots merged in the person of Armada. He hoped that the violent *fait accompli* of Tejero-Milans would oblige the king to give the coup his approval and blackmail the

1 Details of the events of 23 February 1981 have been taken from *El País* and *Cambio 16*. A lively account of the unfolding of the night's drama may be found in Ricardo Cid Cañaveral *et al.*, *Todos al suelo: la conspiración y el golpe* (Madrid, 1981) For a more detailed account of the political origins of the coup, see Paul Preston, *The Triumph of Democracy in Spain* (London, 1986), pp. 196–201.

2 José Luis Morales and Juan Celada, *La alternativa militar: el golpismo después de Franco* (Madrid, 1981), pp. 89–91, 122–5; *Cambio 16*, 17 November 1980; *El Alcázar*, 24 January 1981.

3 *El Alcázar*, 16, 21 September, 2 December 1980; Alfonso Armada, *Al servicio de la Corona* (Barcelona, 1983), pp. 216, 223–7.

political class into co-operating in a government of national salvation under his premiership. At the same time, Milans and some of the hard men of the Tejero plot were encouraged by Armada's supposed proximity to Juan Carlos to believe that their commander-in-chief was actually privy to the conspiracy.[4]

The existence of at least two plots involving different sorts of officers pointed to reasonably widespread support within the armed forces for a coup. Indeed, the complex process whereby the conspiracy was dismantled indicated far-reaching support. The defence of the democratic order was master-minded by a triumvirate of the King, the new Secretary-General of the Royal Military Household, General Sabino Fernández Campos, and the Director-General de Seguridad, Francisco Laína García. It took them eighteen hours to secure the surrender of Tejero. This delay was caused largely by the ambiguity of Armada's position. It was not known until the early hours of the morning that he was in fact a conspirator and in consequence it took longer to secure assurances of loyalty from the other eight Captains-General and other military leaders, many of whom were waiting on events. The coup was seen to be under serious threat only when Juan Carlos appeared on television at 1.10 a.m. on the morning of 24 February.[5]

The coup, the difficulties involved in its disarticulation, and the fact that the king had been obliged to place his personal prestige and safety at risk suggested that Spain's political class in general and the leadership of UCD in particular had severely miscalculated the mood of the army during the transition to democracy. Indeed, 23-F, as the coup came to be known in Spain, brutally exposed the limitations of the government's kid-glove treatment of the officer class. Suárez had avoided injuring its susceptibilities at all costs, in the hope of being able to carry out political and military reforms on the quiet.[6] Thus many of the central figures in the plot turned out to have been involved in previous acts of hostility to the democratic regime without having suffered significant punishment. In May 1979 General Milans del Bosch had absolved an officer who had attacked and insulted the Minister of Defence, General Gutiérrez Mellado. Captain Saenz de Ynestrillas, who was heavily involved in 23-F, had helped Tejero conjure up the *'Galaxia'* coup which had failed in November 1978. For that crime, Saenz de Ynestrillas had been sentenced to only six months' preventive arrest and had been immediately promoted to major. General

---

4 On the role of Armada in the preparation of the coup, see Martín Prieto, *Técnica de un golpe de Estado: el juicio del 23-F* (Barcelona, 1982), *passim*, but especially pp. 88–94; José Oneto, *La verdad sobre el caso Tejero: el proceso del siglo* (Barcelona, 1982), *passim*, but especially pp. 205–35.
5 Pilar Urbano, 'El contragolpe' in Colectivo Democracia, *Los Ejércitos... más allá del golpe* (Barcelona, 1981).
6 Morales and Celada, *La alternativa*, pp. 30, 34–5.

Luis Torres Rojas, who was organizing the participation of the Brunete armoured division in the Tejerazo until the return of General Juste, also had a history of disloyalty. In January 1980, as the commander of the Brunete division, he had been involved in plans for a coup as a result of which he had merely been demoted to the military governorship of La Coruña.[7]

The most flagrant case of government leniency encouraging recidivism was Tejero himself. He seems to have been somewhat deranged by a period of service in the Basque country, during which he saw action against ETA terrorists. Renowned for theatrically embracing the bloody corpses of Civil Guards killed in bomb and sniper attacks, he developed a bitter hatred of the Madrid politicians whom he blamed for failing to smash ETA once and for all. Accordingly, he encouraged his men in the sort of blanket brutality which itself provoked popular support for ETA, and at the same time began to mix with civilian ultra-rightists who persuaded him that he could be Spain's saviour. In January 1977 he was posted away from the North in punishment for an impertinent telegram to the Minister of the Interior, Rodolfo Martín Villa, protesting about the flying of the Basque flag, the Ikurriña, in the region. After the briefest arrest, he was sent to Malaga, where he almost provoked a blood-bath by suppressing, on his own initiative, a legally authorized demonstration in favour of Andalusian autonomy.

It was typical of the cautious treatment afforded army and Civil Guard officers in the post-Franco period that Tejero was punished for his persistently mutinous attitudes merely by being given a desk job in Madrid. There he mixed with Falangists even more nostalgic than himself and, at their encouragement, began to plot. His idea was to kidnap the cabinet in session at the presidential Palacio de la Moncloa, just outside the capital. The plan was to be carried out on 17 November 1978 when the king was scheduled to be out of the country, when many senior officers were to be away from Madrid on manoeuvres and when the city was to be flooded with rightists assembling to commemorate the anniversary of Franco's death on the 20th. In the event, this *Operación Galaxia* as it was known (in honour of the cafeteria where it was hatched), was exposed by military intelligence services. At a time when an increasing number of anti-democratic incidents were being provoked by officers and then virtually ignored by the authorities, it hardly came as a surprise that Tejero was made to serve only seven months' arrest before being given another post in Madrid at the head of a transport unit. Moreover, not only did he now enjoy considerable fame among extreme rightist factions but, as ETA

---

7 Enrique Montánchez, 'De la "Galaxia" al DAC', in Colectivo Democracia, *Los Ejércitos*; Miguel Angel Aguilar, 'La cota del Parlamento', in Julio Busquets, Miguel Angel Aguilar and Ignacio Puche, *El golpe: anatomía y claves del asalto al Congreso* (Barcelona, 1981).

attacks on officers were stepped up, Tejero also came to be looked on benevolently by a growing section of the military hierarchy.[8]

This was not entirely surprising. The constant blood-letting by ETA, the atmosphere of economic decline, the political lethargy of UCD and legalization of the Communist Party had all been played up by the ultra-rightist press to such an extent that military hostility to democracy was greater in 1981 than it had been shortly after the death of Franco. Then, there had been some sympathy for the idea of controlled change under the king's supervision. Moreover, having opted for a policy of avoiding confrontations or purges, UCD had found that the desperately necessary placing of progressive or liberal officers in responsible positions was circumscribed by the inflexibility of the prevailing promotion system. In fact, the democratic regime's urgent need to integrate the armed forces was to run aground on a series of rigidities central to the world-view of the Spanish officer corps.

In any army, but especially in Spain, values normally associated with rightist politics prevail – hierarchy, authority, order, honour, bravery, discipline and patriotism. Equally, values arising from concepts of liberty and equality are unlikely to become part of the praetorian ethos, for reasons of military efficacy. Franco's army surpassed the usual bounds of military conservatism because of the way in which it was forged in a long and cruel war against communism, socialism, liberalism and parliamentary democracy. As a result of the Civil War, the five thousand or so liberal or leftist officers in the Spanish army before 1936 were shot, imprisoned or exiled. At the same time, nearly eleven thousand ultra-rightist Falangists and Carlists were incorporated into the army as *alféreces provisionales*. Thereafter, the military was closely implicated in the running of the country, providing 40 of the dictator's 120 ministers. In particular, the army was involved in the repressive tasks of the dictatorship, the more so as there were no external conflicts to distract its attention.

Moreover, three-quarters of the students in military academies were the sons of officers and were trained by instructors whose primordial task was to transmit the bellicose and anti-leftist ideology of the Civil War victory. For them, the central lesson of the 1936–9 war was that democracy was to blame for the chaos which they believed had made their insurrection necessary. Disorder and the break-up of Spain into autonomous regions were perceived as the Second Republic's most abhorrent challenges to that eternal Spain whose defence was regarded as the army's most sacred duty. Such ideas were nurtured in the hothouse of barrack life, isolated from civil society. Over 50 per cent of officers married the daughters of other officers. They lived, and still live, on separate military housing

---

8   José Oneto, *La noche de Tejero* (Barcelona, 1981), pp. 27–34.

estates, shop at military supermarkets and pharmacies, send their children to special military infant schools and later, at university, to live in separate army-sponsored halls of residence.[9]

As the case of Tejero proved all too graphically, soldiers constantly on the move never made the sort of local contacts that might have helped them understand the society in which they worked. Their intellectual schema was never challenged since the only newspapers and journals read and discussed were the openly fascist *El Alcázar*, *El Heraldo Español* and *Fuerza Nueva*, which were often distributed free in barracks. Little was done by UCD to incorporate the army into the democratic collectivity, other than significant increases in levels of pay and of the budget for equipment. This did increase the professionalism of certain technology-orientated units but had little impact on the more narrow-minded and backward infantry regiments. There was no programme of instruction to persuade officers that it was possible to be both a democrat and a good Spaniard. Thus, while acts of indiscipline, such as those committed by Tejero, went unpunished, declarations in favour of democracy were swiftly and fiercely castigated. Members of the Unión Militar Democrática, who worked to foster democratic ideas within the armed forces were not amnestied until 1988 for sentences passed under Francoist laws in 1976. Officers who made overtly pro-constitutional declarations were arrested for 'meddling in politics'. As late as January 1982, Colonel Alvaro Graíño of the general staff was imprisoned for two months for writing in a Madrid newspaper that some officers held ultra-rightist views; Major Monge, a professor at the General Staff College, was arrested for admitting having belonged to the UMD; Major Perinat was imprisoned for five months for a newspaper article criticizing the fact that military medical staff also held civilian jobs. The same tribunal which sentenced Graíño decreed only one month's arrest for Captain Juan Milans del Bosch, son of the arch-conspirator, after he had been found guilty of calling the king, his commander-in-chief, a useless pig.[10]

Rightists, who were in any case a majority within the army, drew their own conclusions. In fact, given their ideological preconceptions, it is hardly surprising that the army has played the role that it has in the process of transition to democracy. One of Franco's greatest achievements was to maintain the loyalty of the armed forces at the same time as he kept them in penury. Of course, the two processes were inextricably linked. The incorporation of Civil War veterans into the army implied a decision to eschew having a modern army and instead to reward

---

9 Julio Busquets, 'Las causas del golpe' in Busquets *et al.*, *El golpe*; Julio Busquets, *El militar de carrera en España*, 2nd edn (Barcelona, 1971), pp. 198–209, 260–74.

10 Julio Busquets, 'Las Fuerzas Armadas en la transición española', *Sistema* (Madrid), no. 93, November 1989, pp. 22–4.

the politically loyal with secure, if inadequate, salaries. Poor pay was compensated by the wide range of social services, in health, education, housing and even food supplies, which were for the exclusive use of the military. This increased both an officer's sense of belonging to a privileged caste and also his dependence on the regime. Similarly, low salaries were accompanied by considerable free time and the turning of a blind eye to *pluriempleo*. Many were the Spanish firms which used to greet the tax inspector with a colonel in full-dress uniform or send applications to the Ministry of Commerce for import licences in the hands of a general. The middle- and upper-class ranks of the army were subtly corrupted by this process. Since it necessarily involved a deterioration of their professional competence, they compensated by an exaggerated pride in their status as a victorious army, a status which itself implied the continued humiliation of a wide section of the population. Low levels of professionalism and inflated conceptions of political importance were fossilized by slow promotion and late retirement.

Accordingly, the period of the democratic transition saw the army's senior ranks still dominated by veterans of the Civil War and of the División Azul, Franco's expeditionary force which had joined Hitler's armies in Russia. Officers who entered military academies after the Civil War were only reaching the rank of lieutenant-colonel by 1975.[11] This ultra-rightist preponderance was exacerbated by the fact that generals did not retire definitively but rather passed to the reserve, whence they were free to make uninhibited political declarations, usually of an anti-democratic nature.[12] It is, however, necessary to stress that this situation obtained rather less in the navy and air force. This was because of their higher levels of technological expertise and their incorporation into European defence, both of which factors intensified their links with other more liberal colleagues. Nor were they involved in the repressive functions undertaken by the army.

Indeed, the legacy of the judicial role played by the army was to weigh heavily on the transition process. The competence, not to say the obligation, of military tribunals to try civilians for a wide range of political 'crimes' persisted long after the immediate justification for repression after the Civil War. Even after the setting up of the Tribunal de Orden Público in 1963 had taken some of the burden, the military continued to be involved and thus to receive the opprobrium attached to being the instrument of anti-democratic repression. Notable examples were the Burgos trials of 1970, the execution on 2 March 1974 of the Catalan anarchist Salvador Puig Antich and on 27 September 1975 of three militants of FRAP and two

11 Morales and Celada, *La alternative*, p. 24.
12 Carlos Fernández, *Los militares en la transición política* (Barcelona, 1982), pp. 24–5.

of ETA, which led to massive anti-Francoist demonstrations internationally and even within Spain. Even in crisis-free years, such as 1971 and 1972, there were respectively 126 and 151 sentences for political crimes passed by military courts, the largest proportion of which were for 'verbal offence against the Armed Forces'.[13] In the five years following the country's first democratic elections, there were cases of journalists, playwrights and singers falling foul of military justice.

The jurisdictional role of the military within the repressive process was massively backed up by a territorial deployment of forces more appropriate to an army of occupation. This was perhaps understandable after the Civil War and the guerrilla fighting which continued until 1951. However, the system was confirmed and consolidated after 1965 and was only changed gradually by the socialists in the 1980s. For twenty years after 1965, units were divided into two broad operational groupings. The first, the Fuerzas de Intervencion Inmediata (FII), consisted of three infantry divisions: the armoured, the mechanized and the motorized, together with three brigades: the parachute, the airborne and amoured cavalry/artillery. In theory, the FII had an international, defensive function to protect the Pyrenean and Gibraltarian frontiers and to help fulfil Spain's external military treaty obligations. In practice, many of the key units were stationed near major industrial connurbations. The second grouping, the Fuerzas de Defensa Operativa del Territorio (FDOT), consisted of two mountain divisions, eleven infantry brigades and two artillery brigades. Directly under the command of the captains-general of the nine military regions, the FDOT had a much more openly anti-subversive role against *guerrilleros* and political demonstrators as well as possible external enemies.[14]

Another feature of the Spanish armed forces which tended to intensify its anti-democratic political stance was the complex and contradictory network of intelligence services. This became apparent throughout 1974, when the revolutionary activities of the Portuguese army caused some anxiety in the Spanish military circles already worried by the waning health of Franco. Long before the events in Portugal, efforts had been made to combat the possible emergence of political dissidence, democratic or otherwise, within the armed forces. In the early years of the dictatorship, military subversion tended to go no further than jockeying for position by pro-regime factions, usually monarchists but sometimes Falangists. In such cases, punishment rarely exceeded demotion or distant postings.

13 José Oneto, *Arias entre dos crisis 1973–1975* (Madrid, 1975), pp. 63–7; Colectivo Democracia, *Los Ejércitos*, p. 38.
14 César Ruiz-Ocaña, *Los Ejércitos españoles: las fuerzas armadas en la defensa nacional* (Madrid, 1980), ch. XII; José Fortes and Restituto Valero, *Qué son las fuerzas armadas* (Barcelona, 1977), p. 62. See also p. 151 above.

Symptoms of genuine liberalism were, in contrast, punished harshly.[15] In the crisis-ridden twilight of the Franco regime, however, an element of panic became discernible. Just as civilian Francoists were beginning to fear that their plans for a post-Franco *continuismo* might be undermined by the more liberal *aperturistas*, the military hierarchy became prey to similar anxieties.

Indeed, throughout the transition period, events within the army were a faithful reflection of the overall trend of ultra-Francoist politics. In the summer of 1973, the trend of *apertura* among regime forces was apparently squashed by the appointment of the hard-line Admiral Luis Carrero Blanco on 8 June to the post of President of the Council of Ministers. The rightist back-lash of which this was the most visible manifestation soon made its impact within the armed forces. On 9 July four officer cadets were expelled from the Academia de Infantería de Toledo two days before two of them were to graduate as first lieutenants. Their 'crimes' included reading legally published books and magazines on social, cultural and economic subjects; familiarity with other ranks; abandonment of Catholic practice; friendship with university students and conversations with them about social reform; and possession of a questionnaire on army-government relations.[16] The harshness of the reaction to these offences indicated the extent of fear within the military establishment. This was partly a reaction to the discovery in 1973 of a document emanating from 'a group of officers' which called upon the armed forces to defend the real interests of the entire Spanish nation and not just those of a corrupt and narrow clique. That document was the first manifestation of what would eventually become the liberal pressure group of army and air force officers, Unión Militar Democrática.[17] It was largely in reaction to growing signs of democratic sentiment within the officer corps that Carrero Blanco extended the scope of internal intelligence services.

These services, originally set up to hold back the trend to democratization in both the armed forces and society at large, were eventually to play a key role in the various coup attempts of the post-Franco period. Before the dictator's death, however, their greatest triumph was the disarticulation of the Unión Militar Democrática. The revolution of 25 April 1974 in Portugal had raised the spectre of democracy in Spain. The first victim of military paranoia was the Chief of the General Staff, General Manuel Díez Alegría. A liberal, committed to the greater professionalization of the armed forces, Díez Alegría had been sent hundreds of monocles by

---

15 Stanley G. Payne, *Politics and the Military in Modern Spain* (Stanford, 1967), pp. 422–5, 433–4; Jésus Ynfante, *El Ejército de Franco y de Juan Carlos* (Paris, 1976), pp. 111-12; Alfredo Kindelán, *La verdad de mis relaciones con Franco* (Barcelona, 1981), p. 114; Fernández, *Los militares* p.16.
16 Ynfante, *El Ejército*, pp. 113–14; Fernández, *Los militares*, pp. 15–16.
17 Ynfante, *El Ejército*, pp. 118–20.

people who hoped that he might become the Spanish Spinola. On 13 June 1974 he was removed as CGS after an authorized trip to Romania for medical treatment during which he had met President Ceaucescu, then still considered a progressive figure.[18] Nevertheless, any fears surrounding the possible activities of General Díez Alegría paled into insignificance beside those provoked by the discovery by Carrero's intelligence services of a more serious Portuguese-style threat. Clandestine assemblies of young officers comparable to those who had organized the Portuguese armed forces movement were found to be operating in Spain. At a time when Francoists had been hoping for a succession to Francoism without Franco, the destruction of the much admired example of Salazarism without Salazar had come as a bitter blow. The grave illness of Franco in the summer of 1974 could only create considerable tension within the armed forces. The Unión Militar Democrática, the movement behind these assemblies, was democratic and politically moderate. Nevertheless, the brutal reaction of the military authorities, treating them as if they were part of communist efforts to infiltrate the forces with democratic juntas, was an indication of the nervousness inside the Spanish high command in the aftermath of the Portuguese revolution and throughout the death agony of Franco.[19]

The liberal middle-rank and junior officers involved had been meeting to discuss ways of ensuring that the army would not block the increasingly vocal nationwide drive towards democracy. In Barcelona, a group of captains gathered around the seminal figure of Major Julio Busquets Bragulat, in Madrid around Major Luis Otero. By the summer of 1974, the two groups were moving towards issuing the manifesto of what was to emerge publicly in September 1974 as the UMD. The manifesto showed that the UMD's leaders aimed to be truly apolitical, concerned only to prevent the army continuing to be the guardian of the system against the popular will. Accordingly, they called for all forces of the democratic opposition to unite, while themselves refusing steadfastly to be associated with any one group. Their model for how this should happen was the broad political front known as the Assemblea de Catalunya, although they were also influenced by the liberal Christian Democrat Joaquín Ruiz Giménez and, through Busquets, by the Catalan socialist leader, Joan Raventós.[20]

The international and domestic press immediately began to speculate that the UMD was the Spanish equivalent of the Portuguese MFA. The

---

18 Raymond Carr and Juan Pablo Fusi, *Spain: Dictatorship to Democracy* (London, 1979), p. 199; Fernández, *Los militares*, p. 26.

19 Ramón Chao, *Après Franco, L'Espagne* (Paris, 1975), p. 280.

20 Unión Militar Democrática, *Los militares y la lucha por la democracia* (n.p., n.d.) pp. 1–15; José Fortes and Luis Otero, *Proceso a nueve militares demócratas: Las Fuerzas Armadas y la UMD* (Barcelona, 1983), pp. 28, 231–51; Francisco Caparrós, *La UMD: militares y rebeldes* (Barcelona, 1983), pp. 45–60.

leaders of the UMD later denied the connection but it is difficult not to conclude that they were influenced by the events of the Portuguese April. Many of the most influential figures, Julio Busquets, José Fortes and Luis Otero, had contacts in the MFA. Moreover, not only did the UMD emerge suspiciously soon after the upheaval in Portugal, but one of its earliest and most important publications was entitled 'Where are the captains?' and began with the words 'In the aftermath of the military intervention in the Portuguese political scene, many Spaniards are asking themselves "what are our captains up to?" Why do they not rebel against the injustice of a regime which is repudiated by the great majority of the country?'[21] Nevertheless, there was an important difference. The officers of the UMD had no intention of making a revolution themselves as their comrades in Portugal had done. Instead, they aimed only to raise the consciousness of the Spanish army in order that it would not hinder the creation of a democratic Spain by civilian forces.

Almost from the first moment, the various military intelligence services were on the trail of those involved. The high command was outraged at the thought of the army being divided and appalled at the prospect of a significant number of officers joining the democratic cause. The wilder elements in the intelligence services, always given to exaggeration for their own political purposes, reckoned that perhaps as many as 2,000 officers might have been contaminated by the UMD. The UMD itself never had more than 250 active militants although eventually many more were involved as sympathizers. By the time that the UMD held its Second National Assembly in secret in Madrid in December 1974, contacts had been made with the Socialist Party through Raventós and Felipe González, with the Communist Party through Simón Sánchez Montero and Armando López Salinas and with the left Christian Democrats through Joaquín Ruiz Giménez.[22]

The nervousness of the high command was revealed in February 1975 when Major Busquets and Captain José Julve were arrested in Barcelona. The occasion was the anniversary of the foundation of the Academia General Militar de Zaragoza. Every year in each military region, there would be a celebratory lunch and there would be an after-lunch speech by an officer trained in the post Civil War academy. Traditionally, there would then be a reply, either from a senior officer trained in the academy in the days when Franco was director of the AGM or else from the captain-general of the region. In the Barcelona garrison, the occasion had been regularly marked by an incident which had itself become almost a tradition. Every year, Julio Busquets would interrupt at the end of the first speech to say that

---

21 '¿Dónde están los capitanes?', a pamphlet issued in January 1975, reprinted in Fortes and Otero, *UMD*, pp. 252–4. See also p. 27.
22 Fortes and Otero, *UMD*, p. 35.

the, invariably Francoist, first speaker did not represent everyone who had been trained at the AGM. In 1975, however, both traditions were broken. In the light of the ferment surrounding the spread of the UMD, a group of officers including Busquets requested permission for the first speech to be drawn up by a committee. The liberals in the group ensured that the speech would advocate a true apoliticism within the armed forces. However, Busquets and Julve went even further, proposing that the speech should include a declaration of support for Captain Jesús Molina, who had recently been arrested. On secondment to the national railway, RENFE, Molina had been punished for refusing to divulge information about a railway strike. Duly informed of the direction that the draft was taking, the Captain-General of the IV Military Region, General Bañuls ordered the arrest of Busquets and Julve. Bañuls effectively turned the anniversary lunch into a propaganda coup for the UMD. It took place in an atmosphere of great tension, without speeches, and the central topic of conversation was the content of the prohibited speeches.[23] Moreover, the sensation provoked by the arrest of Busquets, who was famous as the author of a widely read book on the sociology of the Spanish officer corps, led to widespread speculation that the army was divided.[24]

Throughout 1975, the UMD grew slowly but solidly, establishing a network of contacts across the major garrisons of the country. A decision was made to set up a 'tactical committee', which was devoted to identifying potential recruits and sympathizers and also to directing UMD members to seek transfer to units where they could best counter the political activities of the ultras. It was known that ultras were concentrating in key operational units. In particular, under the command of General Jaime Milans del Bosch, the armoured division at Brunete was attracting transfer requests from hard-liners. By the same token, the UMD was anxious to prevent the preparation of a coup to forestall democratic reform, and to hinder the use of the army against the civilian population in the event of strikes or demonstrations when Franco died.[25] By the summer of 1975, the intelligence services believed that 10 per cent of the officer corps was involved in one way or another. The prime minister and more liberal senior officers were prepared to keep a discreet eye on events without provoking an incident. However, the ultras were anxious both to smash the UMD as quickly as possible and to derive the greatest political benefit possible. They were aware of the growing debility of Franco and anxious lest the democratic neutrality advocated by the UMD should paralyse the armed forces at precisely the moment when they wanted them united to ensure the survival of the dictatorship beyond the dictator's death.

---

23   Caparrós, *La UMD*, pp. 68–72; Fortes and Otero, *UMD*, p. 36.
24   *Le Monde*, 18 February 1975; *Mundo Obrero*, 4 March 1975.
25   Fortes and Otero, *UMD*, p. 37.

Accordingly, they struck in such a way as to act as a deterrent against the spread of the UMD's political 'neutralism' and at the time which they calculated would do the greatest damage to prime minister Carlos Arias Navarro's tentative drift towards political reform.

The clearly orchestrated sequence of events was set off by General Jaime Milans del Bosch, who in addition to being the hard-line commander of the División Acorazada was also President of the Board of Directors of the ultra-right-wing newspaper *El Alcázar*. Arias Navarro was away in Helsinki at the Congress on European Security and Co-operation, seeking to gain credibility among the western democracies for his timid programme of liberalization. On 23 July 1975, Milans sent a report to the Captain-General of Madrid, the ultra Angel Campano López, informing him that the intelligence services had uncovered the activities of the UMD, which he denounced as a danger to the unity and the objectives of the armed forces. The report had been drawn up by the head of the army intelligence service, the Servicio de Información del Ejército de Tierra, Segunda Bis, or SIBE, Colonel José María Sáenz de Tejada y Fernández Bobadilla, a close collaborator of Milans. It was not properly the province of Milans to forward the report to Campano, other than as a 'concerned' officer. However, with the Milans dossier on his desk, Campano had an excuse to move against the UMD.[26] Seven leaders of the UMD were arrested on 29 July 1975 and two more fell on subsequent days. Spectacular dawn raids were mounted which were more appropriate to the capture of terrorists. The arrests were carried out by large groups of policemen while the buildings where the officers lived were covered by snipers on neighbouring rooftops.[27]

The display of excessive force had the three-fold function of embarrassing Arias Navarro, busy in Helsinki masquerading as a democrat, of humiliating the officers arrested, who were the lowest form of 'reds' as far as the ultras were concerned, and finally of mounting a deterrent to other officers sympathetic to the UMD.[28] The fears of the bunker with regard to the UMD could be discerned behind various public declarations about army unity made by senior hard-liners shortly after the arrests. On 8 August the Chief of the General Staff, General Carlos Fernández Vallespín, tried to play down the importance of the UMD arrests when he claimed that 'the army is fundamentally healthy even if it has just had a slight cold'. However, he went on to talk of the danger of a repetition in the Spanish forces of what had happened in Portugal. Similarly, the Minister

---

26 José Ignacio Domínguez, *Cuando yo era un exiliado* (Madrid, 1977), pp. 23–5, 104.

27 Domínguez, *Un exiliado*, pp. 24, 31–2; Caparrós, *La UMD*, pp. 85–7.

28 The official line subsequently was that Arias had authorized the arrests but it seems more likely that this was merely to cover the fact that he had been taken by surprise. Fortes and Otero, *UMD*, pp. 41–3.

for the Army, Francisco Coloma Gallegos, the Director of the Academia General Militar, General Guillermo Quintana Lacaci, and other senior figures made declarations denying the existence of any divisions within the army.[29]

During the trial of ETA militants in the summer of 1975, the supreme judicial authority under whose jurisdiction the trial was taking place was the Captain General of the VI Military Region, Burgos, Mateo Prada Canillas. He declared on 24 June that 'nowadays when so much is said about reconciliation, the forces of public order do not need to reconcile themselves with anyone'.[30] Coincidentally, Campano as Captain-General of Madrid was to authorize the death sentences on FRAP militants being tried in the capital in mid-September. It was in such an ambience that the preparations were made for the trial of the arrested UMD officers, who were accused of the extremely serious offence of 'military rebellion'. They were refused permission to make use of civilian lawyers and subjected to frequent harassment during their pre-trial detention. Efforts to find a negotiated solution for their plight essayed by José María Gil Robles foundered in early 1976 on the fierce opposition of the newly appointed ultra Captain-General of Madrid, Franco's last Army Minister, General Francisco Coloma Gallegos.[31] (Campano had left the I Military Region to become Director-General of the Civil Guard and been replaced by General Félix Alvarez Arenas. After only a couple of months in the job, on 8 January 1976, Alvarez Arenas became Minister for the Army in the first government under the new monarchy, exchanging posts with General Coloma Gallegos.) Coloma Gallegos's attitude was hardly surprising, since the object of trying the officers concerned was to smash the UMD in the way that would have the greatest impact possible on the widest spectrum of the officer corps. There was an element of damage limitation in the entire process. The intelligence services had the names of hundreds of officers implicated to some degree in the UMD. To reveal them, and therefore expose the extent of sympathy for democracy within the armed forces, would shatter the military unity. Accordingly, a brutal show trial of a few officers was preferred as a way of intimidating the liberals into silence and inertia.[32]

The death of Franco accelerated the retreat into the bunker by the hard-liners. The military ultras worked hard on several fronts to maintain control of the armed forces. While still Minister for the Army, General Francisco Coloma Gallegos captured the mood of the intransigent upper

---

29 *ABC*, 8 August 1975; Fortes and Otero, *UMD*, pp. 88–9.
30 Pierre Celhay, *Consejos de guerra en España: fascismo contra Euskadi* (Paris, 1976), p. 107.
31 Fortes and Otero, *UMD*, p. 117; Domínguez, *Un exiliado*, pp. 134–5, 148–9.
32 Fortes and Otero, *UMD*, p. 126.

echelons when he declared on 15 December 1975 that 'today more than ever before we must stay united to ensure that the torch picked up by the King should not be blown out by those who want to unleash storms'.[33] In the first post-Franco cabinet, the King's advisers had hoped that the Vice-President of the Government with ministerial responsibility for defence matters, and therefore jurisdiction over the three service ministries, would be the liberal commander of the Spanish enclave at Ceuta, Manuel Gutiérrez Mellado, a close friend of General Díez Alegría. A campaign was mounted against Gutiérrez Mellado by ultras infuriated by his moderate stance on the issue of the UMD. He had made strong representations to the Minister for the Army and the Captain-General of Madrid for the UMD to be treated less hysterically. A dossier was drawn up, either by Milans or Campano, purporting to prove that Gutiérrez Mellado was in fact the spiritual leader of the UMD. Arias Navarro was sufficiently moved by the dossier to bow before the strength of ultra feeling against Gutiérrez Mellado, giving the post instead to the fiercely conservative Fernando de Santiago y Díaz de Mendívil.[34] For the moment, Gutiérrez Mellado was promoted to become Captain-General of the VII Military Region in Valladolid. The new Minister for the Army, General Félix Alvarez Arenas was marginally less reactionary than his predecessor, Coloma Gallegos. On the other hand, the Minister for the Navy was a survivor from Carrero Blanco's cabinet, the antediluvian Admiral Gabriel Pita de Veiga. Although Gutiérrez Mellado did eventually take over as Vice-President for Defence in September 1976, after Santiago's resignation in protest at the legalization of trade unions, he was deeply marked by the ultra accusations that he was mixed up with the UMD. Although he worked hard for the depoliticization of the armed forces during the transition to democracy, he continued to oppose the reinstatement of the UMD officers for fear that it would revive ultra intransigence in the delicate process of depoliticizing the army after 1977.[35]

The cabinet as a whole under Arias hoped to bestow paternalistically a mild democratization which would take the steam out of strikes and demonstrations without provoking the bunker. The problem was that while the opposition was stepping up its pressure for a total break with the past, the so-called *ruptura democrática*, the bunker in general and its military members in particular continued to confuse national unity with national uniformity.[36] In fact, the relations between senior military

---

33 Morales and Celada, *La alternativa*, p. 29.
34 Manuel Gutiérrez Mellado, *Un soldado de España* (Barcelona, 1983), pp. 40–3, 47, 132; José María de Areilza, *Diario de un ministro de la monarquía* (Barcelona, 1977), pp. 76–7.
35 Fortes and Otero, *UMD*, pp. 10–11; Gutiérrez Mellado, *Un soldado*, pp. 133–8.
36 Manuel Tuñón de Lara in *El País*, 21 March 1981; interview with Admiral Pita de Veiga in *La Voz de Galicia*, 14 April 1976, quoted by Fernández, *Los militares*, pp. 86–7.

figures and the civilian bunker were extremely close despite regular, and probably sincere, declarations of the armed forces' apoliticism. Typical was the statement by the hard-line General Jésus González del Yerro in May 1975 that 'soldiers who want to stay in the forces should not enter the political arena. The Army would lose its mission and perhaps its essence if it became involved in the actions of such an individual or such a group or in political programmes or tendencies'.[37] Of course, for military hard-liners, loyalty to the principles of Francoism did not involve a political stance but was an unavoidable patriotic duty. General de Santiago was in close touch with ultras such as the retired Director of the Civil Guard Iniesta Cano and José Antonio Girón de Velasco, head of the organization of Francoist ex-combatants. They met, along with the new Minister for the Army, General Félix Alvarez Arenas, in mid-January, to discuss the forthcoming trial of the UMD leaders and long-term strategies for the defence of Franco's fundamental laws against possible reform initiatives.[38]

The trials were held in March 1976 in the hostile atmosphere generated by the invited presence of an overwhelming number of ultra-conservative senior officers, who made threatening comments throughout. The nine defendants received sentences ranging from eight to two and a half years and were expelled from the army.[39] The punishment received by the UMD officers was rather more severe than that which would be imposed upon many of those involved in the attempted coup of 1981 and dramatically more so than for those guilty of the attempted '*Galaxia*' coup of 1979. As a result of various amnesties, they were soon released but efforts to get them reinstated into the army were unsuccessful. That this remained the case throughout the 1980s was a symptom of the continuing strength of right-wing feeling within the armed forces. After all, their crime had been to work by peaceful means for the establishment of democracy.[40] But even after the trial, the UMD continued to function. In mid-May 1976 it issued a communiqué protesting that the annual parade of the army continued to be called the 'Victory Parade', in the Francoist tradition of keeping alive the memory of the Civil War. Despite suggestions from civilian politicians that the *Día de la Victoria* be renamed the *Día conmemorativo de las Fuerzas Armadas*, the view of the ultras prevailed and the parade went ahead as the 'Victory Parade'. Only after Gutiérrez Mellado became Vice-President for

37 *ABC*, 16 May 1975.
38 *Ya*, 13 January 1976; Fortes and Otero, *UMD*, p. 118; Areilza, *Diario*, pp. 81, 118, 152, 216; Fernández, *Los militares*, p. 63.
39 Domínguez, *Un exiliado*, pp. 182–92; Fortes and Otero, *UMD*, pp. 155–79; Colectivo Democracia, *Los Ejércitos*, pp. 60–2; Fernández, *Los militares*, pp. 70–9.
40 Domínguez, *Un exiliado*, p. 161; Fortes and Otero, *UMD*, pp. 10–11, 208–15; Caparrós, *La UMD*, pp. 169–70.

Defence Matters was it possible to turn the 'Day of Victory' into 'Armed Forces Day'.[41]

The trial of the UMD leaders revealed the extent to which the bunker was influencing both the government and the army. However, the rising tide of civilian democratic opposition was causing Juan Carlos to lose patience with the Arias cabinet's slow progress towards reform. Within the space of a month, the balance of power in the armed forces was to tip against the ultras. In the first week of June, General Gutiérrez de Mellado was moved from the Captaincy-General of Valladolid to become Chief of the General Staff. On 1 July, Arias resigned, when it became clear that he no longer enjoyed the king's confidence. Then on 20 July a cabinet meeting presided over by Juan Carlos decreed an amnesty which released the UMD leaders from gaol albeit without reincorporating them into the army. The writing was on the wall for the bunker. Adolfo Suárez's determined adoption of a policy of reforms was to cause first friction then rage among the ultras. The earliest public manifestation of this came in September.

On 8 September Suárez submitted his project before a group of senior officers and asked for their 'patriotic support'. Since they had the backing of Juan Carlos, Suárez's plans were reluctantly accepted, but the officers insisted that the Communist Party be excluded from any future reform. In the event, Suárez was to break his promise and thereby provoke the most intense hatred towards himself. For the moment, however, the most remarkable consequence of his proposals was the resignation as Vice-President of General Santiago y Díaz de Mendívil, on 22 September, after he had tried unsuccessfully to block the legalization of trade unions; in his opinion, they had been responsible for the 'red atrocities' committed during the Civil War. His views were shared by the bulk of the military hierarchy. *El Alcázar*, the ultra-rightist newspaper, whose board of directors, it will be recalled, was headed by General Jaime Milans del Bosch, published a letter from the ineffable General Iniesta Cano thanking Santiago for his 'priceless lesson'.[42]

In fact, Santiago's precipitate act was to speed up the pace of reform. He was replaced as Vice-President for Defence Matters by Gutiérrez Mellado, who was thereby able to take over the urgent task of creating a new generation of officers loyal to the coming democratic regime. Fidelity to Juan Carlos rather than deep-rooted commitment to democracy was the most that the new minister could hope for. However, a loyal nucleus could then be expanded by the addition of those of probable, rather than proven, reliability through the mechanism of strategic promotions. Unfortunately,

---

41 Domínguez, *Un exiliado*, p. 204; Gutiérrez Mellado, *Un soldado*, pp. 83–5.
42 *El Alcázar*, 23 and 27 September 1976; Colectivo Democracia, *Los Ejércitos*, p. 63; Morales and Celada, *La alternativa*, p. 28.

this policy had to be balanced by exaggerated rhetorical acquiescence in the traditional role of the armed forces and the promotion of ultras in the vain hope of neutralizing them. Thus, at the end of 1976, the hard-line Director-General of the Civil Guard, Angel Campano López, was replaced by Antonio Ibáñez Freire, a man close to Gutiérrez Mellado. The fact that, in order to be of appropriate rank to assume his new post, he had to be promoted expressly to lieutenant-general provoked fury in reactionary segments of the military hierarchy, totally devoted as they were to the most rigid seniority system for promotions.[43] The most vociferous critic was Milans del Bosch, who none the less was later to be promoted to Captain-General of the Third Military Region in Valencia. The policy of replacements continued when the Director General de Seguridad, Román Rodríguez, was replaced by Mariano Nicolás García and the Inspector General de la Policía Armada, General Aguilar Carmona, by General José Timón de Lara.[44] With agreement being reached between the government and the opposition, Gutiérrez Mellado and Suárez clearly regarded it as essential that the function of maintaining public order in a nascent democracy be kept out of the hands of bloodthirsty reactionaries.

On the other hand, with continued terrorist attacks keeping military nerves on edge, it was not suprising that in ultra circles Gutiérrez Mellado came to be regarded as a traitor because of his practice of removing committed Francoists who had fought in the Civil War. However, with the exception of Milans, the response of the ultras was initially muted. In part, they were still in some disarray after the death of Franco but even more they were in a state of shock after the massive vote in favour of political reform in the December 1976 referendum. Nevertheless, the ultras were not slow to re-group. With the justification of the kidnapping by the obscure terrorist group GRAPO of Antonio María de Oriol y Urquijo, president of the Consejo de Estado on 11 December 1976 and of General Emilio Villaescusa Quilis, head of the Consejo Superior de Justicia Militar, on 24 January 1977, the bunker was able to assert that Suárez's government was throwing away the achievements of the Civil War. A concerted campaign was launched against the reform process in general and against Gutiérrez Mellado in particular. At first defensive, the campaign went rapidly on to the offensive when it became apparent that the government did not have the determination to take firm measures against increasingly blatant acts of indiscipline. The strategy of promoting liberals while at the same time ignoring challenges from ultras was serving only to embolden the extreme rightists. The first of an escalating series of incidents took place at the funeral of two policemen killed by

---

43 Gutiérrez Mellado, *Un soldado*, pp. 77–82; *El Alcázar*, 28 December 1976; author's interview with General Manuel Prieto López, Feburary 1983.
44 *El País*, 24 December 1976.

terrorists. Ultra slogans were chanted and Gutiérrez Mellado was publicly insulted by the naval captain Camilo Menéndez Vives, who went virtually unpunished.[45]

Everything that the government of Suárez and its Minister of Defence did aroused the anger of the bunker. Gutiérrez Mellado's projected professionalization of the army was greeted as an attack on those who fought the Civil War for Franco. Such attacks hit home sufficiently for the minister to feel himself obliged to make public denials.[46] The rage of the ultras went into an altogether higher gear when Suárez legalized the Communist Party on 9 April 1977. Not only was this considered a vile betrayal of the cause for which the Civil War had been fought, it was also seen as a repellant act of deception by Suárez, who both broke his word and did so in a cowardly fashion by choosing a moment when most senior officers were absent from Madrid.[47] The most dramatic consequence was the resignation of the Minister for the Navy, Admiral Pita de Veiga, and it was also rumoured that the Minister for the Army, General Alvarez Arenas, had had a letter of resignation rejected. The depth of feeling within the army was made public after a meeting on 12 April of the Consejo Superior del Ejército. Its communiqué referred to the general revulsion that the measure had caused, although it also accepted the *fait accompli* in a disciplined fashion.[48]

The legalization of the PCE, unavoidable and a central stage in the transition to democracy, fell right into the hands of the ultras. Massive propaganda was mounted in the barracks and in military housing estates to convince officers of the extent of Suárez's 'betrayal'. Artificial organizations – the Juntas Patrióticas, the Union Patriótica Militar and the Movimiento Patriótico Militar – were set up to distribute cyclostyled and photocopied diatribes against the military reforms of 'Señor Gutiérrez', the deterioration of patriotic values, outrages against the flag, ETA terrorism and the weakness of the government.[49] The effect of this blanket propaganda was to give the impression to those not totally committed to bunker thinking that wide sectors of the army had already reached the conclusion that a military coup was the only solution.

The relative ease with which the propaganda was distributed and the failure to clamp down on its sources raised the question of the political loyalty of the intelligence services. In fact, the role played by these services, both in failing to inform the government of conspiracies and in

---

45 *El País*, 1 February 1977.
46 *El País*, 8 February 1977.
47 Joaquín Bardavío, *Sábado santo rojo* (Madrid, 1980), pp.196–200; interview with General Prieto.
48 *ABC*, 14 April 1977; *El País*, 15 April 1977.
49 Pilar Urbano, *Con la venia...yo indagué el 23-F* (Barcelona, 1982), p.16; Colectivo Democracia, *Los Ejércitos*, p. 71.

actively participating in them, was a crucial element in the development of *golpismo*. Created to eradicate any signs of liberalism in the armed forces, the intelligence organizations were hard-line Francoist in their composition, objectives and methods. After the death of Franco, they were subjected only to a slight cosmetic reorganization. In consequence, the sworn enemies of the democratic regime were provided with an invaluable instrument with which to co-ordinate military plotting and to provide an alternative chain of command during a coup. At the same time as the bunker press, *El Alcázar*, *El Imparcial* and *Fuerza Nueva*, were inciting officers to conspiracy, the intelligence services were failing to report on the success of this propaganda within the ranks.

When Franco died, there were eleven intelligence services, most of which were controlled by the military. The principal ones were administered independently by the Presidencia del Gobierno, the General Staff, each of the three military ministries, the Civil Guard, the police and even the Hermandad de Alféreces Provisionales. The most powerful was the Servicio de Información de la Presidencia del Gobierno set up by Carrero Blanco and run by Lieutenant-Colonel José Ignacio San Martín López. Both San Martín and his second-in-command, Colonel Federico Quintero Morente, were later to be involved in the Tejero coup attempt of 23 February 1981. The SIPG was originally created to maintain vigilance of the universities, the church and the labour movement, but after the Portuguese revolution its activities were extended to include, and indeed concentrate on, the armed forces. In addition to rooting out subversion, the SIPG was rumoured to be involved in directing and subsidizing the violence of ultra-rightist groups against liberal and leftist priests, lawyers, trade unionists and booksellers. Under Suárez, an attempt was made to break the power of the SIPG by subsuming it, together with the independent services run by each branch of the forces, into the Centro Superior de la Información de la Defensa (CESID). Since the CESID, on its creation on 2 November 1977, inherited the personnel of the previous services, the dominance of the so-called 'hombres de Carrero' was unaffected. They were thus able to build up a parallel power structure virtually independent of the military hierarchy, which was loyal to Gutiérrez Mellado and to the king. The Suárez government turned a blind eye to this and regularly issued statements praising the loyalty of the intelligence services. On one occasion, however, the Minister of Defence, Agustín Rodríguez Sahagún, a man normally committed to the policy of ignoring military misdemeanours, did express his dismay that the CESID devoted its energies to spying on ministers and leftist politicians while failing to investigate military conspiracies.[50]

---

50 UMD, *Los militares*, p. 47; Morales and Celada, *La alternativa*, pp. 67–85; Urbano, *Con la venia*, pp. 23–5; Fernández, *Los militares*, pp.190-1.

Ever since the legalization of the PCE there had been an intensification in the propensity of the ultras in the higher echelons of the army to plot. Just how near to boiling point they had been brought by the government's apparent weakness regarding terrorism, regionalism and communism was revealed in mid-September 1977. In Játiva in the province of Valencia, a meeting of senior generals, including three ex-Ministers for the Army, Antonio Barroso Sánchez Guerra, Coloma Gallegos and Alvarez Arenas, the ex-Minister for the Navy, Admiral Pita de Veiga, and the ultras Iniesta Cano, Campano López and Milans del Bosch, was presided over by General Santiago y Díaz de Mendívil. Between 13 and 16 September, they discussed the political situation and finally decided to call upon the king to appoint a Government of National Salvation presided over by Santiago. In the event of his refusing, he was to be asked to sack Suárez and suspend parliament for two years. Behind these requests for what amounted to a bloodless *coup d'état*, there was a clear threat of an outright military intervention.

Civilian support for such subversion went beyond the incitements of the bunker press to the organization of civic support networks. The same ultra politicians, Blas Piñar, García Carrés, Utrera Molina, who were behind the propaganda campaigns of the 'patriotic juntas', were planning for their followers to take over the civil service, local government and communications, in the event of a coup. In the light of both this and the enormous prestige of the generals involved in the Játiva meeting, the government was understandably loath to take dramatic measures which might have precipitated events. Thus, Gutiérrez Mellado persisted with his tactics of trying to control the forces by strategic postings. The most important was the removal of Milans del Bosch from the crucial post of commander of the Brunete armoured division (DAC). The blow was softened by his promotion to be Captain-General of the Third Military Region. Other changes were less positive and merely increased military suspicions that the government was weak, indecisive, meddlesome and vindictive. On 8 October Lieutenant Colonel Tejero came near to provoking a massacre in Málaga, for which he received one month's arrest and the fulsome praise of many ultras. In contrast, on 28 October General Alvarez Arenas was sacked from his post as Director de la Escuela Superior del Ejército in punishment for some extreme declarations by one of his subordinates. On 31 October General Alfonso Armada Comyn was removed from the secretariat of the king's military household for reasons that remain obscure but were connected with his barely concealed political views. On 16 December General Manuel Prieto López was dismissed as Commander of the VI Zone of the Civil Guard for a speech criticizing the government's use of the corps in inappropriate circumstances. All three sackings could be seen

195

as ill-advised over-reactions and they caused intense ill feeling within the forces.[51]

The passage of time was clearly not reconciling the armed forces to the democratic regime. Indeed, 1978 gave the impression that Suárez and Gutiérrez Mellado were skating on ever thinner ice. The precariousness of the situation was underlined on 17 May by the resignation of the Chief of the General Staff, General José Vega Rodríguez, hitherto regarded as a loyal moderate. In fact, contacts with Blas Piñar and a growing anxiety about the terrorist problem had driven Vega to make a stand on the issue of the promotion out of turn of General Antonio Ibáñez Freire to be Captain-General of the Fourth Military Region, Barcelona. The fury which had greeted Ibáñez's earlier promotion to Director-General of the Civil Guard derived from its flouting of the rigid seniority system. Gutiérrez Mellado believed that political considerations should take precedence over strict seniority where key appointments were concerned. Vega and others disagreed vehemently. Vega Rodríguez's resignation was a bitter blow for Gutiérrez Mellado. With encouragement from the ultra press, it seemed to give support to malcontents within the army.

As Vega's successor as CGS, an apparent moderate, Tomás de Liniers Pidal was appointed. The hopes raised by this were quickly dashed when, in a speech in Buenos Aires on 15 June, Liniers praised the Argentine military's 'legitimate' use of violence in their dirty war and implied that similar methods would be appropriate in Spain. No action was taken against him. In fact, in the test of strength between the ultras and the government, the initiative seemed to be passing to the bunker. Massive increases were being decreed in military budgets, with salaries increased by 21 per cent – but this seemed to do little to consolidate military loyalty to the new regime. Increasingly, senior officers were informing the government that the process of regional devolution would have to be slowed down. To do so could only provoke further ETA terrorism. It is hardly surprising then that Suárez's government gave growing indications of paralysis, which in its turn convinced many generals that a firmer, more decisive hand was called for.[52]

The deteriorating political situation was convincing many officers that the time to apply that firmness was near. Moreover, shrewder heads among the ultras realized that, timid though it was, the strategic promotions policy of Gutiérrez Mellado was gradually undermining their power. They were increasingly convinced that the opportune moment had arrived to exploit

---

51 *El País*, 20 September 1977; Fernández, *Los militares*, pp. 181-95; interview with General Prieto.

52 Morales and Celada, *La alternativa*, pp. 40-1; Fernández, *Los militares*, pp. 218–20, 227–8.

their existing strength in the intelligence services and elsewhere, before the reformist line of Suárez received further popular legitimation in the constitutional referendum fixed for 6 December1978. The date chosen for the coup was 17 November. *'Operación Galaxia'*, as it came to be known, having been plotted in the Cafetería Galaxia, envisaged the seizing of Suárez and the entire cabinet at the Moncloa Palace. It was hoped that the ensuing power vacuum would set off a chain reaction that would bring in other units for a nation-wide take-over.

17 November was selected because the king was scheduled to be on a state visit to Mexico, the Minister of Defence and the Joint Chiefs of Staff to be out of Madrid, and a large number of senior generals to be on promotion courses in Ceuta and the Canary Islands. Furthermore, large contingents of fascists were expected in the capital for the third anniversary of Franco's death on 20 November. The actual event was preceded by an orchestrated buildup of tension. Army barracks were once more flooded with the propaganda of the Movimiento Patriótico Militar. Gutiérrez Mellado, on a tour of garrisons to explain the constitution, was virulently insulted by General Atarés Peña, who called him 'a pig and a freemason' to the applause of many officers present. In the event, one of the plotters revealed the plan to the intelligence services, which belatedly informed the government. The two prime movers, Antonio Tejero and Ricardo Saenz de Ynestrillas, were arrested. In general, however, the government gave signs of wanting to brush the affair under the carpet. Thus nothing was done to prevent a series of events almost certainly linked with the projected coup, such as the attendance by five hundred officers at a fascist ceremony in the Valle de los Caídos on 20 November, or the celebration of an international fascist gathering in Madrid on the 18th, at which Blas Piñar called for a military uprising.

The bland response of the government was a reflection of the profound anxiety provoked by the *Galaxia* operation. It was clear, for instance, that many officers had been aware of the plot and were simply waiting on events. Moreover, the intelligence services had played a disturbingly ambiguous role. Some officers had reported that something was being plotted but the information was not passed on. In their basic function, the intelligence services had failed either to discover the conspiracy or to inform the government if they had. It was only at the last minute, on 16 November, that Suárez was told, after the head of the CESID had himself been informed by another officer. It appeared that units in Burgos, Valladolid, Seville and Valencia were involved and that only the fortuitous intervention of the liberal General Pascual Galmes prevented the Brunete armoured division joining in.[53]

---

53 *El País*, 17, 19 November 1978; Colectivo Democracia, *Los Ejércitos*, pp. 78–85; Morales and Celada, *La alternativa*, pp. 43–9.

'*Galaxia*' was in most respects a rehearsal for what was to become the 23-F plot. That its failure could be followed less than two and a half years later by a more thoroughly planned repeat performance can be attributed to the weakness of the government's response in 1978. The minimal punishment was meted out only to those whose involvement was too conspicuous to be ignored. Official statements presented the events of November as the wild schemes of an unrepresentative minority, '*cuatro locos*'. Nor was the policy of appeasement confined to the government. All sides of the political spectrum, including the socialists and communists, were accomplices, in rhetorical wishful thinking about military loyalty. Increasingly, the government was forced to make concessions to a military hierarchy which pushed for a slowing down of the autonomy process and for recognition of its own independence of political control.

Accordingly, the tide of military agitation and insubordination gathered momentum throughout 1979. Funerals of ETA victims were virtually institutionalized as occasions for military insults to Suárez and Gutiérrez Mellado and for calls for an army take-over. The continuing problem of ETA rendered it easy for the ultras to whip up support against the government and democracy in general. The success of ultra pressure was reflected in the cabinet reshuffle of April 1979. Although for the first time a civilian, Rodríguez Sahagún, was appointed as Minister of Defence, many of the reforms of Gutiérrez Mellado were rolled back. The authority which he managed to concentrate in his ministry was now effectively devolved back to the general staffs of the three services. Gutiérrez Mellado was pushed upstairs to be vice-president of the government with overall responsibility for defence and security. The new civilian Minister of Defence was to take to unprecedented extremes the policy of concession to the military hard-liners, particularly in terms of silencing the pro-democratic minority within the forces.

Needless to say, all such concessions were inadequate to pacify hard-liners who were keen to unleash an Argentinian-style 'dirty war' in the Basque country. In May 1979 their hostility to the government reached a new peak. The post of Army Chief of General Staff fell vacant. An appointment by strict seniority favoured the ultras who dominated the upper echelons of the army, while the government saw the vacancy as an opportunity to further its own ambition of liberalizing the forces. The logical candidates by seniority were both hard-liners, Milans del Bosch and González del Yerro. The normal appointments procedure called for the consultation of the Consejo Superior del Ejército, which duly pronounced in favour of Milans. It is hardly surprising then that furious indignation greeted the appointment of General José Gabeiras Montero, an associate of Gutiérrez Mellado. Gabeiras had to be promoted from major-general to lieutenant-general and then leap-frog five other generals to qualify for the post. The need for distortion of the promotion machinery highlighted the isolation of the liberals around Gutiérrez Mellado. It is reported that on one occasion Suárez upbraided his vice-president for occasionally promoting ultras and was told that in order to fill all senior posts with liberals it would have been necessary to look among the ranks of majors.[54]

The verdict of the military hierarchy on the achievements of Gutiérrez Mellado was made abundantly clear at the trial on 28 May of General Atarés Peña. The court's decision of not guilty was a judgement on Gutiérrez Mellado rather than on the defendant. Significantly, both government and opposition were silent about the acquittal of Atarés. Instead politicians chose to pay heed to frequent declarations by generals that the army would always adhere to article 8 of the constitution, wherein its role as defender of Spain's constitutional order and territorial integrity was enshrined.[55] It seemed to have escaped their notice that the sudden enthusiasm of the high command for this article of the constitution was not unconnected with the fact that it provided them with a justification for intervening in politics. Parallel with the increasingly open and confident statements by generals about their readiness to defend the existing order however and wherever necessary, 1979 saw an intensification of incitements to military intervention from the extreme rightist press. The fact that terrorists had killed ten active and two retired generals in the course of the year facilitated the provocation of military indignation by the ultra media.

The fact that something was in the air might have been deduced from the stepping up of anti-democratic declarations by the three most senior ultra generals still on active service, the Captains-General Milans del Bosch, González del Yerro and Pedro Merry Gordon, respectively commanders of the III (Valencia), Canary Islands and II (Seville) military regions. Their outbursts against the crisis of authority were met by silence and embarrassment on the part of the government. Meanwhile, *El Alcázar* and the rest of the ultra press was converting Tejero, Saenz de Ynestrillas and Atarés into heroic figures. Rage about terrorism and the progress towards regional autonomy could be more easily converted into *golpismo* after the ludicrously light sentences passed after the '*Galaxia*' affair. Indeed, the conviction was growing that if an important Madrid-based unit were to give the lead then the rest of the army would follow. Accordingly, the thoughts of *golpistas* began to centre on the Brunete armoured division, the key to the capital and currently commanded by an ultra, General Luis Torres Rojas. In fact, Torres Rojas was merely the latest stage in a long process whereby the DAC of Brunete had become an ultra stronghold. Practically from the beginning of the democratic transition, right-wingers had been requesting and obtaining postings to the DAC.

---

54 Morales and Celada, *La alternativa*, pp. 49–53.
55 *El País*, 6, 10 June, 1979.

Under the command of Milans del Bosch, who had a remarkable facility for generating the unquestioning loyalty of subordinates, the DAC had been brought into the bunker.

Within a month of Torres Rojas taking command in mid-1979, a series of unauthorized manoeuvres began, with patrols carrying out exercises in the control of the nerve centres of Madrid, armoured vehicles dominating the main access roads and troop carriers patrolling the industrial belt. It appears that Torres Rojas was at the heart of a planned coup whereby the Brigada Paracaidista (BRIPAC), supported by helicopters, would seize the Moncloa Palace while armoured vehicles of the DAC neutralized the capital. Having forced the government to resign, the conspirators would then proceed to the formation of a military directory under either Santiago y Díaz de Mendívil or Vega Rodríguez. The Cortes would be dissolved, the Communist Party banned and regional autonomy reversed. The continuity with the Játiva meeting and the *Galaxia* coup was obvious. All that was needed to convert normal manoeuvres by the BRIPAC on 21 October into a full-blown coup attempt was the difficulty of obtaining sufficient fuel and munitions. That missed opportunity did little to stem the tide of agitation. Indeed, on 20 October, *El Alcázar* had published an appeal by General Santiago for military intervention to solve the country's problems, and thereafter pressure from the ultra press reached ever more hysterical levels. In the event, the conspiracy around Torres Rojas came to an abrupt end on 24 January 1980 when he was removed from the DAC and sent to be military governor in La Coruña.

The way the government handled the Torres Rojas affair significantly paved the way to the 23-F attempt. It was announced that the transfer had been planned even before Torres Rojas had taken over the DAC. This was patently absurd and did nothing to mitigate the indignation felt in military circles that Torres Rojas had been dismissed while he was away from the unit on holiday with his family in Las Palmas. The fact that the Minister of Defence, Rodríguez Sahagún, hid the real reasons for the dismissal led many politicians to think that the government merely raised the spectre of military threats to avoid difficulties in other spheres. This impression could only be confirmed by the appalling treatment given to Miguel Angel Aguilar. One of Spain's most distinguished journalists and the best informed expert on military questions, he was then editor of *Diario 16*. He had published the real reasons behind Torres Rojas's transfer, which were met by government denials, which led to his being tried for insulting the army and forced from the editorship of the paper.[56]

The playing down of the Torres Rojas affair was followed in May by the trial of Tejero and Saenz de Ynestrillas. Despite having been

56 Colectivo Democracia, *Los Ejércitos*, pp. 85–91; Morales and Celada, *La alternativa*, pp. 57–61.

involved in a mutinous conspiracy, they received sentences of seven and six months respectively, which meant their immediate release. A greater encouragement for conspirators could hardly be imagined. A week later, the Joint Chiefs of Staff rejected a petition for the reincorporation of the UMD leaders and the Captain General of Madrid, Quintana Lacaci, a supposed liberal, commented ominously, 'the Army should respect democracy, not introduce it into its ranks'.[57] The failure of the government or press to revindicate the UMD was a further sign of weakness that helped to convince the right within the armed forces that it could act with impunity. Thus, as soon as he was released from custody, Tejero entered into conspiracy with Milans del Bosch and Torres Rojas. They enjoyed widespread support as was indicated by growing military pressure for the departure of Suárez. The 23 February 1981 coup was just around the corner.

Like previous rehearsals, the Tejerazo was to lead to a further coup attempt. However, two crucial aspects of its failure were decisive. Its technical errors and the undignified behaviour of Tejero and its other leaders both during the coup and their subsequent trial constituted a public humiliation for the armed forces. Secondly, the determined resistance of the king backed some days later by mass demonstrations created a sense that the army was isolated within society at large. The ultra conviction that 'Spain' was with them took a heavy blow. Thereafter, the long trial of the conspirators did nothing to enhance military prestige, but rather projected a picture of petty-minded, brutal and arrogant men whose behaviour belied their rhetoric about the national interest. Paradoxically, despite the military phobia about socialism, this background made many sectors of the army readier to obey a socialist government. This tendency was confirmed by the fact that the socialists in power tended to be authoritarian rather than falling into the sin of *desgobierno* – which had characterized the UCD period and infuriated the officer corps.

However, there were still large numbers of officers hostile to democracy. This was revealed in the starkest form at the beginning of October 1982 when plans for a coup were exposed. Scheduled for the day before the 28 October elections, the coup was to be a more thorough version of 23-F. The Royal Palace of the Zarzuela, the Moncloa Palace and the head-quarters of the Joint Chiefs of Staff were to be bombarded by artillery; communication centres and access roads were to be occupied and the capital sealed off. Technically well prepared, it seems to have been inspired by the imprisoned Milans del Bosch and supported by civilian ultras. There were, however, some grounds for optimism. The CESID intelligence service, reorganized since 1981 by Colonel Alonso

---

57 *El País*, 13 September 1980; Colectivo Democracia, *Los Ejércitos*, pp. 91–3.

Manglano, acted efficiently and swiftly to expose the plot. Moreover, the fact that the coup included provision for the liquidation of many senior officers contributed to the process of isolating the ultras. Equally, there were disturbing elements in that the UCD government arrested only three officers despite having documents incriminating about two hundred.[58] However, the era of UCD appeasement was about to give way to a more equal relationship between the army and the PSOE. The risks were high but, by dint of firmness and a policy of rearmament and modernization, the socialists made remarkable progress after 1982 towards inducing the military to a firm acceptance of the democratic regime.

---

58   *El País*, 3, 4, 5, 6 October 1982.

Further reading

Notwithstanding the comments made in the Preface about the relative lack of studies of the right in comparison with the abundance of work on the left, there is still a substantial body of available material. Detailed references to the sources used in each chapter are given in the footnotes. The purpose of this short essay is merely to provide a guide to the labyrinthine bibliography on the Spanish right before the Civil War and on the Franco regime after it. Almost all of it tends to be monographic since there is no overview of the parties and organizations of the right as a whole. The only such work, Ricardo de la Cierva, *La derecha sin remedio (1801–1987): de la prisión de Jovellanos al martirio de Fraga* (Plaza y Janés, Barcelona, 1987) is a self-opinionated exercise in special pleading – on behalf of Manuel Fraga – which is provocative and exasperating by turns. Accordingly, it is necessary to sample specialist works on various aspects of the subject.

The Spanish right in the 1950s and the subsequent Franco dictatorship can only be explained adequately in the context of the political and economic development of Spain in the previous hundred years. The best introductions remain Gerald Brenan's beautifully written and deeply felt *The Spanish Labyrinth* (2nd edn, Cambridge University Press, 1950) and the immensely thought-provoking and solidly reliable work by Raymond Carr, *Spain, 1808–1939* (Oxford University Press, 1966). The political positions of the Catholic Church, which was so often a reference point for ultra-rightist attitudes, are brilliantly analysed in Frances Lannon, *Privilege, Persecution, and Prophecy: The Catholic Church in Spain 1875–1975* (Oxford University Press, 1987) and also in Stanley G. Payne's *Spanish Catholicism: An Historical Overview* (University of Wisconsin Press, Madison, 1984).

The crucial role of the army is described in Stanley G. Payne's highly informative narrative, *Politics and the Military in Modern Spain* (Stanford University Press, 1967); in the monograph by Carolyn Boyd, *Praetorian Politics in Liberal Spain* (University of North Carolina Press, Chapel Hill, 1979); and in a series of recent works produced in Spain in the wake of the attempted military coup of 1981. Manuel Ballbé, *Orden público y militarismo en la España constitucional (1812–1983)* (Alianza Editorial, Madrid, 1984) is a fascinating account by a constitutional lawyer. Carlos Seco Serrano, *Militarismo y civilismo en la España contemporánea* (Instituto de Estudios Económicos, Madrid, 1984) is a judicious conservative account of civil–military relations before the Civil War. Gabriel Cardona, *El poder militar en la España contemporánea hasta la guerra civil* (Siglo XXI Editores, Madrid, 1983) is a masterly critical survey by an army officer turned historian. Joaquim Lliexá, *Cien años de militarismo en España: Funciones estatales confiadas al Ejército en la Restauración y al franquismo* (Editorial Anagrama, Barcelona, 1986) is a brilliant, albeit somewhat cryptic, essay in interpretation.

The Primo de Rivera dictatorship, an arcadian interlude longingly evoked by most Spanish rightists, is discussed as a pre-fascist experience in Shlomo Ben-Ami's difficult but significant book, *Fascism from Above: The Dictatorship of Primo de Rivera in Spain 1923–1930* (Oxford University Press, 1983). Javier Tusell, *Radiografía de un golpe de Estado: el ascenso al Poder del general Primo de Rivera* (Alianza Editorial, Madrid, 1987) is a controversial but important interpretation of the reasons for the emergence of the first dictatorship. María Teresa González Calbet, *La Dictadura de Primo de Rivera: El Directorio militar* (Ediciones El Arquero, Madrid, 1987) examines the nature of military authoritarianism in practice.

The Carlist movement, touchstone of reactionary attitudes, and its relations with other right-wing groups, especially fascist ones, are analysed with learning and clarity in Martin Blinkhorn's *Carlism and Crisis in Spain, 1931–1939* (Cambridge University Press, 1975). The other radical authoritarian movement, Acción Española/Renovación Española, is presented as the central precursor of Francoism in my article 'Alfonsist monarchism and the coming of the Spanish Civil War', *Journal of Contemporary History*, vol. 7, nos. 3–4 (July-October 1972). A similar approach is adopted by the Spanish political scientist Raúl Morodo, in his *Los orígenes ideológicos del franquismo: Acción Española* (2nd edn, Alianza Editorial, Madrid, 1985). Not without interest for its wealth of detail is an immense doctoral thesis recently made available, Julio Gil Pecharromán, *Renovación Española. Una alternativa monárquica a la segunda República*, 2 vols (Editorial de la Universidad Complutense de Madrid, 1985). A startlingly original and lucid study of this area of the extreme right is to be found in Ismael Saz Campos, *Mussolini contra la II República* (Edicions Alfons El Magnànim, Valencia, 1986).

The most hotly debated area of the Spanish right is still the authoritarian Catholic party, Acción Popular, later the Confederación Española de Derechas Autónomas. Its many ambiguities and its flirtation with fascism are admirably revealed in its semi-official handbook, José Monge Bernal, *Acción Popular* (Saez Hermanos, Madrid, 1936), and in its leader's fascinating and voluminous memoirs, *No fue posible la paz* (Editorial Ariel, Barcelona, 1968). The most favourable scholarly study is Richard A. H. Robinson's *The Origins of Franco's Spain* (David & Charles, Newton Abbot, 1970) which stresses the CEDA's Christian Social rhetoric. The opposing view is to be found in José Ramón Montero's massive, and intensely critical, *La CEDA: el catolicismo social y político en la II República*, 2 vols (Ediciones de la Revista de Trabajo, Madrid, 1977). Broadly in agreement with Montero, but placing the CEDA in the context of its battle with the Socialist Party for control of the apparatus of the state, is my own *The Coming of the Spanish Civil War: Reform, Reaction and Revolution in the Second Republic 1931–1936* (Macmillan, London, 1978).

For obvious reasons, there is less disagreement about the Falange. The standard work is Stanley G. Payne's sweepingly titled pioneering study, the extremely readable *Falange: A History of Spanish Fascism* (Stanford University

Press, 1961). It has recently been joined by Sheelagh Ellwood's short but comprehensive *Spanish Fascism in the Franco Era* (Macmillan, London, 1987), which manages to get under the skin of Falangist convictions. A stimulating and original approach, with stress on Falangist imperialism, is to be found in Herbert R. Southworth's 'The Falange: an analysis of Spain's fascist heritage', in Paul Preston (ed.), *Spain in Crisis: Evolution and decline of the Franco regime* (Harvester Press, Hassocks, 1976). A thoughtful Marxist interpretation, Javier Jiménez Campo, *El fascismo en la crisis de la II República española* (Centro de Investigaciones Sociológicas, Madrid, 1979), amply repays careful reading. A crucial recent monograph is that by Ricardo Chueca, *El fascismo en los comienzos del régimen de Franco. Un estudio sobre FET-JONS* (Centro de Investigaciones Sociológicas, Madrid, 1983). There are many works by Falangists which tend to hagiography of the movement's leader, José Antonio Primo de Rivera. One which goes beyond that is Maximiano García Venero, *Falange en la guerra de España: la unificación y Hedilla* (Ruedo Ibérico, Paris, 1967), which faithfully recounts the version of José Antonio's proletarian successor Manuel Hedilla. It should be read in conjunction with Herbert R. Southworth's mordant commentary, *Antifalange* (Ruedo Ibérico, Paris, 1967). Two recent memoirs by Falangist notables are Pilar Primo de Rivera, *Recuerdos de una vida* (Ediciones Dyrsa, Madrid, 1983) and Raimundo Fernández Cuesta, *Testimonio, recuerdos y reflexiones* (Ediciones Dyrsa, Madrid, 1985). Unfortunately, they are more notable for what they do not say than for what they do.

The Franco regime is constantly examined for evidence of fascist features. Analytical accounts may be found in Paul Preston, *Spain in Crisis* (see above); Raymond Carr and Juan Pablo Fusi, *Spain: Dictatorship to Democracy* (George Allen & Unwin, London, 1979) and Sergio Vilar, *La naturaleza del franquismo* (Ediciones Península, Barcelona, 1977). Max Gallo's *Spain Under Franco* (George Allen & Unwin, London, 1973) is vivid but not free of inaccuracies. The best overview is Stanley G. Payne's splendidly comprehensive *The Franco Regime 1936–1975* (University of Wisconsin Press, Madison, 1987). Amando de Miguel, *Sociología del franquismo* (Editorial Euros, Barcelona, 1975), examines the various pressure groups within the Francoist élite and makes an important contribution to the debate on the nature of the regime. Two stimulating, original and entirely opposed interpretations are by Juan J. Linz, 'An authoritarian regime: Spain' in E. Allardt and Y. Littunen (eds), *Cleavages, Ideologies and Party Systems* (Westermaarck Society, Helsinki, 1964), and by Eduardo Sevilla Guzmán and Salvador Giner, 'Absolutismo despótico y dominación de clase: el caso de España', *Cuadernos de Ruedo Ibérico*, 43–5 (January–June 1975).

The regime's openly fascist period is not really disputed. Its imperial ambitions and their authors' quest for promotion and preferment are expressed in many works of which the most explicit is José María de Areilza and Fernando María Castiella, *Reivindicaciones de España* (Instituto de Estudios Políticos, Madrid, 1941). Franco's relations with the Axis are studied in Klaus-Jörg Ruhl, *Franco, Falange y Tercer Reich: España durante la segunda guerra mundial* (Ediciones Akal, Madrid, 1986) and in Xavier Tusell and Genoveva García Queipo de Llano, *Franco y Mussolini: la política española durante la segunda guerra mundial* (Editorial Planeta, Barcelona, 1985). However, by far the shrewdest and most subtle analysis of Franco's policy during the war is to be found in Denis Smyth,

Diplomacy and Strategy of Survival: British Policy and Franco's Spain, 1940–1941 (Cambridge University Press, 1986). Franco's Russian adventure is described in country-and-western style by Gerald R. Kleinfeld and Lewis A. Tambs, *Hitler's Spanish Legion* (University of Southern Illinois Press, Carbondale, 1979). The alleged architect of pro-Axis policy, Ramón Serrano Suñer, has defended his record and shifted the burden of Nazi sympathies on to Franco in his *Entre Hendaya y Gibraltar* (Ediciones Españolas, Madrid, 1947) and *Entre el silencio y la propaganda: la Historia como fue, Memorias* (Editorial Planeta, Barcelona, 1977), as well as in numerous articles and a compelling set of interviews with Heleno Saña, *El franquismo sin mitos: conversaciones con Serrano Suñer* (Ediciones Grijalbo, Barcelona, 1982). An interesting biography of Serrano Suñer is that by Fernando García Lahiguera, *Ramón Serrano Suñer: Un documento para la historia* (Editorial Argos Vergara, Barcelona, 1983). Altogether more gripping, and controversial, is Ramón Garriga, *Franco-Serrano Suñer: un drama político* (Editorial Planeta, Barcelona, 1986).

Important studies of Francoist attempts to regiment labour and the economy are Miguel A. Aparicio, *El sindicalismo vertical y la formación del Estado franquista* (Universidad de Barcelona, 1980), and Joan Clavera, Joan M. Esteban Marquillas, M. Antònia Monés, Antoni Monserrat and J. Ros Hombravella, *Capitalismo español: de la autarquía a la estabilización* (Edicusa, Madrid, 1973). On the Falangist Youth Front and its Women's Section, see Juan Sáez Marín, *El Frente de Juventudes: política de juventud en la España de la postguerra (1937–1960)* (Siglo XXI Editores, Madrid, 1988) and María Teresa Gallego Méndez, *Mujer, Falange y franquismo* (Ediciones Taurus, Madrid, 1983). On press censorship, see Javier Terrón Montero, *La prensa de España durante el régimen de Franco* (Centro de Investigaciones Sociológicas, Madrid, 1981) and Justino Sinova, *La censura durante el franquismo* (Espasa Calpe, Madrid, 1989).

Despite the striking similarities between many of the instruments of his regime and those of Hitler and Mussolini, easy identification of Franco with fascism has been rendered difficult by his cousin's publication of his table-talk, Francisco Franco Salgado-Araujo, *Mis conversaciones privadas con Franco* (Editorial Planeta, Barcelona, 1976). A similar impression is inadvertently conveyed by the massive biography, based on Franco's private papers, by Luis Suárez Fernández, *Francisco Franco y su tiempo*, 8 vols (Fundación Nacional Francisco Franco, Madrid, 1984). The stifling mediocrity portrayed in both of these works could not be further removed from the veneer of anti-establishment novelty conventionally assumed to be central to authentic fascism. In this context, it is instructive to read Dr Vicente Gil, *Cuarenta años junto a Franco* (Editorial Planeta, Barcelona, 1981) and Alfredo Kindelán, *La verdad de mis relaciones con Franco* (Editorial Planeta, Barcelona, 1981).

Index